Connecting WITH Coincidence

The New Science for Using Synchronicity and Serendipity in Your Life

Bernard D. Beitman, MD

Health Communications, Inc.
Deerfield Beach, Florida

www.hcibooks.com

Cataloging in Publication Data is available through the Library of Congress

© 2016 Bernard D. Beitman

ISBN-13: 978-07573-1884-9 (Paperback)
ISBN-10: 07573-1884-3 (Paperback)
ISBN-13: 978-07573-1885-6 (ePub)
ISBN-10: 07573-1885-1 (ePub)

Publisher: Health Communications, Inc.
            3201 S.W. 15th Street
            Deerfield Beach, FL 33442–8190

Cover design by Dane Wesolko
Interior design and formatting by Lawna Patterson Oldfield

Bob and
mamie

**Coincidences alert us
to the mysterious hiding
in plain sight.**

a delight to 1!
see you
Bernie
Portsmouth   7/29/16
NH

Contents

PART 3: A New Theory of Coincidences

Introduction

At some point in our lives, all of us have experienced a fleeting moment when a weird coincidence made us smile and wonder. It could have been a song that came on the radio just as it went through your mind or a phone call from a long-lost friend the very day you thought of this person. Or, it could appear as it did for Saundra—in black and white letters. Saundra was enjoying Chinese food at her father's house and texted her sister to let her know that one of their favorite movies, *The Wizard of Oz*, was on television. Her sister texted back that she remembered watching the movie with their mother, who was now deceased. "Mom would always fix popcorn . . ." she typed as she fondly remembered their treasured times together.

While Saundra was reading her sister's text message, she grabbed a fortune cookie and opened it. Much to her delight, her fortune greeted her with the word *popcorn*.

Something special had just happened to Saundra, and when she texted her sister to tell her, they both felt the presence and comfort of their mother.

I've been deeply interested in coincidences like this most of my life—trying to make sense of them, to understand how best to use them, and how best to explain them to skeptics and believers alike.

I had experienced coincidences many times before, but none was more startling than what happened at 11:00 PM on February 26, 1973, when I was thirty-one years old. Suddenly, I found myself bent over the kitchen sink in an old Victorian house on Hayes Street in the Fillmore District of San Francisco. I was choking on something caught in my throat. I couldn't cough it up. I hadn't eaten anything. I didn't know what was in my throat. I'd never choked for this long before. Finally, after fifteen minutes or so, I could swallow and breathe normally.

The next day, my birthday, my brother called to tell me that our father had died in Wilmington, Delaware, at 2:00 AM Eastern Standard Time. He was three thousand miles and three time zones away; 2:00 AM in Wilmington was 11:00 PM in California. My father had bled into his throat and choked on his own blood at about the same time I was uncontrollably choking. He died on February 27, my birthday.

Was this just a coincidence? No. The timing was too perfect. The experience was too visceral. I loved my father, but I had no idea that our connection could transcend time and space in this way. I began to wonder if other people had had similar experiences.

A man riding a train back to his home in Zurich, Switzerland, was suddenly overtaken by a frightening vision of someone drowning. Upon arriving home, he discovered that his grandson had almost drowned in the lake by his house around the time of the terrifying vision.

The man in this story was psychiatrist Carl Jung, who invented the word *synchronicity* for a wide spectrum of weird coincidences. He personally experienced many strange events, but his writings focused more on theoretical speculation. Known as the preeminent theoretician of coincidence, he developed the synchronicity theory using complex ideas from quantum physics and ancient philosophies, along with his own concepts of the collective unconscious and archetypes. He also clearly documented that meaningful coincidences have been recognized throughout human history in many different cultures. I've explored much the same forest as Jung but followed a different path.

I grew up in Wilmington, Delaware, the headquarters of the DuPont Company, where chemistry was king. During some school assemblies, we watched movies depicting the history of this onetime gunpowder company, which started on the banks of the Brandywine River that runs through Wilmington. I liked chemistry and majored in chemistry at Swarthmore College. If I'd continued on in this major, I would've been faced with a choice of becoming either a chemist or a chemical engineer. The chemist comes up with new ideas and molecules. The chemical engineer figures out how to use them. I chose the practical path, but not in that discipline. I became a psychiatrist, a profession in which chemicals are often used to help people.

As one whose profession revolves around the life of the mind, I also began to notice the weird coincidences in my life, as well as those in the lives of my patients. My fascination with the subject eventually led me to conduct research on coincidence at the University of Missouri-Columbia, the results of which appeared in two issues of the journal *Psychiatric Annals*, for which I was the editor.[1] Now the engineer in me is using the results of that research to put coincidence to practical use. I see myself as an engineer for Jung's theoretical ideas.

As demonstrated by my research at the University of Missouri-Columbia, at least a third of the general population frequently notices weird coincidences. Friends, colleagues, patients, acquaintances, and strangers standing in line at a coffee shop—many people seem to be talking about, if not experiencing, coincidences these days. "What a coincidence!" "What are the chances of that happening?" "Let me tell you about this coincidence." In our modern technological culture, there are even smartphone apps to help you track your coincidences.

But what do people mean by "coincidence"?

For some people, coincidences represent random chance at work. To these rationalists, the universe runs like a clock, and the laws of probability describe how the Grand Machine runs. They are "just" or "mere" or "only" coincidences. Others believe that meaningful coincidences are the work of a personal God who is guiding and nurturing them. In between God and probability lies a broad spectrum of theories. The emerging field of coincidence studies, a field I'm helping to develop, proposes closer connections between mind and environment than are currently accepted in psychiatry and psychology.

Our perceptions of coincidence emerge from swirls of information in our minds juxtaposed with swirls of events in our surroundings. Like two dials being spun by separate hands, the active mind and a pattern of events briefly coincide, causing the mind to note an odd correspondence. The match is often surprising because it seems improbable. But coincidence is more than the unlikely juxtaposition of similar events—the two events must also be meaningfully connected, and the meaning is personal and intricately linked to the person involved. Many books offer compilations of amazing coincidence stories, and there is no shortage of books advocating specific theories. This book is different. I've tried to pull apart the coincidence reports from many different sources to see

But coincidence is more than the unlikely juxtaposition of similar events—the two events must also be meaningfully connected, and the meaning is personal and intricately linked to the person involved.

how and why they could've happened the way they did. In the process of examining these stories, I've come to discover the essential features that make coincidences happen, including the personality characteristics and situational factors that serve to increase their frequency. These characteristics and factors have proven to be so consistent that I realized we actually do—and can—make our own coincidences.

Part 1 shows how meaningful coincidences occur in all aspects of life: relationships, health, money, and spirit. It introduces several possible uses and explanations. Part 2 outlines concrete suggestions about how to use coincidences, particularly "instrumental" coincidences. These coincidences provide practical assistance in daily life in two different ways. The first kind delivers just what is needed—a person, information, or money. The second kind provides a comment about a question or a decision. Part 2 also describes how to increase the frequency of coincidences. Part 3 introduces the psychosphere, our mental atmosphere. Just as we exchange oxygen and carbon dioxide with the atmosphere, we exchange subtle forms of energy and information with the psychosphere. These subtle exchanges of energy-information may form the basis for many otherwise unexplainable coincidences, including my simultaneous choking while my father was dying.

Part 1

Weird Coincidences
Commonly Occur

CHAPTER 1

Closer Than Close

The simultaneous choking as my father was dying, as well as many other personal weird coincidences, drove me to research how common these experiences might be. They turn out to be very common. In fact, I discovered that psychiatrist Ian Stevenson had collected at least two hundred similar stories.[1] I became convinced that something more than random chance was occurring in these "coincidences." But what exactly was happening here? I decided to find out.

As a psychiatrist, I marvel at the importance and complexity of our relationships to other people. Sitting in my office, day after day, week after week, year after year, I observe and listen to people trying to understand and improve their connections to others.

Like you and me, each of my patients is trying to manage the confusing paradox of being a separate, evolving, growing individual while also desperately needing to feel emotionally connected to someone else. Some want to deny the need for others, to stand strongly alone, to be self-reliant. Others are afraid to be without someone else defining them. My job is to help them all find a balance.

There also exists a mysterious undercurrent between my patients and me. Through a combination of their words, the tone of their voice, their facial expressions, and something more, I join my patients in their lives. Each time they come to the office, I experience their world with them and become, for a time, part of them. My mind mirrors theirs with the help of familiarity and what are known as *mirror neurons*—that remarkable collection of nerve cells in our brains that are activated both when we perform an action and when we observe that same action. Mirror neurons probably help us empathize with the other person. We become attuned to each other. We resonate. And, I believe, in our attunement to other people and to the world around us, we sometimes go beyond the standard understanding of brain function. We enter a currently mysterious realm in which people experience the distress of a loved one at a distance.

According to Stevenson, the majority of these resonating experiences take place among immediate family members. For example, a woman suddenly feels deeply distressed and feels impelled to run home. She finds her husband in the midst of a heart attack. Because she gets there in time, he recovers. Among family member pairs, the most common connections occur among mothers and children. For example, a daughter suddenly starts crying uncontrollably. Her mother has just died suddenly in a distant location. The daughter only later receives the confirmation.

A psychiatrist told me that he and his brother couldn't get into trouble without their mother knowing. When they came home on time but had gotten into fights, she knew before they walked through the doorway. He insisted that no one had alerted her by phone.

Julia Altamar, from Tuscaloosa, Alabama, told me this story concerning the death of her son: "At the exact time my son died, I was standing under a full moon looking up, with Coco, our German shepherd, on a leash, as I'd taken her outside. I could feel my soul being pulled from my body, and I knew something horrible had happened. I wanted to come inside and call my son, but the fear was overwhelming. I didn't even take my clothes off prior to lying on the bed, as if I knew someone would be coming to tell me. It took me only seconds to race to the door when the doorbell rang. And although no one is ever ready for such horrific news, somehow my inner mind had been prepared; how, I cannot explain, but otherwise I may not have survived the shock."

Altamar knew in ways we have yet to understand that her son had been killed. She received the necessary information in an extraordinary way and was then better prepared when the awful news was delivered in a conventional way.

Family members are most likely to experience simulpathity but so can close friends. Jungian psychiatrist Jean Bolen tells the story of Judy Vibberts, "who had been having an uneventful, pleasantly relaxed afternoon in San Francisco's Golden Gate Park, when precisely at 4:30 (she unaccountably noted the time) she was suddenly struck by excruciating, doubling-up abdominal pain, accompanied by a splitting headache. That evening, she found out that a good friend had been in a terrible accident. Her car had been smashed, causing severe abdominal and head injuries. She had been taken immediately to a hospital, needed emergency surgery to remove her ruptured spleen, and was on the critical list in the intensive care unit. The accident had occurred at exactly 4:30 PM."[2]

One of my patients sometimes abruptly awakens in the middle of the night feeling upset and knowing her friend in another city is going through a big loss, probably a relationship breakup. She then calls the friend, and her impression is confirmed.

Occasionally even strangers find themselves connected to each other.
One of our research participants wrote, "I was separated from my abusive husband. While he was gone on a business trip, I'd decided to reunite with him. He missed his return connecting flight. That night an unknown woman who was being abused by her boyfriend mistakenly dialed a number and got me. [The study participant didn't report the reason for the woman's call.] The fear in her voice made me realize that reuniting with my husband was a mistake. I met him at the airport the next morning to tell him that my plans had changed and he wouldn't be returning to my house. Many things have happened to me like that. I wasn't a believer in God until I paid attention to these things. I am a strong believer in God today."

The reflection on the unexpected phone call clarified her feelings about her marriage and what to do about it. How to explain this coincidence? Here, the woman attributed the coincidence to God. Others would say it was a random event. I would like to explore an additional possibility. The two women were synchronicity sisters, temporary emotional twins, each suffering from abusive men and needing to break away. This similarity created a resonance that helped to connect them. As many of these stories show, the research participant's intense need and high emotion—and being in transition to pick up her husband—helped to set the stage. How the other woman's fingers "just happened" to find the wrong but right telephone number becomes an important question. As meaningful coincidences become more increasingly studied, I believe we will see how, to varying degrees, probability, God, and personal responsibility play roles in their creation. Some coincidences will be

Some by personal responsibility. Others by Divine Mystery. Many will be best explained by a combination of all three.

best explained by randomness. Some by personal responsibility. Others by Divine Mystery. Many will be best explained by a combination of all three.

Therapist-patient pairs also seem to develop the capacity for one to feel the other's distress over distance. Robert Hopcke, a Jungian therapist in Berkeley, California, reports having had an eerily similar coincidence with an ex-patient named Jerry. Hopcke had a disturbing dream in which Jerry was lying very still in a beach house, breathing very slowly. Their therapeutic relationship had ended a year before, yet the anxiety of the dream was thick and almost palpable. Hopcke wondered if he should call Jerry, but he didn't. Months later, Jerry unexpectedly called to set up an appointment. It was then that Hopcke learned that several months earlier Jerry had given up because of a failed relationship and had checked into a hotel near the ocean where he took an overdose. For three days he lay unconscious and then woke up feeling terrible. Nobody seemed to miss him. Jerry told Hopcke the date. When Hopcke checked his dream journal, he discovered his dream had taken place a week *before* Jerry's suicide attempt. Hopcke told Jerry that the dream was evidence that Jerry was connected to at least one person, even though he felt he wasn't connected to anyone. Jerry was *not* alone.[3]

Currently we have no accepted scientific explanations for such coincidences. So, in an attempt to learn more, I instituted a research study on coincidence at the University of Missouri-Columbia in 2007. Approximately 700 people—faculty, staff, and students—responded to our request to rate the frequency of common meaningful coincidences (see the Weird Coincidence Scale in the Appendix). The participants rated among several things how frequently they had experienced strong emotions or physical sensations that were simultaneously experienced at a distance by someone they loved. The group as a whole told us they "occasionally" had such experiences. About 15 percent of the 681 participants, or 102 people, reported that they frequently had such experiences. This finding strongly confirmed the reality of this strange phenomenon. A few told us detailed stories of knowing when their wives, who were halfway across the world, were about to deliver their child. Several others told us how a sibling sensed that something was terribly wrong and later discovered that their brother or sister had been greatly distressed.[4]

The most common triggers for these experiences are death or dying and major illnesses or injury.[5] These reports of "feeling the pain of a loved one at a distance" suggest that *something* out of the ordinary is going on. I call this experience *simulpathity*. The word comes from the Latin word *simul* meaning "at the same time" or "simultaneous," and the Greek word *path*, meaning "suffering or emotion," as in sym*pathy* and psycho*path*ology.

Twins have been most often studied for evidence of simulpathity. Although it would seem to be more likely that twins would experience simulpathity, the most important variable seems to be the degree of connectedness, no matter what the relationship. British writer Guy Playfair reviewed the research on twins and concluded that the likelihood for nonordinary communication between twins increases if they are identical (come from one egg), strongly bonded, and extroverts.[6]

In Christchurch, New Zealand, anthropologists Brett Mann and Chrystal Jaye interviewed adult twins in depth about their illness experiences. Of the twenty twin pairs Mann and Jaye interviewed, fifteen were identical twins, including one set of conjoined twins separated at birth. The group reported that the illness or injury of one twin was commonly experienced by the other. The twenty pairs reported more than fifty incidents in which one felt the pain of the other at a distance. Some pairs reported more than ten incidents while others only one or two. These parallel events often occurred during major life crises.[7]

Accidents also trigger simulpathity coincidences. Eighteen-year-old nursing assistant Diana was dishing out meals to patients when she suddenly began shaking like a leaf. She could barely stand up. She knew something awful and shocking was happening and was filled with terrible dread. When she called her mother, she learned that a car had hit her twin brother; his spleen was ruptured and his kidney was damaged. The doctors were very worried because they couldn't stop the bleeding. She later discovered that she had started shaking around the time his motorcycle was hit.

How does this happen? We might get a better idea of how simulpathity operates by looking at the experiences of twins joined at the head. These are called craniopagus twins, a condition that occurs in about one out of 2,500,000 births, or about 2 percent of conjoined twin births. The twins usually die young. In one case, when Canadian craniopagus twins Krista and Tatiana were born, they were not only connected at their skulls but also via a thin link of nerve tissue that connected each other's thalamus.

The thalamus functions as the major switchboard for the brain and connects our lower brain with our higher brain, coordinating inputs and responses. All sensory inputs except smell go to the thalamus; directed movement and emotion also travel through it. So Krista and Tatiana could pick up sensations from each other, as well as emotions and intentions. If one drank something, the other seemed to taste it.

When the twins were two years old, their neurosurgeon covered Krista's eyes and glued electrodes to her scalp. While a strobe light flashed in Tatiana's eyes, Krista's visual cortex was firing. They reversed roles and got the same response in the blindfolded Tatiana. This was strong evidence that the twins were connected through the thalamus. The light went into one set of eyes and out to both visual cortices.

The family wasn't surprised by the results. When one girl's vision was angled away from the television, she seemed to be laughing at the images in front of her sister's eyes. The sensory exchange extended to the girls' taste buds as well. Krista liked ketchup, and Tatiana didn't. So when Krista ate ketchup, Tatiana, who wasn't eating ketchup, tried to scrape the stuff off her own tongue.[8]

These twins felt each other's feelings, which is explained through the connection of the thin strand of nerve tissue they shared. But we know that ordinary, separated twins can sometimes communicate emotions without this physical, neuronal link. They appear to do it "wirelessly."

Is there a good theory that fits the existing information?

Tatiana and Krista had a nerve "wire" between each of their thalami that allowed them to receive some of the sensations of the other. Their skulls were also fused. Their brains were functioning within one large piece of bone. Here, we come closer to the truth of what happens with non-conjoined twins and what I experienced with my father. We don't have a neuronal wire between our thalami, but we seem to share a very flexible, invisible mind envelope. We share a special consciousness with those we love; we are part of their minds and they are part of ours. Our identity exists *in relationship to them.* Like Tatiana and Krista, we are both individual and connected, separated and fused, with those we love. What happens to them sometimes happens to us.

These stories tell us that we share minds with each other. The implications are enormous. But what is it that fuses our minds together? Is it love?

There are many kinds of love—parent-child, sibling-sibling, lovers, husband-wife, partner-partner, friend-friend. The love that breeds the fusion of minds is love that melts boundaries between self and other, making identities overlap. Perhaps Leon Russell, the piano player and singer, had a sense of just where they overlap: "I love you in a place where there's no space and time," he crooned. Our interconnected minds may each wander along separately through ordinary space and time, but under the right conditions, often in times of great distress, the limits of space and time are breached and loving minds find each other again. Like many twins, we may come to accept these connections, this simulpathity, as part of ordinary reality. When we do, the hidden reality that supports these connections will become better known.

But why is it that only the negative, painful emotions are most likely to be acknowledged and received? Why is joy not shared at a distance in the same way? Maybe it is, but we don't notice it. If emotions are like the wind, a warm, gentle breeze is less likely to get our attention than a blast of cold air. It's these awful emotions surrounding dying or pain that drive us to move, rescue, or help. Joy experienced by a loved one makes us smile and feel content, happy to share the feeling, but painful emotions call out more loudly to do something.

Quantum physics provides a more speculative possibility. Think of a pair of electrons. As they circle around each other, each electron is itself spinning but in a direction opposite the other. Now separate these two electrons at a great distance. Although they are no longer circling each other, they continue to spin themselves. Change the spin of one electron and, instantaneously, the other electron will reverse its spin. The time for this change in the spin of the other electron is not limited by the speed of light. It's faster. It's instantaneous. The particles appear to be separate, but they act as if they are one. Physicists use the term "nonlocality," which means that the particles are actually connected despite their distance from each other. The electrons are "entangled." Are twins entangled like this? Was Altamar connected to her son like this? Was I connected to my father like this? Can we generalize from the extremely tiny world of electrons to our much larger human world? Quantum physicists are trying to develop theories and experiments to demonstrate that the principles governing the microscopic particles also apply to our macroscopic world.

Though we should be skeptical about the generalizability of quantum entanglement to the larger human world, to be skeptical about the truth of these simulpathity stories is not as easy. Some people view each story on its own and dismiss it. Others see a series of anecdotes as evidence—a reason for more systematic study. This happens frequently in the field of psychopharmacology, for example, which often proceeds from individual stories to new principles and treatments. We go from a single case study, to a case series, to a controlled trial, and then to several controlled trials. For example, while testing the supposed antituberculosis drug isoniazid in the 1950s, researchers noticed that tuberculosis patients given the new drug became happier than those given a placebo. Subsequent research studies on the drug resulted in a new antidepressant called iproniazid (which was similar in chemical structure to isoniazid). Iproniazid was pulled from the market because it caused liver damage, but the research led to other antidepressants with less severe side effects.

Other researchers who were testing a new antihypertensive drug were told by the men in the study that they were more easily able to have erections. The researchers formally tested the anecdotal reports and now we have Viagra and its cousins. So single cases, then strings of single cases, can and do lead to important new knowledge.

Twins, family members, friends, therapists, and patients are much more connected and entangled with one another than we have previously recognized. Some people will claim that these stories are romantic fabrications driven by a wish for ethereal energies, but the sheer volume of similar, heartfelt, amazing experiences argues otherwise.

These stories suggest that each of us is part of an intricate web of emotions that exists both inside and outside our bodies. Our participation in this matrix of feelings, which I call the psychosphere, depends on our time together and the degree of shared emotion. It could result from a relatively short time together with highly intense emotion or a long time together with modest emotion.

> *Each of us is part of an intricate web of emotions that exists both inside and outside our bodies. Our participation in this matrix of feelings, which I call the psychosphere, depends on our time together and the degree of shared emotion.*

And age does not seem to matter.

While serving in Italy in 1944, a soldier was knocked unconscious by shell splinters. "Back in Monmouth, England, that day," he wrote, "my wife was washing up after lunch. My daughter, aged 2½, to whom I was only a name, as she was born after I joined up, was playing with some bricks on the kitchen floor. She suddenly got to her feet, went over to my wife, and said, 'Daddy's been hurt' and went back to her bricks."[9]

The "how" of the experience needs further explanation. But the fact of these emotional currents connecting us at a distance is indisputable—and can be lifesaving. One of our research participants reported this story: "Last weekend I was waiting at a red light, and as it turned green, my cell phone rang. I looked down to answer the phone, thereby delaying my acceleration into the intersection. When I looked back up, a truck ran the red light through the intersection just where I would be if I'd started at the change of the light. This was meaningful because it was a call from my older brother with whom I hadn't spoken in months, and I've always felt like he was a protector of mine."

This extraordinary timing again looks like simulpathic sensitivity by a brother for a sister, which led to the phone call. A mere coincidence, some might say. Just random chance. Probability has to play a role, but something else is also at work.

Another study participant described how her brother once saved her life: "There was a very dark period in my late teens, a confused time, to say the least. I cannot explain the rationalization, or rather, I should state, there was none. I couldn't seem to withstand all of the suffering in the world . . . and one afternoon, I took my dad's gun, got in my car, and drove to an isolated place on the lake. The intention was to end my own life. I sat there, with gun in hand, without truly understanding why. . . . It was as if I didn't have any clue how I managed to arrive at this moment in time. But, as tears slowly came down my cheeks, I heard the sound of another car pulling up beside me . . . and my brother stepped out of the car, asking me to hand him the gun. I was breath-less; I was totally shocked. All I could do is to ask him how on Earth he knew I was feeling this way; how did he know I even had this gun, and, most important, how did he find me? He said he had no answers. He didn't have any idea why he got into his car; he didn't know where he was driving, nor why he was going there; or what he was supposed to do when he arrived."

How did her brother know that she needed him? What made him make these complex decisions without a conscious intention? He seemed drawn to his sister by her distress, without consciously know-ing that she was about to kill herself. Simulpathity coupled with an uncanny knowledge of where to go helped to save her from taking the next step.

My mathematically inclined colleagues would tell me these coinci-dences are examples of random chance at work. They would say that in large populations, many unlikely events like this have to happen. I wouldn't be able to argue with them because theirs is a fixed belief in the "laws of probability." But the timing of that call was too precise for randomness. The brother showing up just when he was needed calls for a better explanation. And there are too many coincidences like these to simply claim random chance. These coincidences sug-gest we live in a matrix of unbounded links to one another, especially those we love, especially those with whom intense emotion has forged a bond beyond our current understanding.

These connections between us exist. In themselves they are neither good nor bad. It depends on how we use

These coincidences suggest we live in a matrix of unbounded links to one another, especially those we love, especially those with whom intense emotion has forged a bond beyond our current understanding.

them. Sometimes they can also cause problems and need to be broken. But their value is demonstrated by their life-sustaining nature. I never knew how attached I was to my father until he died. I now have some idea about how attached I am to my children and to my wife, and it's far more than I ever thought. We must deeply respect the power of these connections.

These coincidences, as reflected in these meaningful resonances of feeling states between two people at a distance from each other, offer clues to new ideas about relationships. Many people write and talk about how everything is connected, how we are not separate from one another but are one. Simulpathity tells us about the variations in these connections and how it may play an unrecognized role in helping, separating from, or coming together with those we love, the subject of Chapter 2.

 THINK ABOUT YOUR LIFE HISTORY. When have you felt the pain of another at a distance from you? Has anyone let you know they have just tuned in to you? Has anyone ever shown up just when you needed without knowing why they had come?

CHAPTER 2

Finding Romance

Few of life's adventures compare to the thrill and adventure of romance. Songs and poems celebrate its wonder and its pain. Movies and novels are often spiced with tantalizing possibilities of love fulfilled and love lost. Although Hollywood endings and their fairy-tale counterparts usually conclude with "and they lived happily ever after," life often stands in stark contrast. The beginning of romance is usually energized with the most optimistic possibilities, much like the future that enthusiastic parents envision for their newborn babies.

Most of us hold that one true love in our imaginations. To find someone to match that imagined person inspires amazement and gratitude for one of life's most dramatic coincidences. Romantic love requires that each of the potential pair be together in space and time. The two have to see each other and feel the presence of the other. They need to be able to touch each other.

A common path to enduring relationships begins early in life. Perhaps the couple has been in the same social circles for years—high school, college, and work—and talk to each other regularly. Then one day one of them realizes that he/she is the other's best friend. Mutual commitment follows. They know each other organically, fundamentally, realistically.

The probability that two people will meet is directly related to the number of friends and acquaintances they share in common. Social researchers call this the *social proximity* effect—people looking for dates meet people through people they both know—friends and family.[1] Then after they meet, they can swap stories about the people they both know. They can get to know each other by knowing how they each relate to someone in common. And by being part of a shared social network, they are already in some sense compatible.

These days, face-to-face social networks are shrinking, largely because of the ever-evolving lure of Internet social networks. But the Internet has also provided a way to solve a problem it helped create—through online dating.

Dating sites on the Internet generate high volumes of potential contacts. Their TV ads show happy couples wrapped in warm music and sunshine, glowing with the delight of having found that perfect complement. But reality and academic research combine to puncture these beautiful images. Why? Because the lists of characteristics date seekers use to describe themselves are usually irrelevant to the necessary interpersonal chemistry—that special feeling that sets the stage for commitment.

To examine online dating, the *Washington Post* took on the persona of a matchmaker. In their popular section called Date Lab, they asked readers to send the newspaper information about themselves for a personal matching by the Date Lab staff. They asked many questions, sought photographs and bios, and used their algorithms and intuition to make matches. The lucky couple got a free dinner at an upscale restaurant, and each was asked to give a report right after the date. The reports were usually glowing—great match, much fun, good-looking, delightful evening, wonderful person. But the follow-up? They rarely saw each other again. Something was missing. Some "click" didn't happen—the click that generates an e-mail invitation and desire to accept. They've met, but in an artificial way.

The 2013 Pew Research Center reported that 5 percent of Americans who are in a marriage or committed relationship say they met their significant other online. During the years 2008–13, when Internet dating began surging in popularity, 12 percent of people in marriages or committed relationships met online. Despite the wealth of digital tools that allow people to search for potential partners, and even as one in ten Americans are now using one of the many online dating platforms, the vast majority of relationships still begin offline.[2]

Yet the two people did meet. Computer algorithm matching sometimes does work. How it works is more basic than the alluring photographs, the upbeat self-descriptions, and the promise of that perfect person. It offers more contacts and more intersections with other lives which increases the number of possible opportunities to meet that one special person for you.

Increasing Opportunity

"Speed dating" provides an increase in contacts and does so with face-to-face rather than webpage contacts. Speed dating focuses on meeting a lot of people in a short period of time. In contacts lasting several minutes, participants talk about whatever they choose. After each contact, the participants note whether or not they would like to meet this person again. A day or two later they are informed of matches and contact methods.

The key here is increasing opportunity. Spanish gypsies offered advice about how to find what you are seeking—"the dog that trots about finds a bone." Dating sites and speed dating offer the possibility of trotting about where there might be some bones.

In 2012, the *New York Times* profiled an ultrarich businessman named Edward Conard, who advocated an extremely rational approach to social networking: "Conard applies a relentless, mathematical logic to nearly everything, even finding a good spouse. He advocates, in utter seriousness, using demographic data to calculate the number of potential mates in your geographic area. Then, he says, you should set aside a bit of time for 'calibration'—dating as many people as you can so that you have a sense of what the marriage marketplace is like. Then you enter the selection phase, this time with the goal of picking a permanent mate. The first woman you date who is a better match than the best woman you met during the calibration phase is, therefore, the person you should marry. By statistical probability, she is as good a match as you're going to get."[3] Conard used this system himself, and while there is much to criticize in Conard's approach, it got him trotting about, much as going to parties, speed dating, and getting on websites do.

While at a local hospital for a cardiovascular screening exam, I struck up a conversation with the vascular lab technician. She led a very organized life—so organized that it strangled her marriage, and she soon found herself divorced and very lonely. She had one good woman friend she saw every day after work and regularly on the weekends. She felt very close to her, but this friend also wanted a man. In her very systematic way, the technician analyzed the online dating sites, evaluating them by their methods, cost, depth of questions, and online reviews. She selected one site. She then replied to the offers from men who seemed most suitable to her, only to find that each and every one wanted to have sex with her on the first or second date. She wanted more time to get to know them, to trust them, to feel comfortable with them. She would tell her friend the details of each disappointing date.

When her friend looked at some of the men the technician had selected, she saw one she found interesting. The friend made contact with this man, liked him, and began to spend all her free time with him and not with the technician. Within two months they were planning to be married. Not only did the organized technician not find a man online, but she also lost her best friend through her dating site.

The friend, who had been scouting for a partner as well, found a connection using her own social network in a unique way. The technician was forced to endure what so many friendships must endure— when the marriage partner appears, the old friendships begin to wither away. "Wedding bells put an end to that old gang of mine." It's often very sad for the friends left behind.

The technician lost contact with her friend. But their relationship didn't have to be this way. Had she made an effort to keep up with her friend and her new partner, he could've helped connect the technician with some of his single friends—expanding her range of possibilities of finding a partner. The technician simply had to open her eyes to this possibility. Peering over the technician's shoulder, the friend was alert to possibilities from a source she didn't create. It unfolded in front of her and she seized the moment. Luck favors the prepared mind.

Luck favors the prepared mind.

Increasing Randomness

Many of us are like the technician—enacting the same patterns day after day—going to the same stores, the same gym, the same paths, the same friends' houses, the same daily routine. There's comfort in routine. Children require organized lives. Adults relax in them. Routines create our comfort zone. But for the seeker of almost anything—a partner, ideas, job, self-understanding, wisdom, better health, friends—a leap into disorder, outside the comfort zone, offers new possibilities. In randomness, in chaos, even in crisis, there is opportunity.

A leap into disorder, outside the comfort zone, offers new possibilities. In randomness, in chaos, even in crisis, there is opportunity.

Breaking out of repeated routines and constricted social contacts opens the gate to randomness, to the unexpected, to adventure. Squire D. Rushnell, in his book *When God Winks on Love*, tells the story of Karen Gold, who led a dazzling New York life as a high-profile model and was sought after by the rich and famous of the highest-flying social circles.[4] She was also the divorced mother of two young children. She felt stuck. Wanting freedom, she jumped on a jet to Freeport in the Bahamas. After checking in to her hotel, she asked the taxi driver to take her to a quiet beach. She settled into the peace of the surf, the wind, and the hot sun. Then the loud roar of a dune buggy interrupted her quiet.

Franco Ferrandi was also living an ideal life as a maître d' of the luxurious Princess Hotel in the Bahamas. He worked in a beautiful setting that provided him the continuing opportunity to select an evening's date from the countless beautiful women who were attracted to this handsome, charming man. But, as with Karen, the wonder of his fairy-tale life was beginning to fade. On one of his days off, he hopped onto his dune buggy and headed down the beach.

That's when he saw Karen. He stopped to talk. She responded. Something clicked between them. She let him know she had small children. He welcomed the idea of small children in his life. That pleased her. More than three decades later, they have three grown children and live a fabled life together, with summers in Martha's Vineyard and winters in Palm Beach. Their romance started with each being drawn to the same deserted beach in Freeport in the Bahamas.

Karen had rushed off to a romantic island, a place more likely to attract people looking for partners for a few days, not a lifetime. She did something different by breaking out of her daily routine. She went to an island where love is in the air. She was ready for an enduring relationship. Franco, too, broke out of his routine at the right time. But he wasn't one of those tourists coming for a brief visit and quick romance. He was ready for someone special. And he seemed to know that someone on the beach was waiting for him. Their meeting looks like a date they had planned . . . the narrow time window, a specific place. It's as if he had said, "Meet me there at two or so," and she did. They seemed to know without knowing that they knew.

Psychotherapist Robert Hopcke wrote a bestseller called *There Are No Accidents*, in which he takes a Jungian perspective on coincidences.[5] He emphasizes the "acausal" nature of coincidences, or that there are no apparent causes. He focuses on the highly charged emotions associated with meaningful coincidences. The meaning embedded in the feeling becomes the "acausal connecting principle." The two elements of the coincidence—one in the mind and one in the surroundings—are also connected through the activation of an archetype that is associated with the intense feeling. Jung thought of archetypes as universal patterns, forms, or ideas that channel emotion and experience. The most common archetype is the idea of motherhood. Romance is another archetype.

Hopcke shared this romance story in his book: Pete and Mary first met at a hot tub party in Marin County, California. They were interested in each other but were also involved with other people. They exchanged first names and left the party. Mary managed to get Pete's address and phone number from the host of the party, and then left California for Texas with her boyfriend. Pete would see the party host on occasion and usually asked about the "hot tub" girl he had met, wanting to know when she might be available. But the host knew Pete wasn't really interested—he never committed to any woman. Mary kept Pete's phone number but never called him.

Years later Pete dutifully booked a flight from San Francisco to Las Vegas to attend his aunt's funeral. When he got to the airport, he discovered that all flights were grounded because of dense fog. Impulsively, he rented a car to drive the nine hours to Las Vegas. On the way he remembered that an old friend lived in the desert town of Mojave, so he decided he would visit him and stay overnight. Unfortunately, his friend wasn't home, so he checked into a local motel. At this point, he criticized himself for doing things so impulsively, not planning and never committing to anything. He realized that he needed to change that aspect about himself. As he walked into the motel office to register, he bumped into Mary, who was returning to San Francisco to find a place to live. She had broken up with her boyfriend because he refused to commit to their relationship.[6] Pete and Mary were both ready to commit to someone, and they did. How could this chance meeting have happened? They seem to have planned to meet without knowing it. We seem to have the ability to know things beyond our conventional senses.

Rushnell tells the story of Melanie Hohman, who seemed to have mysterious access to important information.[7] Her story begins with Ray Masterson rotting in prison after being caught high on drugs and robbing people in a parking lot with a toy gun. After a year of trying to be like the other prisoners, he prayed for a way out. He remembered his grandma Hattie threading her needles to create little flowered napkins. He remembered the University of Michigan football stadium, the games he watched, and their yellow and blue colors. He looked around and saw an inmate two cells down hanging a pair of striped socks up to dry—they were yellow and blue. A thought came to his mind: "the thief . . . steal no more . . . something useful with his hands . . ."

Using the prison sewing kit, he imitated Grandma Hattie by embroidering a blue and yellow "M." Soon the other inmates began giving him clothing to make other emblems for them—Harley logos, Puerto Rican flags, and other university and sports team emblems. After an older prisoner gave him a book about Impressionist paintings, Ray went on to create Bible scenes, Shakespeare scenes, and images inspired by songs and his own life. His sister, who lived in Albany, New York, two hours away, took some of Ray's artwork to art shows and shops. She sold some pieces. He was thrilled. He then prayed for a woman to enter his life.

One was about to do just that. After years of depression, despair, and alcoholism, Melanie Hohman, also living in Albany, tried to pull herself out of it by going to Alcoholics Anonymous (AA). There a woman befriended her who recognized her discomfort with being in the AA spotlight. The woman invited Melanie to her home to discuss the next steps. As Melanie entered her home, she recalled, "My eyes were drawn across the room to a small frame of art. It was so strange. Everything else seemed to melt away—the only thing I could see was that piece of art. I actually became physically dizzy as a result."

The kind woman was Ray's sister. Melanie began a correspondence with Ray, helped him sell his art, and visited him. Three years later they were married and had two children of their own, for a total of three (Melanie had one from a previous marriage).

Prayer can alter consciousness to create new states of mind from which creativity can flow. Ray's prayer for a way out of prison propelled him back into his past for clues to finding a way out. He remembered his grandmother and Michigan and then saw the socks. He experienced a creative coincidence where his thoughts met their mates in his surroundings. Rushnell believes that God provided Ray an answer to his prayer for a woman in his life. But from the details Rushnell provides, an additional possible explanation emerges. Ray's sister knew that he wanted a woman in his life. She found someone to bring home who could be a possibility. Melanie broke her routine—she had gone to an AA meeting—and took a chance on the hospitality of a stranger. Breaking out of patterns increases coincidences. Melanie then recognized—intuitively, viscerally—a compatible soul through Ray's artwork. She knew without knowing she knew. Because she, too, was ready to establish a relationship, she took the initiative to write to this man whose art had touched her so deeply.

Breaking out of patterns increases coincidences.

As a religious scientist, I believe psychological science attempts to understand the principles by which we use our God-given abilities to influence the way we, and others, live. I look first to personal responsibility—our own potential to know and to act.

Other romance stories are not all that different.

Jerry was lucky to meet Rita. In January 1970, he was flying back to Los Angeles after attending a memorial for his father at the college where his father had worked. He had delayed the return trip by a day to visit an old high school friend who was about to go to prison for a major protest against the Vietnam War. The flight was routed through Chicago. In six months his cardiology fellowship would be over, and he had no plans after that. Jerry's seat was on the aisle, and when passengers boarded the plane in Chicago, an attractive woman sat down in the window seat in his row; the seat in between them was empty. They introduced themselves, and Rita said that she was returning to Los Angeles from her widowed mother's wedding in Evanston, Illinois. Throughout the flight, they talked nonstop, but when they were landing, she declined his offer of a ride home, though they did trade phone numbers. Upon arrival, Rita gave him a good-bye hug and asked him to wait for her call; she was in the midst of a relationship that was ending, and she had to take care of it first. Rita's middle name was Theresa. Jerry's mother's name was Theresa. His father's girlfriend in Italy was named Rita. Growing up he had heard his father call any girl he found attractive a "Rita." Jerry thought these connections might be important but not enough to suggest that their relationship was meant to be. He had to know more about her. As she had said she would do, Rita broke up with her boyfriend and two weeks later called him. After a rocky beginning filled with romance and misunderstanding, Jerry found Rita to be a warm and loving person who seemed to really like him. She wanted to be with him. They were married in 1973.

How had Jerry and Rita "arranged" to meet in those assigned seats? For many years, Jerry thought his father had arranged it—that it was truly a marriage "made in heaven." Or perhaps the respectful acts of attending the memorial and visiting his high school friend had somehow contributed to their coming together, and that Jerry had decided to take the plane a day late to visit his high school friend. How had the seat selection been decided? Back then all you could ask for was an aisle or window seat. *What did they know that they didn't know they knew?*

Looking back, Jerry now believes that Rita and he had more to do with their meeting than they could ever imagine then. He was at a place in his life where he was open to possibilities: he was finishing his training, was now able to earn a good salary (which he had demanded of himself as a prerequisite to getting married), and could go almost anywhere and get a job. Rita was ready to leave an unsatisfying relationship. When Jerry and Rita met, their emotions were in a heightened state: each of them was returning from a major family event—commemorating his father's death and Rita's mother's second marriage. High emotions often open the gates to useful coincidences. They were in transition both literally—in a plane—and in life. Transitions open up new possibilities. They were ready and the events of their lives had set the emotional stage. But the same plane? The assigned seats? They were offered a choice, and they were aware enough to take it, but the mystery in the details still remains.

 HOW DID YOU MEET YOUR IMPORTANT PERSON OR PERSONS? How do you explain your meeting? Are conventional explanations enough or is there more? What is the "more" to you?

Instrumental Coincidences

How were the seats assigned? Probability, random chance? Or divine intervention? I choose to believe that our individual will makes a difference in these outcomes. That, in ways we are now beginning to understand, we help steer our lives without being consciously aware that we are doing so. Our need creates the coincidence. For this reason,

I call these types of coincidences "instrumental coincidences." These are the coincidences that are instrumental in helping us find people, solutions, useful information, and new possibilities.

The people in the preceding stories didn't consciously know who their future partners would be. But if we can find stories about people who had some conscious indication of a future loved one, that would lend support to the idea that many more people really *do* know who they will meet but don't consciously know that they know.

Joseph Jaworski has such a story. He was running to catch a plane at Chicago's O'Hare airport when he noticed a "very beautiful" young woman walking toward him. As she passed him, he stopped and looked into her eyes, which were "absolutely gorgeous." He was certain he knew her. At that moment, he saw his future life with her. He ran after her and caught up with her. As she was about to hand her Dallas-bound ticket to the agent, he pulled her back and insisted they talk right then.

"Are you married?" he asked.

"No" she replied. "Are you?"

"Of course not," he said.

He told her that he felt that they'd met before, although he knew they hadn't. He insisted that she give him her name and telephone number. Without hesitation, she did. Jaworski later wrote about meeting Mavis. "In her presence, I felt this warmth. When my eyes met hers, it was a spiritual thing. When I ran after her, it was as if nothing else mattered. I can hardly describe any of this. It is very mysterious. But it feels like love."

They were married within the year. The rest of their life together is described in Jaworski's book *Synchronicity: The Inner Path of Leadership*. Love at first sight. He knew, and she, too, seemed to know—right then.[8]

SOME COINCIDENCE OPPORTUNITIES NEED TO BE SEIZED NOW! Have you acted quickly with a person, idea, or thing? Has someone seized you during a coincidence?

Do some people consciously know beforehand? Can some of us envision the romantic partner of our future? To do so would be an ultimate form of romantic coincidence: a consciously held mind image finds its partner in the world.

Julia Altamar told me how she knew the man she would marry:

> It was a dream, very vivid . . . and in the dream I met a man with salt-and-pepper hair, handsome, and several years my senior. I described him in great detail to my mom the next day and told her that I would marry this person, but I didn't know him. Also in the dream, my mother and I decided to refinish the downstairs of her house so I could live there, which would assist her in many ways. Two weeks later, I met the man I'd dreamed about. He looked identical to the person in my dream. He asked where I lived, and I told him, and I in turn asked the same question of him, yet, prior to his answering, I announced, "I know," and said the street name, the actual apartment complex name, the building number, and the apartment number. He didn't say a word and just stood there. I was amazed that I'd told a complete stranger something so absurd, and I immediately began apologizing and laughing, saying not only how sorry I was, but that I also had no idea, whatsoever, where he lived, nor did I know why I'd made this statement to him. By this time, still without uttering a single word, he had his billfold in hand and was removing his driver's license and placing it in my hand. At this point, nothing could be said. His address was exactly as I'd told him. We were caught in the wonder of this moment. Two months later, we were married, and within the following year, we had refinished the downstairs of my mom's home and moved in.

Altamar explained the origins of this relationship:

> I would have to say that in my world, when you dream something such as this
> and see it come to be in such a way, it is as if it is more destiny (or it has already
> happened) than intelligence. At that time there was no one else in my life and my
> son was still young; his son lived with him as well. The attraction was there from
> the beginning, and before you could hardly blink, we were married. It was as if
> we had known each other for a long time, even though we hadn't, and as it was,
> the marriage was good for both of us at the time, and for the time—something
> that was meant to be for whatever reason. And right or wrong, much of my life
> has existed in this mode.

The marriage ended several years later. Marriages may begin with
predictive dreams or strange coincidences, but they must be maintained
through trust, commitment, caring, and consistency. Coincidences open
doors, encourage possibilities, and link us to grander connections. Yet
in the house of marriage, each of us makes decisions to keep the relationship flourishing. Marriage for Altamar and this man seemed to help
both of them for a while, but then they were no longer good for each
other. They had to separate and go their own ways. Many relationships
are temporary aids in our journeys through life.

Some would argue that this conscious vision of her future was not
the "real deal" because the marriage did not last forever. Destiny does
not necessarily seal relationships to the ideal of departing at death.
To Altamar, who later remarried, this short marriage aided her in her
life's journey.

If Jaworski could instantly recognize the woman in his future and
Altamar could see the image of a man in her future, then others might
also know who is coming into their lives but not be aware that they

know. So much depends upon whether you can trust your subconscious for information about the future. Altamar could trust her intuition because previous experiences had told her that she could know things in ways that seem unbelievable to most scientists. Much conventional scientific thinking lags behind the general population in accepting these other ways of knowing.

Confirming Commitment

Commitment to a long-term relationship can be frightening. The uncertainty leads many people to use coincidences to support their romantic decisions.

Rushnell tells the story of Christopher and Marion, who felt the desire to be together, but because of recent, painful divorces, both of them were very cautious about another deepening relationship. Besides, Christopher lived in San Francisco and Marion lived in Youngstown, Ohio. How could they manage work and family obligations and be together? Their feelings seemed to be pulling them toward marriage, but was it the right thing to do? Were they simply trying to escape from loneliness and put the pain of divorce more quickly behind them? Christopher jokingly said that they needed a sign.

For some reason, Christopher found himself standing trancelike, looking at a bookshelf in his home, and came to focus his attention on one book: *The Nature of Love* by Kahlil Gibran, author of the internationally known book *The Prophet*. When he randomly opened the book, he read these words: "Give your hearts, but not into each other's keeping, for only the hand of Life can contain your hearts." To him this meant they must jointly commit to God while giving their hearts to each other.

He called Marion and read the lines aloud to her. She became silent for a while and then said, "Christopher, you're not going to believe this. I am, right now, holding the same book in my lap, and the only part of the book I have read is the part that you have just read to me!"[9]

They were looking for a sign and found it. The circumstances of this useful coincidence included several of the usual qualities—searching for something, high emotion, and transition, each of which seem to help create coincidences. Also, Christopher reported that he stood "'trancelike' in front of the bookshelf" for no particular reason. He had entered an altered state of mind. Altered states of mind seem to both increase the recognition of coincidences and help to create them. Then he "randomly" opened the book, an action that also helps produce coincidences.

Altered states of mind seem to both increase the recognition of coincidences and help to create them.

The timing and similarity of the experience between Christopher and Marion seems like a form of simulpathity—experiencing the same feeling at a distance without knowing it. While it is easy to think that this is a mystery and move on, this coincidence could be thought of in this way: two people afraid of commitment needed some external validation of their decision. Like the people meeting in the motel in the Mojave Desert, they arranged to read the same passage from the same book at the same time without knowing it. They could then surprise themselves with this sign, which they seemed to have created, and then use it to do just what they wanted to do—get married.

And so they did. The simultaneous reading showed each of them how closely connected they actually were. But the story does not end there. Three weeks later in a small church in Westminster, Pennsylvania, without rehearsal, the ceremony began. As part of the ceremony the pastor had, on his own, selected the same passage from Kahlil Gibran!

How did that happen? They never asked the pastor why he'd decided to use this passage; each of them had assumed the other had asked the pastor to read it. This coincidence is harder to explain. The pastor's independent decision to read the same passage even further confirmed their decision to marry. Somehow he had registered the importance of this passage to the couple.

How a meaningful coincidence helped confirm a marriage decision is described in a story from *Small Miracles* by Yitta Halberstam and Judith Leventhal.[10] Carol's husband Ralph had died at age thirty-five, and Bob's wife had been killed in an auto accident. After many lonely years, they met and married, each deeply appreciative of the other. They differed on how to deal with the past—Bob wanted to talk about it and Carol wanted to forget it. For ten years Carol won out until she decided it was time to remember her husband Ralph and learn about Bob's wife. She pulled out photos from her honeymoon, some of which were taken on their trip to Lourdes. Bob and his first wife had also gone to Lourdes. As they were looking through the photos together, Bob suddenly stopped their photo journey. He was staring at a picture of Carol and Ralph—and the couple behind them. In the picture it looked as if the couple in the background were posing with Carol and Ralph. That couple was Bob and his first wife.

For Bob and Carol, this evidence that they had been at the same place at the same time further strengthened their belief that they were meant to be together. Without the amazing timing of the camera's shutter click, their paths crossing would've been lost. The two couples were together in time and space and photo positioning, all without apparent planning. Perhaps Carol and Bob had been drawn together at Lourdes, a place of holy healing, because each knew something about their futures that they didn't know they knew at the time. But they now know even more that they were meant to be together: they had visible evidence.

The next story, which comes from one of our research participants, illustrates how coincidences can be used to support a decision when other realities may be pointing in the opposite direction. "Right after my grandmother died, my boyfriend and I were driving home. Right when we got out of the car, 'our' (my grandmother's and my) song came on. I truly believe my grandmother was telling me that she really liked my boyfriend. That meant a lot because she knew that my parents were not very fond of him."

This briefly told coincidence of the timely appearance of the favorite song she shared with her grandmother strengthened her belief in the relationship with her boyfriend. We don't know what happened to this relationship. The ambiguity remains. Perhaps her parents were right, perhaps not. She took what she wanted from the coincidence. Would her grandmother actually have approved? Care needs to be taken in coincidence interpretation. Most writers of coincidence stories emphasize their positive effect on the people who experience them. But her use of this coincidence could've turned out negatively. She may have taken the song as a sign because it quelled doubts that she herself was having. Coincidences can offer possibilities, not certainties. The responsibility for interpreting coincidences falls on us.

Coincidences can offer possibilities, not certainties. The responsibility for interpreting coincidences falls on us.

That people subconsciously create coincidences to help confirm romantic decisions may be obvious to an outside observer but not to the woman in the next story, who was also one of our research participants. "When I was widowed, I looked back at the previous week and saw many meaningful coincidences leading up to that point. For example, my husband's birthday was on a Wednesday, the day of his car accident. He passed away the next day. When I began dating again, I was concerned with what my late husband would think. One day while visiting his grave, I accidentally cut my ring finger with some grass clippers. I had to go to the Emergency Department, where they removed my wedding ring. My boyfriend and I took it as a sort of sign that it was okay to proceed in our relationship."

She had cut her own finger! Yet she felt the necessary removal of the ring at the hospital was a sign from her husband. Many other romance stories suggest to us that the people involved are directly creating their own coincidences while not being aware of doing so.

 WHEN HAS A COINCIDENCE SEEMED TO INDICATE THAT you should commit yourself to someone, to trust in the future with someone? You may need to learn that coincidences only deserve a seat at the table of your romance—they don't deserve to be the decider-in-chief.

TRY TO DETECT THOSE COINCIDENCES you have subconsciously created.

Love Triangles

Love sometimes blossoms under the tension of the impossible. Perhaps Freud and his followers were right about the Oedipal conflict and the Electra conflict—little boys and little girls compete for the love of one parent against the other parent, and these conflicts play out in adult life. These high-intensity, triangular relationships can evoke some strange and problematic coincidences.

Love sometimes blossoms under the tension of the impossible.

The 1942 Academy Award–winning movie *Casablanca* revolved around a love triangle and a dramatic coincidence. When nightclub owner Rick (played by Humphrey Bogart) heard a song that was linked to his broken romance, he looked up and saw his lost love with her husband. Says Rick, "Of all the gin joints, in all the towns, in all the world, she walks into mine." With that coincidence, the plot thickens.

It doesn't just happen in the movies. A surgeon ducked into my office one day with a very worried look on his face. "I am a married man," he said. "I love my children and my wife. But a coincidence appeared to me, and I took it as an opportunity, much to the possible pain of my family. My wife and I had a terrible fight right before I left town. She made it clear to me that she was glad I was going. She told me not to bother calling her. During the conference I sat in a restaurant sipping a drink, feeling sorry for myself and feeling very lonely, when in walked my high school girlfriend. I hadn't seen her in years and not heard from her. All I knew was that she lived in another town hundreds of miles from this one. What was she doing here? She was going to another conference! I had been thinking about her more frequently recently, and she told me that she had been thinking about me. We had a few drinks and you can guess the rest. I am hoping that by telling you this, I will stop this from going any further."

This looks to me like another date arranged between two people who wanted to be together but knew that they should not be arranging it at all. By interpreting their coming together as unintentional, they could convince themselves that the "coincidence" somehow gave them license for their behavior. They didn't have to take responsibility for meeting because "serendipity" arranged it. To take full responsibility for helping to create this illicit union might be terrifying (Am I really that unhappy with my spouse? Do I have that level of power?).

But the surgeon did know that he was responsible for what had happened—or didn't happen—next. I don't know what he ultimately decided, but hopefully he did the right thing for his family and himself.

Some coincidences offer temptations that need to be resisted for ethical, moral, and family reasons.

As this story illustrates, some coincidences offer temptations that need to be resisted for ethical, moral, and family reasons. By taking this opportunity toward what appeared to him to be a logical conclusion—an affair—he would create major difficulties for his family. Was he prepared for the turbulent consequences? This is a perfect illustration of how careful we need to be when interpreting coincidences. Just because we have a serendipitous moment doesn't mean we always have to act upon it. We need to wisely decide the purpose of its meaning.

The usefulness of some coincidences can be difficult to untangle. One of my patients, whom I'll call Odette, knew of my interest in coincidences and asked me to help her figure out one that involved her boyfriend, Morris. "I was leaving your office yesterday," she said, "and returned a phone call from Morris that I had received while we were in session. Morris told me that he had been to the bank to deposit a check, and that as he was leaving he looked at his deposit slip and noticed something was wrong. He went back to the teller and realized that he had reversed two of the numbers in the middle of the account number by accident and deposited the check into someone else's account. It turned out that the account that he deposited it into was his ex-wife's account. What are the chances of that? He got the mistake corrected, but he was a little thrown off by it. And to be honest, I'm weirded out by it, too, because I believe that those sorts of coincidences carry some significance. I can't figure out what it means, but it's too big of a coincidence to not mean something. I wonder if subconsciously he accessed her account because she is still on his mind. That's the only thing I can think of."

"Too big of a coincidence to not mean something," Odette said. The feeling that Odette articulates compels many of us to search for meaning. This wasn't Odette's coincidence though. It was her boyfriend's. Morris dismissed it as just a mistake. He didn't want to go down Odette's jealousy path because he knew that in some way he still wanted to give to his ex-wife. But that didn't necessarily mean, as Odette thought, that he wanted to get back with her. The coincidence served to help Odette "own" her intense jealousy and work with me to resolve it. However, later, Odette came to understand that this coincidence fit too well into Morris's pattern of being distracted by other women to ignore it. Eventually she left him after he became involved with yet another woman. The coincidence helped her to more clearly accept Morris's inability to commit.

THINK ABOUT A TIME WHEN someone else's coincidence affected you.

Since the telephone is an essential medium of human communication, it's no surprise that it should sometimes provide a coincidence connection in love triangles. Hopcke tells the story of Yvonne and Gert.[11] During a difficult time in her marriage, Yvonne began a friendship with Gert, a fellow teacher in her school who was also in a committed relationship. Their attraction to each other grew, but they were determined to keep the relationship nonsexual. They began to meet regularly in Gert's office, which was more private than Yvonne's. Many times when Yvonne's husband called her at school, the switchboard operators mistakenly put the call through to Gert. (Then again, perhaps the switchboard operators knew she was in Gert's office.) In this way, through a dozen or so "wrong numbers," the two men developed a relationship with each other. To Yvonne, these apparent accidental calls from her husband to Gert accelerated her decision to enter an even more intimate life with Gert. She viewed the crossed lines as a crossroads and decided to take a new path. Her merely platonic relationship with Gert became a memory.

One evening they decided to find an out-of-the-way restaurant for a quiet dinner where no one they knew was likely to appear. They didn't know that Yvonne's husband and some colleagues had impulsively decided to eat at this very same out-of-the-way restaurant on that same night. They missed running into each other by only a few minutes. Yvonne learned about the near-coincidence the next day. A narrow time window allowed Yvonne and Gert to avoid public discovery. But this possible embarrassment accelerated their decision to make their relationship public, which they did.

Yvonne's husband had impulsively decided to go to that restaurant. These intuitive, nonrational acts are motivated from some part of our minds. He knew, but didn't know that he knew, that Yvonne and Gert had planned to have dinner there, too. Perhaps his decision to eat at the same out-of-the-way restaurant emerged in his conscious mind as a way to accelerate the inevitable divorce.

The path of true (and not so true) love can run on some twisted paths that are very difficult to explain. The next story comes from a participant in our Weird Coincidence Survey: "My boyfriend was cheating on me with this girl named Ashley. A couple of days after I found out about her, somehow my phone line and her phone line got crossed, and every time someone tried to call my cell phone, it went to her cell phone. It was so weird that it was the girl my boyfriend had cheated on me with and not anyone else."

Had the boyfriend somehow engineered the switch? I couldn't find a way to do it, but that doesn't mean he didn't manage the trick. Nevertheless, the message was clear. The boyfriend's affection was no longer going to his old girlfriend but to his new girlfriend—as were all his phone calls. The diversion of the phone calls mirrored the diversion of her boyfriend's affection. In ways we are just beginning to understand, perhaps the intense emotion of the betrayal activated a switch in cell phone connectivity. Yes, that does sound impossible. Or is it? We could argue that out of all the phones in the world, sometimes phone numbers are accidentally mixed up. But the phone line switch took place shortly after she found out about the new girlfriend, so the timing suggests a cause. Intense emotion may have contributed.

Then again, maybe someone other than the betrayed girlfriend could've gotten the betrayed one's cell phone, punched in a forwarding code, and put in the number of the new girlfriend. The most likely culprit would be the old boyfriend, but what is the likelihood that he would do such a thing? Skepticism provides good company for us on this journey through coincidences. It helps to sharpen our thinking. Perhaps the old boyfriend had his reasons.

How Romance Coincidences Are Created

These stories tell us that we know things that we don't know we know. This conclusion extends our understanding of our subconscious and unconscious minds. Freud introduced us to our personal unconscious with enlightening observations about dreams, slips of the tongue, and neurotic behavior. These events have meanings and intentions that people didn't appreciate until they reflected back on them. The Freudian unconscious holds a storehouse of early upbringing experiences that play out in adult life. Before Freud, few people considered the possibility that in adulthood we repeat patterns established in childhood. Now this idea is well established.

Jung, as a onetime student of Freud, expanded his teacher's concept of a personal unconscious by proposing the existence of an unconscious that is shared by all of us. This collective unconscious contains fundamental symbols common to all human beings. Jung called these fundamental symbols archetypes, some of which include Mother, Father, Romance, Marriage, and Death. He believed that during meaningful coincidences, archetypes are activated. He also believed that meaningful coincidences, or synchronicities, provided evidence for the existence of the collective unconscious.

Many romantic coincidences point to a layer of the unconscious that lies between the Freudian personal and Jungian collective unconscious. Like the personal and the collective, this intermediate unconscious contains useful knowledge about us. It shares with the personal unconscious information about how to better understand our own abilities to function in our relationships with those we love and others. Simulpathity abilities lie in this intermediate unconscious, which shares with the collective unconscious information about how we are connected to the people and environment around us by its potential to help guide us to what we need. Just as the repetition of childhood patterns into adulthood had been ignored before Freud, the functioning of this intermediate unconscious has also been ignored. We are closer than ever to recognizing its usefulness.

What do the romance stories teach us about the functioning of this intermediate unconscious?

1. Like other layers of the unconscious, it tells us that we know things we don't know we know. We may be able to know who we will meet as well as how to meet that person.

2. For romantic (and, as you will see, other) coincidences to occur, emotion is usually involved, as well as some kind of need. The need is usually accompanied by a sense, perhaps a vision, of what is needed.

3. The person must be actively going about their world trying to make the needed person, thing, or idea appear.

4. The person often enters an altered state of consciousness. Usually an altered state of consciousness implies a mind change caused by a drug, hypnosis, or dreaming, but it also includes more subtle changes in consciousness. An altered state of consciousness increases access to this intermediate unconscious. Going on a vacation; stopping at a strange hotel in the desert; going to a graveyard, a party, or to a friendly stranger's home—stepping out of our regular routine, in other words— breaks our everyday perceptual filter, that standard way we think about ourselves, and opens our minds to new ways of connecting to people and the environment. In that altered state, like Christopher in San Francisco standing in front of a bookcase, we do something for no reason, something that helps to create the coincidence between the need and its fulfillment. This action without conscious intention is a direct result of knowing something we don't know we know.

5. Alertness and quick response may be required. The opportunity may present itself in a narrow window of time. Joseph Jaworski in the airport dramatically seized the moment and the woman of his dreams. He acted without knowing why.

Expecting the unexpected makes coincidences a regular part of daily life.

Those who know that useful coincidences commonly occur come to expect them as part of daily life. The rational mind learns to anticipate and accept the once unexpected. Expecting the unexpected makes coincidences a regular part of daily life.

CHAPTER 3

Family Ties

Families form a fundamental role in all societies. The family not only feeds and houses children but also teaches them how to behave socially, primarily by parental modeling. The child's fundamental need for love, security, and sustenance, and the parental need to love and nurture, creates our most emotionally charged human relationships.

Coincidences occur among and between family members because of the high emotional charge that family membership generates. Mothers and children, fathers and children, husbands and wives are deeply connected to each other through the friction of conflict, as well as through common experiences, altruistic sacrifice, and love. Within the human family, the idea of mother, father, sister, brother, son, and daughter reverberates with ancient feelings.

In addition to high emotion within them, families go through transitions—the life cycle events that include birth, coming-of-age rituals, marriage, and death. Within each of these events lies opportunities for coincidences because of their high emotional charge *and* because they hurl people into major transitions. Many less predictable events also rock families (sickness, divorce, handicaps, and accidents) while others boost family pleasure (vacations, holidays, and visits with close relatives and friends). All such events are breeding grounds for coincidences.

Transitions destabilize our everyday routines; they "de-automatize" our thinking by breaking automatic responses and introducing novelty into our lives. With suspension of our usual ways of looking at ourselves and the world around us, we see with new eyes and fresh perspectives, making us more likely to notice the things, situations, and people around us. With the sense of wonder and curiosity built into us from childhood, transitions enable us to more readily connect the patterns around us with the patterns in our minds.

Parents and Their Children

Mothers just seem to know things about their children. Sometimes this knowledge is extraordinary. The mother of six-year-old Ruth went into town to shop, when she suddenly had the feeling that she must return home. "Where's Ruth?" she demanded of the babysitter. "She's at Ann's." Ann was her six-year-old playmate. The mother rushed over to Ann's house, but Ann's mother thought she was at Ruth's! On auto-pilot, Ruth's mother drove down the street, over the railroad track, parked, ran through a gate, up a little hill, and down to an old quarry now filled with water. There at the edge sat both children with their shoes off ready to go wading. Had they stepped into the water, they likely would've drowned because the sides of that old quarry were very deep. Ruth's mother acted upon, and was guided by, some instinct that she couldn't explain.[1]

Ruth's mother not only knew her daughter was in danger but also where to find her. She moved automatically as if guided by something external to her. I believe she had a kind of map of the territory with her daughter in the center of it and a route to find her way. Here was the power of need in transition once again. Ruth's mother knew that her daughter was in trouble, felt it in some form of resonating need, and, like a bird heading for its summer nesting grounds, went right to her.

A telephone call at just the right time can connect parent and child.

In a PhD dissertation, Mark Cameron described Kelly, a twenty-eight-year-old member of Alcoholics Anonymous. She was struggling with a great deal of anger and resentment focused on her father, an active alcoholic with whom she had been living from the age of ten. They were now estranged. She described their relationship as one of emotional turmoil and "dysfunctional." One day, as she was reading Alcoholics Anonymous *Big Book*, she came across a passage that described alcoholics as sick people who, like a cancer patient or someone suffering from another serious medical illness, should not be treated with disdain and resentment. She suddenly had a "revelation" about her father and felt her anger and resentment melt into empathy and concern. She realized how he was suffering and was ill from his alcoholism, just as she had been suffering from the same illness: "I felt like all those feelings that I carried around about my dad were gone. I guess I see this now as God removing my resentments." She suddenly "felt a sense of peace." As she pondered these new feelings and perceptions, her cell phone rang; it was her father calling. The two had been so alienated that she didn't even think he knew her phone number. Surprisingly, he confessed to her how important she had been in his life, how sorry he was, how he cared about her and would do anything to help her. He wept as he spoke openly about their troubled relationship. Kelly later told the interviewer that the coincidence of her father calling just at the moment when her heart was opening up struck her as "amazing."[2] Simulpathity in action!

Although they were estranged from each other, they were still connected to each other by those remarkable bonds we first saw in the earlier simulpathity stories. Through those subterranean tunnels, subconscious webs, and strange warps in time and space, Kelly's father felt her readiness to hear from him, and, without knowing why, he contacted her when she was most open to embrace him.

Fathers are increasingly learning and accepting their important role in raising children. We offer our children not only financial support and a knowledge of how to do things but we also provide emotional support simply by being with them. Sometimes, as in the following story, fathers need help to be fathers.

Caught in the throes of a problematic marriage, author Robert Perry had begun to neglect his thirteen-year-old son Adam. Feeling a little guilty, he took Adam to a local football field to throw a Frisbee. After a while, Adam decided to just lie down, so Robert played the game of trying to throw the Frisbee to land on Adam. His inability to engage Adam made Robert feel that he was inadequate as a father.

Later that evening Robert was watching an episode of the cartoon series *The Simpsons* in which Krusty the Clown (a combination of entertainer and disgusting old man) discovered he had a daughter. She begs him to play Frisbee with her down at the beach. After a while, Krusty just lies down and asks his daughter to try to hit him with it. Krusty then realizes he is not a good father and, glancing at Homer Simpson playing with his children, decides to ask Homer to help him become a better father.[3]

The cartoon story mirrored Robert's failures as a father. One of the two participants in each story stopped playing and required the other one to do all the work of playing. Although it was Adam who hit the ground in real life and it was Krusty in the cartoon, Robert could see himself as the lazy one. Both men felt inadequate as fathers. Like Krusty, Robert needed help to become a better father. Television, movies, songs, and novels are based on stories about people—and not just any stories. These tales, both fluffy and enduring, often reflect ongoing patterns of people navigating through life. As the great movie director Alfred Hitchcock once said, "Movies are like real life with the boring parts taken out."

Media stories can become mirrors for our lives. The most enduring stories stay with us over the years because their messages have become timeless commentaries on human foibles, pretensions, inadequacies, and needs. As Krusty the Clown, the inadequate father, did for Robert, these media commentaries can help us to change for the better. How did Robert find himself in front of his television set on this particular channel? He believes that complex coincidences like this are signs of God's beneficent intentions.

 THINK OF AN EXAMPLE IN YOUR LIFE when a scene in a movie or on a TV series reflected a problem in your life and offered a possible solution.

Spousal Relationships

Coincidences also demonstrate the special resonance that exists between husband and wife. In a case described by Sally Rhine Feather in her book *The Gift*, retired judge Stanley Peele was struggling in law school to come up with a court case that provided a precedent for a particular problem. The specific question was, "What is the name of the case that controls a boundary dispute with a squatter?" It was 11:30 PM, and his wife, Carolyn, was asleep in their bed. He was sitting in the corner of the bedroom, surrounded by papers, when he softly whispered this specific question. Suddenly, Carolyn sat up in bed and in a very clear and confident voice said, "Housten and Gallagher, 1927." When he asked her how she knew, she answered with a snore. She was sound asleep. He looked up the case. She was right.[4]

Now how did that happen? My skeptical friends will claim that he answered himself and had become so tired that he thought Carolyn had answered instead of him. If we are to believe Stanley's story, then Carolyn had somehow accessed information in a way that we don't ordinarily think people do. She was in an altered mental state (sleeping), and her husband had a great need, which she seemed to have felt. These two ingredients helped her find what he needed.

Stanley and Carolyn show us how two minds can interlace with each other. Living together, being together, and loving together seems to fuse us into partially overlapping beings. These coincidences open us up to accepting how we are not as separate as we think. These mergers of minds signal our enjoyable closeness.

In the next story, a woman named Janine, a friend of a friend of mine, had a difficult marital problem. She was confronted with a problem she had been ignoring. An instrumental coincidence jolted her into realizing how far apart she had grown from her husband.

At age forty-six, Janine was flying high. As the vice president for finance at a major international company, she was earning a six-figure income, deeply respected for her shrewd understanding of numbers and company politics, and an often-sought-after advisor. Her job took her to major cities on four continents, always first class, usually followed by successful business outcomes. Yet, something was gnawing at her. Her daughter and son, soon to be teenagers, were growing up so fast she hardly knew them. Her very patient husband looked sadder and sadder each time she packed her suitcase. But she shrugged off the feeling and refocused on the company balance sheet and her next major business meeting.

On a busy day at Chicago's O'Hare airport, she ran to get into the first class boarding line, got out her ticket, and handed it to the agent. When she looked up, she saw her husband coming off another plane through a nearby gate. She tried to call to him, but he didn't hear her. She hadn't known he was traveling. Puzzled, she thought of the image of two ships passing in the night. She and her husband hardly knew each other anymore. The coincidence shocked her into thinking about their family. The ache she had suppressed now became more obvious. She missed her children and him. She couldn't do this corporate adventure anymore.

So she quit her job and started a nonprofit organization in her home city to help people develop skills that would make them more employable. She dismissed the full-time nanny and housekeeper, taking over as the wife and mother of her home. Her political and financial abilities helped the nonprofit thrive.

This airport coincidence evoked and clarified the feeling that she was ignoring. Coincidences like this one resemble the clarifying statements I use with my psychotherapy patients. In her description of her marriage, I could've easily confronted her with an apt metaphor for their lives—two ships passing in the night, going in opposite directions. She saw her marriage in this way and acted to change it for the better. Here again are the markers that seem to increase coincidences—she was in transition (boarding a plane), a situation that puts us in a state of mind different from the usual. Yes, she traveled regularly, but boarding and deplaning are each transitions, just as going to lunch or coming home at a different time or by a different way are slight variations in daily routines. She was also carrying around a heavy emotion, an empty feeling with no clear name. When transition is coupled with strong emotion and need, the stage is set for a meaningful coincidence. I'm willing to guess that the two of them subconsciously arranged to pass each other to demonstrate what they were doing to their marriage and their family. Like two dancers moving across a room, gyrating alone to the rhythm of their song, their emotional bond twirled them back together in an embrace. I'm guessing that if I could talk with Janine, she'd be able to explain how she choreographed this dance. Somehow she knew when her husband was arriving but "forgot."

When transition is coupled with strong emotion and need, the stage is set for a meaningful coincidence.

Relationships are characterized by repeated patterns of communication. Sometimes these patterns need to be examined and changed. Coincidences can reflect these patterns back to us. Just as a mirror can visually suggest to us that we need to get a haircut or lose weight, coincidences can usefully mirror our psyches.

Just as a mirror can visually suggest to us that we need to get a haircut or lose weight, coincidences can usefully mirror our psyches.

My patient Bart was heading for divorce. He and his wife kept arguing. She talked too much. She was too ready to offer advice and not hear the advice he offered. Their last child was about to leave home. Couples therapy did little good. As the idea of divorce percolated in his mind, Bart went to the local mall and saw five friends and acquaintances, each of whom just happened to be in the midst of divorce. Several weeks later he independently heard from three old friends, each of whom were divorced. This series of other people divorcing made him realize: *I don't want to be one of them.*

Was it just because he was thinking about divorce that he noticed all the divorcing men? Skeptics easily and correctly suggest that if you are looking for yellow Honda Accords, you will see them. If it is on your mind, you will notice. Yet, five divorcing men appearing in one outing? Three divorced old friends calling within a short period of time? The message pounded home. Without looking, he wouldn't have seen them. He had positioned himself to find this series of divorces. They were out there and he found a way to experience them live, in 3-D reality. Like Janine, he found in his environment a reflection of his conflict. I call it counseling by coincidence.

Encountering the series of divorced men led Bart to recommit to maintaining his own marriage. When he and his wife left town, they were better partners than ever before, though they still had much work to do with each other.

Divorce doesn't necessarily end ongoing contact between ex-spouses. Coincidences can continue to play a role in settling child custody conflicts. A divorced man in our research study was trying to gain custody of his daughter: "I was taking my ex-wife back to court to gain custody of my daughter (as per my daughter's wishes). I have addiction issues and, of course, my ex made sure the court was well aware of them and used them as the main argument to prevent me from gaining custody. Coincidently, my twelve-step group in Arkansas selected me to represent them at the fellowship-wide annual business meeting that happened to be in the same county in California and at the same time as the custody hearing. This provided me transportation and lodging for the custody hearing and demonstrated to the court that I was making good progress in my recovery. I was awarded custody."

Was the timing and location of the annual twelve-step business meeting and the custody hearing just another turn on life's roulette wheel where he won (and his ex-wife lost)? What was his role in creating this opportunity? He did his part by working his way up his local twelve-step program. His preparation helped to create this opportunity. His daughter's desire could only help create this coincidence. Right action can help to create the timing and placement for desired coincidences to take place.

More Transitions

When a woman is considering having a baby, coincidences can help make that very important decision. As told by author Jean Bolen, a therapist had reached the time in her life when she needed to decide to have a baby or not. She loved her work with patients and enjoyed the financial independence from her husband, but she yearned to realize her youthful potential in art. She had begun painting again, enough to rekindle her love for it, and she was ready to have a baby, though she didn't want to give up her professional life and financial independence.

While attending an all-day symposium, she happened to sit next to a colleague she hadn't seen in many years. Over lunch she heard how her colleague had left her profession of six years to be a nonworking, at-home mother. She had become an avid gardener, learned to bake bread, and had become a potter. Now she was back in her professional role and doing volunteer teaching at a medical school.

The therapist found herself responding with joy and a feeling of liberation from her immobilizing conflict. She left the meeting early, lured her husband home, threw away her contraceptives, and aimed to become pregnant.[5]

This therapist had left her usual routine by going to a conference. She happened to sit down next to someone who provided the synchronicity she needed—a reflection of her current state and a suggestion about how it could play out. She felt an intense emotion that drove her to use the coincidence to finally decide what she should do. How she found the "right" place to sit could again be called random, divine guidance, or her own sense that this seat in the audience was most likely to be of help to her. Here is more evidence for a person's ability to find his or her helpful place in homing pigeon–like fashion.

Pregnancy itself becomes a journey into new territory; another person is about to enter the mother's life. As with other transitions, coincidences are more likely to appear during pregnancy and are likely to involve the fulcrum of the transition: the growing being inside.

A pregnant couple was informed that their unborn child had a high risk of Down's syndrome. They had to decide whether to terminate the pregnancy or risk having to assume the extra responsibility of a special needs child. They each took a day off from work to decide what was best for them. How would a child with Down's syndrome change their future? Could they have another child? What about the upcoming need to care for their elderly parents?

During their outing, they happened to sit close to a couple with a Down's child and were given a glimpse of a possible future for them. They later asked a friend what this coincidence meant. Did it mean they should have the child or not have the child? The friend didn't know.

This couple was presented with an opportunity to ask the parents of that child what it was like for them. They also had the opportunity to play with the child to experience what it might be like to have a child like this one. They could've further understood the pros and cons of the decision they were considering on their day off. But they didn't act. Opportunities can arise in narrow time windows. This couple wasn't ready to seize theirs.[6]

Coincidences can also help people find a home, a task that often requires luck and quick decisions. The emotional need, and the clear transition accompanying the anticipated move, helps to increase the likelihood of useful home-finding coincidences.

A sales representative for a drug company told me about her home-finding adventure: "My husband and I decided to buy and fix up the house we were currently renting. It was an okay place and seemed like the easiest thing to do. We drove to the bank and started the process of taking out a loan. On our way back to the house, my husband decided to go a different, longer way back. He said later he just felt like taking the alternate route. I spotted a woman putting up a "For Sale" sign for her house right as we passed by. We stopped. It was just what I wanted. We bought it! It was just the right place for our family."

Her husband just "felt like it." Here was a man with a mildly dis-satisfied wife who may have sensed a solution to her dissatisfaction and took the route that led him to just the right house for them. On the other side of the coincidence was the woman putting up the "For Sale" sign. She was signaling her request just as the husband *Getting lost* was turning the car in her direction. It seems as if the *may help you* two beams of need connected and drew the buyer and *find what you are* seller together; they picked up information for each *seeking.* other and from each other. We all have this capability, which is increased during high emotion and shifted contexts (like taking a different way home). Getting lost may help you find what you are seeking.

 DURING MAJOR LIFE TRANSITIONS, what coincidences have you noticed?

Family Lost and Found

Loved ones get lost, and through what seems like miracles, some of them are found. Yet, a closer look tells us that persistence, transition, resonance, and need—these very human qualities—play a large part in creating the outcome. These qualities, along with hope, continued movement, and searching and believing, can, at least sometimes, help to create monumentally unlikely coincidental reunions. A powerful need can draw two separated people back together. One story from the book *Small Miracles of the Holocaust* illustrates how coincidences fueled by love can reunite separated family members.

Louis Kopolovics was drafted into the Hungarian army in 1943, while his family remained in their home in the Carpathian Mountains. Somehow he survived the deliberate risks Jewish soldiers were ordered to take, like picking up land mines and doing the harshest physical labor. He was later arrested by the Germans in Budapest and forced to march the length of Austria to the Mauthausen concentration camp, where he was liberated by Patton's army on May 6, 1945.

Like so many other teenagers and young adults, he began the hunt for his family. He kept moving between safe havens for refugees, hoping to run into someone who knew something or to find some information on a bulletin board. One day, someone tapped him on the shoulder

...ather is dead. I was with him in Buchenwald until the

...polovics continued to search. False leads, huge disappoint-

...ents, yet he kept going.

On a crowded train to Budapest, he wearily sought an empty seat. He was so tired. He thought that maybe it was time to stop looking. He found a vacant bench but realized why it was vacant. It was covered with mud, but he didn't have the energy to find another seat. He looked for something to wipe the seat. He spotted a piece of paper that appeared to be a page torn from an official document. Suddenly, a name on the page caught his attention: Lenka Kopolovics. His sister! There were dozens of other names on the list, but his sister's name had leaped out at him. The document bore the official seal of the Swedish Red Cross and recorded the names of people sheltered by them.

He telegraphed the Swedish Red Cross and somehow his sister received the message. His sister told him that their family had been sent to Auschwitz where all but their brother, Bernie, had died. Kopolovics returned to their hometown looking for his brother and ran into him crossing a bridge. The three siblings finally reunited.[7]

Persistence was rewarded. A torn piece of paper lying on the floor of a crowded train provided the crucial clue to his search. How did that document shard find its way to a place near that muddy seat? How did Kopolovics, in his tired stupor, scan that page of numerous names to find his sister's? Such a series of necessary events has the look of orchestration, of planning, yet there is no known source for this active knowledge, except mystery or God. Or is there? Kopolovics had to be looking, seeking. Without his active scan of the document, however tired he may have been, the final result would've eluded him. How had the seat been muddied as if waiting only for him? How had the document been located so conveniently for him to grasp? And the timing, that fortunate timing! The crowded train left only the muddied seat. The paper had arrived some brief time before, and it would've been removed a brief time later. We can add another potential source: the intense desire of one desperate man to construct a situation that provided him the answer he sought. Mystery remains about just how it all happened, but some of the contributions to this apparently orchestrated event become more accessible: desire and action were clearly involved.

The act of sitting down next to the person you are seeking is a regular theme in the creation of some very useful coincidences. Rushnell tells this moving story: Mavis Jackson had driven past the same Anaheim church for twenty years, each time muttering to herself, "Someday, I'm going in there." One Sunday she decided to go in and take a seat in the middle of this three-thousand-seat church that was filled with people. She was thrilled with the service and excitedly said to the woman sitting next to her, "I'm so glad I came today. Wasn't it wonderful?" The young woman nodded, and said, "I'm from the Midwest. I'm actually here on a mission. To find my birth mother."

Mavis had some idea of how she felt, since she had had to give up her little girl for adoption many years ago. "What's your daughter's birthday?" the young woman asked.

"October 30," Mavis replied.

"That's my birthday!" gasped the young woman.

Yes, they were mother and daughter.[8]

After twenty years, Mavis had picked the right day and the right place to sit in that massive church to find her long-lost daughter. Her daughter had also picked the right place to sit. Like unknown lovers seeking each other on a beach, mother and daughter were drawn to each other by similarity and need.

As with mothers and daughters, so, too, with fathers and sons. In 1969, during the Vietnam War, twenty-year-old USAF sergeant John Garcia and a young Thai woman, Pratorn Varanoot, lived together and had a son named Nueng. Her family discouraged her from moving away from Thailand, so John left for the United States without Pratorn and Nueng. She then married another US soldier, who returned all of John's letters, which prevented John from retaining contact with his son.

In 1996, John was driving down a highway in Pueblo, Colorado, when he noticed that his gas tank was half full. Although he didn't need gas at that moment, for some unexplainable reason he decided to stop at a service station he didn't normally use. Although he had thirty dollars in his wallet, he decided to pay by check, which he wouldn't ordinarily do either.

"Are you John Garcia?" asked the young man behind the counter after looking at the check.

"Yes," John replied.

"Have you ever been in the Air Force?"

"Yes."

"Have you ever lived in Thailand?"

"Yes," John replied, with increasing surprise.

"Do you have a son there?"

"Yes," John again replied.

"What was his name?"

"Nueng," John responded.

"I'm your son," the man behind the counter revealed.[9]

Perhaps Nueng, even more than John, was looking to be reunited. Did Nueng radiate a beam of information, drawing his father to him, and leading him to respond without knowing why? Resonance, similarity, and need joined forces for another instrumental coincidence.

Family members find each other in all sorts of ways, under all sorts of conditions, sometimes to fulfill important needs. In each case, the coincidence provides them the opportunity to comfort each other at their time of need. In this case, each needed a strong, familiar soul, and they coincidentally found the person they were seeking. Again we see two primary accompaniments of many coincidences—need and transition.

Of course, today there is no better technology than the cell phone to "find" the other person. But it wasn't always that way. There was once a time when we had to depend on payphones hanging inside a glass-enclosed closet on the street or on a wall or post. In those days, some pretty funny coincidences took place, several of which have been collected at a site called "Understanding Uncertainty," which is run by mathematicians in Cambridge, England, who study probability.

One story reads: "I was 15 and shopping in town with a friend when I should have been working on a school project with the same friend. I walked past a public phone box just as it started ringing. I 'dared' my friend to answer the phone. She 'double-dared' me. I opened the door, answered the phone 'hello?' and my mum said '[H]ello, Charlotte. Are you coming home for dinner?' I was so surprised I confessed all. It turned out that the phone box had the same number as my friend's home number bar one digit. My mum had misdialed and inadvertently called the phone box that I just happened to be walking by."[10]

Here we not only have the wrong number—that happens regularly—but the wrong number during a narrow window of time. This timing suggests a connecting beam of information between the two. The mother had "mistakenly" dialed while trying to find what she suspected: that her child was with a friend and not doing what she was supposed to be doing.

Here is another story of a random phone call hitting its mark: "When I was a teenager, a group of us went to Liskeard in Cornwall for our first holiday together without our parents. Whilst out visiting the local beauty spots, we walked beside a public telephone box and could hear the phone was ringing. First of all we just laughed and ignored it, but on passing, I felt the sudden urge to go back and answer it. I picked up the phone and somebody said 'Is that you, Carol?' Well I was stunned, but I answered, yes. It was my aunt on the end of the phone who was trying to contact my father to advise him there had been a death in the family. I have puzzled over this all of my life. My family lived in Wallington, Surrey, and my aunt lived in Sutton, Surrey. How did that call get through to a public phone box in Cornwall just as I was walking by?"[11]

Because the aunt needed to make contact, Carol was willing to follow her sudden urge to answer the phone.

Family Pets, Too

Boys and their beloved dogs can lose contact with each other, but something in one or both of them draws them back together. I loved my dog. He got lost one day, and we found each other. This early event in my life was the first to open my eyes to the usefulness of coincidence.

When I was eight or nine years old, my father quit his job as manager of a dime store to buy and sell cattle in the farming communities surrounding Cleveland, Ohio. He knew I desperately needed a dog, and one day he brought home a six-week-old puppy, black with tan and white splotches, who liked to chew on trees. I named him Snapper, and we became best buddies. By example, he taught me bad habits that are with me still, like scratching his back when nervous and making smacking noises while eating. One day, Snapper disappeared. I became frightened and asked my mother where he was. She didn't know and suggested I go to the police station near my elementary school.

I rode my bike the usual route to school, cut across the playground, crossed the big street, and pushed the bike up the stairs and the long walk to the front of the police station. A man in uniform sat behind the large entrance desk. He shook his head. "Sorry, son, we haven't seen your dog."

Tears flooded my eyes as I left. I wasn't paying attention to where I was going. I went down the stairs. Instead of recrossing the big street, I mistakenly rode on the sidewalk on the right side of the street. Sobbing, sobbing, sobbing, I looked up and coming toward me was a black dog walking in Snapper's sideways style. Could it be? Could it be? Yes! It was Snapper! He was casually happy to see me, jumping up on my legs, letting me pet his head. He seemed to be asking me why I'd taken so long to find him.

I got lost and found my dog. What was going on here? Were we drawn together because we loved each other so much? Or was our finding each other just one possible event out of many others and we just got lucky, a chance event? I believe we were drawn to each other, but I also wanted to look at the probability of running into each other by examining Snapper's tracks on a Google Earth map. He left our house on Menlo Road in Shaker Heights sometime before I got home. Coming out of our driveway, I turned right and he had to have turned left. A few houses down, he had a choice to go right or left at the fork. Left would've taken him away from me, while right would be toward the police station and me. Then he would've gotten to the big road. There he could've turned right, or left, or gone across. Had he gone left or right, we would've missed each other. I couldn't have seen him all the way across because the big street was actually three roads: two streets for cars paralleling the tracks of Cleveland's Rapid Transit commuter rail line between them. He had to have crossed the big street. On the other side, he could've gone straight, left, or right. Only right set him on the path toward trotting into me.

We had a discrete time interval to find each other on the police station side of the big street. He could've trotted past the police station before I got there. But we found each other about halfway between the police station and his final right turn.

Snapper had four decisions to make to find me. He made all of them correctly. His actions, coupled with my tear-filled wrong turn, were to me more than dumb luck or random chance. This very helpful coincidence reunited us. He was a much-needed companion for a lonely boy for several years afterward. I still miss him.

The Snapper story takes its place among the many, many stories about dogs finding their masters or finding their way home. Rupert Sheldrake has conducted some simple experiments demonstrating Dog Geospatial Information Acquisition. He and Pamela Smart studied the behavior of a mongrel terrier named Jaytee, owned by Pamela. Her parents, who lived next door, noticed that Jaytee would go to the window around 4:30 PM, around the time Pamela left her job as a secretary. He usually waited there for thirty to forty-five minutes, the time it took for her to come home. After she lost her job, her returns home were more unpredictable, yet her parents observed that Jaytee seemed to anticipate when she had begun her journey home.

Sheldrake and Smart devised a formal study of this ability to anticipate. They wanted to see if Jaytee depended on something other than simple routine, subtle cues from her parents, or sounds from her car. With careful record keeping and then videotaping over many months, they concluded that Jaytee acted as if he knew she was coming home between ten to forty-five minutes before she arrived. The farther away she was, the earlier he anticipated.[12]

Some of our animal companions know exactly where we are!

 WHAT STORY DO YOU KNOW of a beloved dog or cat finding its way home?

How Can That Be?

Let's first assume that these stories are true. I can vouch for only the ones I have personally experienced and the ones my patients and friends have told me.

The stories in this chapter add to the growing evidence for an as-yet-unnamed sense that allows us to know things we don't know we know, or, more accurately, to know things we shouldn't be able to know, according to conventional scientific understanding. The question, then, is *how* some people gain this knowledge.

I can offer diagrams that can lead to theories. The diagrams provide ways to visualize the information acquisition without explaining how the diagram works. This way of thinking is similar to instructions about how to drive a car but without knowing how the engine moves the wheels.

A hint about how to do this comes from a story told by Sally Rhine Feather (whom we met earlier in the book) about a woman named Natalie, who was romantically interested in a certain psychotherapist. She needed to find him, to put a note on his car windshield. In her search she found herself in a part of town where she had never been—and there was his car.[13] How did she get there? She said she had a map in

her mind of where to go. Of all the stories in which people find someone they are seeking, only in this one have I found a direct reference to
a kind of mapmaking by an internal Global Positioning System (GPS).

We can look to migrating birds for a clearer understanding of what
might be going on. How do they know where to go? They fly thousands
of miles north and south to find the very same place each year. The
birds seem to be navigating by using the earth's magnetic field. Birds
must first have a way to detect a magnetic field; some part of their
brains has to register that information. Then another part of their brains
must compare the incoming information to a stored map.[14]

Migrating birds have sensors, probably in their inner ears, to pick
up electromagnetic waves pulsing around the earth's atmosphere. The
magnetic field has distinctive patterns in different locations, which
the birds can sense. This information is then sent to their brain stem.
Researchers have identified a group of cells in the brainstem of pigeons
that record both the direction and the strength of the magnetic field.
This information can then be compared to maps stored elsewhere in
their brains—probably the hippocampus. By comparing the brainstem's
present location with the already stored map, they can detect where they
are in relationship to where they are going. The frontal cortex uses this
information to correct the course, if necessary.

This is only one model of how migratory birds manage their
flight patterns. Much more is yet to be learned. Do they use smell or
landmarks?

This magnetic field migratory bird paradigm sets the groundwork
for a possibly more complicated human diagram, which requires flexibility in the mapping based upon needs. The birds simply need to find
familiar ground in different seasons. The human must find the needed
"other" who is moving around in space.

How does the human brain know where the lover, the child, the sister, or the cousin might be? The simulpathity stories tell us that we do know what is going on with loved ones at a distance. Like a GPS locator in a cell phone, we can, when needed, tune in to that position in space and call up a map to lead us there. Need (of either one or both), coupled with transitions from usual routines and behaviors, helps us tune in to the maps that guide us to the right seat on a train, the patch of sand on the beach, the chair in a coffee shop, or the pew in a church. Love, that mysterious, hard-to-define, cherished, difficult, intense, and sometimes confusing emotion, often has an important influence.

The human GPS idea takes us closer to imagining how someone can know about and find another person or thing. We can also find situations in which patterns "out there" in our environment mirror internal problems and can help to resolve them, like Janine passing her husband in the airport or Bart seeing multiple divorced men in a short period of time.

Some "hard scientists" want to call this "magical thinking." They think we are searching for patterns of connections that don't exist. But the evidence from these stories indicates the existence of innate potential beyond what is commonly accepted by the scientific establishment. We each have within our grasp an ability to find our way to people, things, and situations that most of us don't know we have. This capacity lies within our intuition; it's our subconscious ability to locate needs in our surroundings. It is aided by strong emotion, transitions from the web of habitual patterns, and the willingness to scan and seek.

 YOU ARE LIKELY TO INCREASE YOUR COINCIDENCES during times of high emotion, transition, need, and seeking.

CHAPTER 4

Friends, Colleagues, and Acquaintances

Who is a friend? Of all the words about people in relationships, this word has the most flexibility and ambiguity. A friend can be someone in your social group, past or present, or someone you know/knew well or not so well. A friend can be someone who did you a favor, or someone with whom you worked and had dinner. Usually friends know something personal about each other, have shared major feelings and adventure together, or helped each other through a difficult time. You can be thought of as a friend if you belong to the same club, group, or organization. Because you share the same interests, go to the same meetings, or believe in the same ideas, someone may consider you a friend. You can be called a friend simply because it is to the advantage of that person to have a third person think of you as their friend.

Facebook has further stretched the meaning of friend. A person becomes a friend if you accept their request to be your friend. You may never have met them in person.

For our purposes, a friend is someone you like very much and with whom you have had both good and bad experiences and still maintain a connection. Friends resemble well-liked and loved family members except for one very big difference—the relationship is chosen by each person and is not by birth. Friendships are strengthened and maintained by frequent contacts and shared interests. Good friends often know details of the lives of each other's parents, siblings, children, current work, and other friends and may visit and share meals in each other's houses.

Another characteristic of deep friendships is the ability to discuss problems one person has with the other, to be able to say something like "What you did/what you said hurt me." This ability to "meta-communicate," to comment on communication, characterizes strong friendships.

New Friends

The strong emotions and transitions of friendships create breeding grounds for coincidences. Discovering a new friend provides one of life's special pleasures. Friends want to be together not because of our built-in biological need for romance, sex, procreation, or potential life partnership, but for softer, more self-determined, optional reasons. We like each other for who we are. We are not necessarily trying to make money from each other or develop business arrangements. We like talking together, doing things together, and being together. We support each other not out of family obligations, legal requirements, or moral injunctions, but because we sincerely care about the other's well-being.

Some strong friendships start in the strangest way.

In June 2001, ten-year-old Laura Buxton of Staffordshire, England, was attending her grandparent's golden wedding anniversary and needed a friend. Her grandfather thought she could find a pen pal by writing her address on a label with the message "Please return to Laura Buxton," and release it on a helium balloon.

Ten days later a farmer in Milton Lilbourne, Wiltshire, about 140 miles away, pulled the balloon out of the hedge that separated his pastures from the neighbor's. He noticed the name Laura Buxton. Since this was the name of his neighbor's daughter, he brought the balloon to her.

Laura Buxton from Milton Lilbourne, who was also ten years old, wrote to Laura Buxton in Staffordshire. As this was such an interesting coincidence, their parents arranged for them to meet.

The parallels in their lives were quite startling.

The girls, both tall for their age, were the same height and both decided to wear pink sweaters and jeans for their first meeting. Both had brown hair, which they wore in the same style. Both girls had three-year-old black Labrador retrievers and gray pet rabbits. They also had guinea pigs, which were the same color and even had the same orange markings on their "bums."

The girls quickly became friends and spent hours together talking. By age nineteen, they had remained very good friends. Laura Buxton from Staffordshire got more than the pen pal she was seeking.[1]

Perhaps the similarities between the two girls influenced the balloon's trajectory. A well-known psychological principle known as "assortative mating" captures the tendency for people with similar characteristics to be drawn together. From schizophrenics, Asperger's, and the religiously orthodox to the wealthy college-educated and those with similar jobs, people like finding people like them. They become friends and sometimes marry based on their shared similarities. Most of these pairings are carried out by feet-on-the-ground meetings or sometimes Internet matches. The windblown balloon eliminates these more easily accepted mechanisms. The story evokes the possibility of "like attracting like," that somehow similarity creates resonance, and resonance draws the two people together. Biologist Rupert Sheldrake has created a compelling theory around "morphic resonance," that shapes and forms (morphs) influence and perpetuate each other. Similarity may predispose the two people to come together in this unlikely way.

In 2009 the two young Lauras in the story appeared together on National Public Radio's *Radiolab*. The hosts asked what caused them to come together like this. The girls thought that it was maybe "fate" or a "lucky wind" and believed that they might find out how it happened when they were "old grannies." The hosts wanted listeners to take a scientific look at this odd coincidence. They rolled out statistics professors to demonstrate that strange events do happen with some regularity, and sometimes the probability of these strange events happening could be calculated.[2]

The statisticians went to that standard image for understanding probability—flipping a coin for heads and tails. As everyone knows, if you flip the coin one hundred times, you are very likely to get fifty heads and fifty tails. The more flipping you do, the more closely you will get to the 50/50 result. However, during the flipping sequence, there is a certain probability, a low one for sure, of getting a run of seven heads or seven tails. So in a trial of one hundred flips, there is a probability of about 16 percent for getting a run of seven tails. If you want to flip a coin just seven times, then the probability of getting seven tails is just 1 percent. The reason the probability is so much higher in flipping one hundred times is that there are about fourteen opportunities for runs of seven (100 divided by 7 = 14). Focusing on the single event, the string of seven tails, ignores the background activity, which is made up by the other coin flips that create the whole series of flips. Similarly, looking at some coincidences without noticing the surrounding events that can be influencing their occurrences can make a coincidence appear far more unlikely than it really is. The example of double lottery winners illustrates this idea.

What are the odds that someone, somewhere, wins the lottery twice? This strange event happens, although the odds are one in a trillion. In large populations, the very, very unlikely will happen. With all those people buying all those lottery tickets, someone will hit it twice, just as lightning sometimes strikes the same person twice. The statisticians warn us that we may find meaning when "it is just coincidence." Like other skeptics, they used the word *coincidence* with the word *just*, which is intended to minimize its significance. The background activity for the double lottery win is made up by all the other lottery tickets purchased, just as a run of seven tails is much more likely in the context of one hundred flips than with just seven flips. The lightning hitting the same person twice happens in the context of all those other lightning bolts hitting someone.

Let's look closely at these "hard" statistical positions. In flipping the coins or studying lottery winners, we know the base rates. Base rate refers to the known probabilities for an event to happen. To determine a base rate requires knowing the total population involved and the number of times that event happens—like the two-time lottery winner. In a specific period of time, the number of people buying a lottery ticket divided into the number of people winning it twice gives the base rate.

The base rate for getting a run of seven tails in one hundred coin flips is 16 percent or one out of six.

What, then, is the base rate for setting off a helium balloon to go more than 140 miles and land near the house of a girl with the same name? The experiment could be run, but it would take a huge number of trials. Millions of helium balloons with randomly selected names would fill the air. Then they would have to be found and turned in by a willing populace. Some balloons would be hung up in trees, while others might be chewed up by dogs, eaten by goats, or sunk in a lake or the ocean. In the midst of those trials, our statistician friends would tell us that this very, very unlikely event would take place. The trouble with this reasoning is that once *any* event takes place, statisticians can dismiss it with a wave of their hands saying, "In large populations, very unlikely events will happen," or "Any odd event has a certain probability of happening." Translated into simple English, both these statements mean "If it happened, it could've happened." Of course!

Some events, like the meeting of the two Lauras, are just too unlikely to have a known base rate. Some unknown human element could be playing a part in their creation.

The statisticians on the program also criticized the story by pointing out several differences between the two girls. The storyteller picked out the similarities between the two and ignored the differences. For example, one of the Lauras likes pink and the other blue. In college they had different majors. And when they first met, one of them wasn't quite ten. Yes, the girls didn't match on all possible characteristics.

So, yes, they're not *exactly* the same. They're not identical twins, but when they met, it was as if each was looking into a mirror. And no identical twin exactly matches the other. Most important for this coincidence, the girls each needed a friend and they found one! No one on the *Radiolab* program mentioned this crucially important *need* that each of them felt. The first Laura's need was expressed during a celebration of a family transition—the golden wedding anniversary of her grandparents. Her grandfather wanted a friend for her. Once again *need* and *emotion* and *transition* are associated with helping to set the stage for a coincidence-inspired, enduring friendship.

There would be no story without the parents. If they hadn't found the coincidence compelling, no opportunity for friendship would've existed. Coincidences offer opportunities. Someone has to decide to seize that opportunity.

While the Laura Buxton story stands out as wildly improbable, other friendships begin with less unlikely circumstances and yet have the same ring of something more than "just coincidence" helping them to happen.

My son Arie is amused by my interest in coincidence and is rather skeptical. On Father's Day 2012, a few months before his marriage to Liza, he told me this story: Arie and Liza had been in Minneapolis, Minnesota, for almost one year. Arie was ready to make some new friends. They had settled in but not met enough compatible people. They received an invitation from a local Minnesotan to attend a big concert downtown. As they wandered around this ten-thousand-people gathering, Arie bumped into someone he knew from high school in Columbia, Missouri. They had run together on their Hickman High School cross-country team. He greeted Arie enthusiastically and offered to introduce him to some other locals he knew. Suddenly Arie was expanding his circle of friends.

A little later another person around his age approached him, asking, "Are you Arie from Hickman High School?" Arie didn't recognize him. He turned out to be a tennis player from another Missouri high school who had beaten Arie in the district semifinals in Hannibal. He, too, offered to get together with Arie and introduce him around. He needed some more people to play tennis and other sports with. They got together for a tennis match, then weeks later, they played again.

Although skeptical about coincidences, Arie was emphatic about the strength of his need for friendship and the bumpiness of being in transition. He needed some grounding in Minneapolis. He and Liza did something unusual for them—they broke their routine and went to a rock concert. The need for friends, their state of transition, and the breaking of routine all contributed to increasing the likelihood of a meaningful coincidence. The probabilities were pretty low of running into the right people among ten thousand, yet their chances were better in this dense crowd of like-minded, similar-age people than on the streets. Unlike the red balloon story, the odds of finding old connections in this setting could possibly be calculated. But two of them? His need for new friends helped to create this double hit. The human ability to detect and move toward a needed someone or something seems to be more common than we realize. My son may be a little less skeptical of coincidences.

Rob Hopcke tells the story of finding himself in a desperately lonely life. Friends had died of illness and accidents so often that he had to adjust to going to the gym alone, biking alone, and attending the opera alone. Among the people at the gym was a sullen-appearing new guy, muscular and not very friendly. He didn't seem to fit in with the rest of the crowd. This coincidental friendship involves Rob and this man, Phil.

When another one of his friends died, Rob agreed to sing at the service. Anxious about his performance, Rob made an appointment with the masseur at the gym, whom he had seen several times before.

But the masseur never showed up. The staff member noticed the problem and offered him a free massage with someone else the next day. The loss of both the massage and the friend accentuated Rob's sense of isolation and abandonment. The next day the new masseur also failed to appear; his car had died. Once again Rob was left without the expected comfort. That evening he was met with yet a third masseur, who turned out to be that sullen, muscular guy who didn't look at all like a masseur to Rob.

But Phil turned out to be quite different from the dumb jock he appeared to be. He was very intelligent and well read; Rob had much in common with him. Among other things, Phil was planning to become a therapist and was an avid cyclist. He became Rob's cycling buddy, workout partner—and his best friend.[3]

The Chinese "Book of Changes," the *I Ching*, advises, "perseverance furthers." Rob kept pushing on from one disappointment to another. A more Western phrase suggests, "One door closes and another opens." I would add "so be sure to open the next door." Rob had a need, and so, presumably, did Phil. Rob's story suggests that people can scan their surroundings for potential need fulfillment and bounce their way to a best friend.

 TO INCREASE COINCIDENCES, keep moving! Try to find coincidence-rich environments.

Friends at Play

Friends are in our lives for many reasons—help, support, understanding—but the best thing about good friends is playing with them. Some games are more serious than others, however.

At age nineteen, Deidre, a patient of mine, was caught between two worlds—the wealthy social class of her divorced mother and the newly discovered middle-class world of her current friends and boyfriend. She had grown up with butlers and maids, exotic foods and clothes, luxury hotels in the world's most fancy resorts, and apartments in Paris and Rome. Yet with her current friends, she found simpler entertainments: first-time love and acceptance without massive displays of manners and clothes. Now she had to choose between staying in the town where she had spent her childhood and adolescence with these middle-class friends and starting community college there or beginning her first year of college at an exclusive university in England where she would be caught up once again with the wealthy elite. She didn't want to leave this local group of people, especially her boyfriend. She'd finally found love and acceptance.

As she was tormenting herself with this decision, she and her boyfriend and several other friends went to a bar in town. While there, in walked her best friend from elementary school, a wealthy, beautiful young woman who had been living in Europe for many years. They'd not seen each other in ten years. The friend was accompanied by an even wealthier Londoner. They had flown in for a few days from Italy, where they'd been vacationing.

Deidre was struck with the differences between her friend's wealthy young man and her own boyfriend. The wealthy young man was very well dressed, elegant, had exquisite manners, and spoke in a charming way. Her boyfriend was sloppily dressed, interrupted others, and cursed regularly. And the young women in her group often cursed, while the young women in her upper-class circles never did. Deidre felt embarrassed by the clothes her friends wore, their ill manners, and her boyfriend's failure to work or go to school.

In the bar that day, she became the sole audience member for a personal play contrasting two future social circles. It seemed as if the scene had been produced just for her. She heeded its message. With deep regret she realized what she had to do—return to the upper-class life and become the socially prominent young woman she was raised to be.

How was this play "produced"? People her age do go to bars regularly, and this bar was one of the popular places to go. Her elementary school friend still had ties to the town, so she was bound to return sometime. The friend was from a wealthy family, so she was likely to have a boyfriend from the same class. So there was a certain likelihood for this meeting to take place. But just why at this particular time, just when Deidre was tormented by this crucial decision? Of all the bars in town, her old friend walked in with a boyfriend to directly compare hers with? What is the base rate for this improbable event? It's very difficult to calculate.

There is more than "just a coincidence" going on here. Once again, high emotion comes into play—Deidre's anguish about possibly leaving her friends and her boyfriend. The period was also one of transition —either go or stay. She was faced with a crucial decision. I believe that in some way she alerted her childhood friend to come to the bar to stage the scene for her. The friend, for her own reasons, had come to town, open to possibilities. In ways we are beginning to understand, that old friend timed her entrance to help bring Deidre back into the aristocratic fold. The scene enabled Deidre to see—outside her worry-absorbed mind—clear representations of the two options involved in her decision.

My conventional science friends will once again accuse me of "magical thinking." To Matthew Hutson, science writer and author of

The 7 Laws of Magical Thinking, there is no science to back up the conclusions these coincidence stories suggest. He can't accept ideas that haven't been substantiated by scientific research. More specifically, he cannot accept that minds might interact with each other at a distance or that mind and matter can connect. Yet, as Hutson points out, many ideas that were once thought to be magical have later become true. Take "magical contagion," for example, which was the belief that something invisible carried something infectious. Bacteriology has shown that we have reason to fear that something invisible can be transmitted. Bacteria are the causes of magical contagion.[4]

Just look around us now. We possess telepathic-like capabilities: we can know the thoughts of others through telephones, e-mail, texting, and social networking. We can also be clairvoyant, seeing what is happening at a distance right now through television and webcams. Coincidences are pointing the way to our recognition of new ways of understanding and using innate human abilities. Within what Hutson would call magical thinking lie visions of the near future. Hutson concedes that magical thinking, when done in moderation, helps enhance the meaning of our lives. It helps us find solace and support by believing we are surrounded by invisible energy and assistance. Magical thinking also provides new ideas for us about the potential interactions between our minds and our surroundings. If there is to be a science of coincidence, then it begins with stories like those in this book, one after another, the next one and the one after that.

Playing with friends is not only a celebration of life but it can also be lifesaving, which Laizer Halberstam discovered during the Nazi scourge. At age five, he violated an unspoken rule in a Polish village by playing with a non-Jewish friend. The two of them traded stamps, coins, and toys. One day they decided to teach each other prayers.

Their parents would've been horrified but never knew. Laizer taught his friend a Jewish prayer, and in turn he learned a Christian prayer.

Ten years later he was fleeing the Nazis disguised as a Christian. A Nazi soldier, examining his forged papers, became suspicious. "You say you are a good Christian? Well then, why don't you recite a Christian prayer for me now, one that all good Christians should know by heart?" The prayer the soldier selected was the one he had been taught by his friend.[5]

The Nazi must have selected a well-known prayer, one that five-year-olds could learn. Most important, Laizer had remembered it. The life-saving coincidence was created through the playful sharing of two little boys. We can again raise the question of base rates. How many little Polish boys had exchanged prayers with each other? Then how many Jewish Polish young adults who were fleeing the Nazis were asked to recite a well-known Christian prayer?

Without ever being able to calculate the likelihood of this happening, my statistical friends will say that there was a probability that this prayer coincidence would happen. And something similar may have happened several times but has not been recorded. Perhaps. To Laizer, who later became a rabbi, and to his daughter Yitta, something else seemed to be going on. They believed it was God. I attribute more responsibility to the risk-taking Laizer and his playful friend, his very good memory for prayer, and a good sense for survival. Luck happens when opportunity meets preparation.

Luck happens when opportunity meets preparation.

Next comes the story of a German, named Rainer, who many years later was traveling in the United States. Ray Grasse, author of *Waking Dream*, e-mailed me the story, which he heard from Rainer, whom he met in Nepal in 1982:

In Germany a friend asked Rainer if he'd like to travel to Los Angeles with him for a week, all expenses paid. Apparently, his girlfriend just backed out of the trip they had been planning for some time, so rather than travel by himself, he decided to ask Rainer if he wanted to use the ticket, so that he'd have company. The two of them flew to Los Angeles and stayed at an associate's house. One afternoon, Rainer was in the house by himself when the doorbell rang. On answering it, he was shocked to discover another one of his friends from Germany—his very closest friend, in fact—standing there equally astonished. Neither one had known the other would be traveling to the United States, since both of their trips had been impulsive. His friend had been driving around the city that afternoon and got lost, and decided to pick a house at random to ring the doorbell to ask for directions—and there stood his friend Rainer answering it.

The knock on an apparently random door to find help forms a subtype of useful coincidences. In his autobiography, *My Early Life,* Winston Churchill tells of fleeing enemies in South Africa and "randomly" knocking on the door of the only house in which a British sympathizer lived in an otherwise hostile territory.[6] The book *Small Miracles of the Holocaust* tells of a man fleeing the Nazis who escaped deep into a dense forest he had never traveled in before and knocking on a cabin door to find a Christian whose life he had saved years before.[7]

Like sitting down next to strangers, chancy knocks when in need can yield surprisingly useful results. What is it about the seeker that helps him identify the needed resource? This personal GPS-like system seems quite real. But, yes, many desperate knocks don't yield desired results. And many strangers sitting in the next seat may be boring or unapproachable. Need, transition, and timing play important roles in helping to create these useful coincidences.

In her small town in New York, Susan Watkins carefully observed coincidences and recorded many of them in her book *What a Coincidence!*

Among the recurring themes was thinking about a friend and then running into that person. She recorded several of these stories. Thinking of Lonnie and running into her, thinking of Sharon and seeing her. These were people she hadn't seen in quite a while.[8] Similarly, our research participants reported that they, too, sometimes thought of a person and then saw them. These simple coincidences can draw your attention to the connection between thoughts and events in everyday life. If you want to see more coincidences, look for and remember the common ones like these. Noticing and thinking about them will sensitize you to the more complex ones.

Coincidences Between Counselors and Clients

Psychotherapy and counseling provide breeding grounds for coincidences because the patients are emotionally distressed and seeking some kind of change. The participants become colleagues in this interior adventure. Sometimes their experiences mirror each other in ways that are mutually beneficial.

Counselor Rolf Gordhamer described one client-counselor experiential mirror: "During the Iran-Iraq war in the mid-1980s, I was counseling an Iranian college student, who was very worried about his family. They had to leave their home, which was in the war zone. Over a few sessions I searched for a way to ease his emotional pain. Thinking I could bring some spiritual flavor into the sessions, I showed him the book *Autobiography of a Yogi*. He reached into his satchel and, to my amazement, pulled out the same book. We were both practically on the same page. This synchronicity seemed to bring a calm to the student. He knew that destiny was controlled by an essence greater than ourselves."[9]

What was the likelihood that they were both reading the same book? Not an easy calculation to make. First published in 1946, the book describes the author's search for a spiritual teacher. Translated into more than twenty-five languages, it became one of the most popular spiritual books of the twentieth century. Both counselor and client were searching spiritually for meaning in their lives, so this book was a likely choice, although there are thousands of other popular books on the subject that they could've been reading. The fact that they were on almost the same page made the mirror highly improbable and struck each of them as significant.

The student could've interpreted the coincidence as suggesting that the counselor and he were very much tuned in to each other, but that wasn't what he wanted to feel. He wanted to believe that a greater power guided human destiny and, by implication, that power was benign and his family would survive. The student was searching for an external confirmation of his belief, and he found it.

Coincidences are open to interpretation at both the personal and transpersonal levels. They can be applied to current decisions, and they can be used to confirm or challenge our beliefs about reality. The student was seeking confirmation of a cherished belief in a loving God in the hopes that this belief would help ease his concern for his family. For the time being, the counselor had helped him to accomplish this aim. I maintain that the counselor somehow tuned in to the client and selected just the right thing—the book—that would calm the client. In the search for a means to help, he displayed a unique form of empathy.

Then we have the story of psychotherapist Erica Helm Meade, who was feeling miserable because of a recently diagnosed intestinal parasite. She was heartsick that her beloved cat had also been infected, perhaps by some contaminated water, and was fighting for his life.

A client arrived also feeling quite sick. "I found out yesterday that my bird and I are both infected with intestinal parasites." The therapist was astonished by the similar situations—intestinal parasites in both human and pet at the same time in the same office? They lived more than thirty miles apart and were on separate water systems.

This client was in therapy to help regain contact with her own spirituality, which was lost to her many years earlier. As the therapist heard the client describe numerous failed veterinary treatments, she imagined the client praying for the bird. *Whether it lived or died, was healed or languished, she would have to make a plea to the spirit world*, thought the therapist.

She asked the client if she had prayed about it. The client burst out crying. That day marked the beginning of her return to spiritual practice.

The therapist, too, had let her spiritual practice languish. This client's return to daily prayer encouraged her to also begin praying for her cat. Both animals hovered near death, but much to the surprise of their vets, both animals fully recovered. The mirrorlike coincidence renewed their shared passion for daily prayer, for which the therapist thanked both sets of parasites.

The mirrored pairs of pet-owner intestinal parasites can be difficult to explain. Within many coincidences lies mystery. What emerges from this story is support for a little-known adage about why people are drawn to become psychotherapists: "Being a therapist is the only way to be in psychotherapy without being the patient." We learn so much about ourselves in helping others.[10]

PSYCHOTHERAPY AND COUNSELING HAVE ALL the ingredients that foster coincidences: high emotion, need, transition (the desire for change), and seeking the resolution of emotional difficulties.

Look for Conventional Explanations First

From the narrow confines of a therapist's office to the broad landscape of world travel, intriguing coincidences emerge. Neighbors can cross paths in surprising ways far outside their neighborhood. In the following "small world" story from Great Britain, there is a hidden note of caution for coincidence finders:

> My wife and [I] were holidaying in Vilamoura, Portugal, last year. One day we decided to take the bus along the coast to Albufeira for the day; we walked through the town and along the beach, then took the large lift at the far end to the top and sat on a viewing platform looking back towards the town. We then remembered a former single neighbour, who had said they were hoping to spend more time in the Algarve, and we wondered which part? Then casually glancing to the next seat . . . Yes, you've guessed it . . . he was sitting on the next bench also looking back towards the town!! He also was speechless when we made our presence known to him.[11]

After thinking of the neighbor, there he was. Surprise! By the responses received from our research participants, it appears that running into someone you know in a faraway place is a common occurrence. The statisticians point out that those who travel are likely to know a large number of people, many of whom are also likely travelers. In looking at this small-world example, this vacationing couple could've run into any number of people in any number of places. The gate for meeting someone you know in a far-off place swings fairly wide. These coincidences tend to be surprising but rarely personally significant.

They remembered him, though, before they saw him. This case didn't involve an arbitrary acquaintance. They had just thought about him and mentioned him to each other. How had it happened that they had both just thought about him? Better to answer questions like this in the simplest, least controversial way by first seeing if conventional science can offer a reasonable explanation. For this story, what we currently know about how the brain works is the best place to look.

Our eyes are constantly scanning our environment. Although the scenes in front of us appear stable, we see things out of the corners of our eyes. These peripheral sightings reach awareness when they are unique, special, threatening, or potentially useful. Otherwise the scanning results continue to register subconsciously. Most likely, the vacationing couple saw this friendly neighbor out of the corner of their eyes. He wasn't unique or threatening but familiar in an unexpected place. The thought of him registered in one of their brains. That person mentioned the connection to the other. Then they both looked around and spotted him. One of them had subconsciously seen him, thought of him, and then brought him up before consciously registering his presence. The appearance of the neighbor seemed to be an inexplicable mind mirror when more likely it was created through normal subconscious scanning.

This point first came home to me when a patient described himself as guided by angels. He used the following experience to support his belief: "I was stoned on marijuana," he told me. "Really stoned. I got into my car and started to drive down this narrow street with cars parked on either side with a narrow margin for error as I drove.

Suddenly without knowing why, I slammed my foot onto the brake pedal. I looked up from the shock of the quick stop and saw a child run right in front of my now stopped car. Had I not slammed on the brakes, I would've hit that child and ruined my future."

He sat back satisfied with himself and his heavenly help.

I offered a different explanation, one grounded in brain science. Information coming through the eyes is routed to two different circuits —a fast one and a slower one. The slower one goes to the occipital cortex (the visual cortex in the back of the brain) and then is analyzed for identification and significance. The faster route goes directly to the amygdalae, the almond-shaped structures deep inside the brain, which are best known for their role in fear reactions. For example, if a person is afraid of snakes and sees something on the ground that looks like one, the amygdalae trigger a flight response. The slower circuit simultaneously but more slowly analyzes that thing on the ground and later determines that it is a gnarled stick. Better to have run and then asked questions than to have stuck around and chanced being bitten by a snake.

The same is true for my patient. His foot hit the brake before he consciously recognized the perilous situation he was about to face. He was saved, not by an angel but, in my opinion, by the quick-reacting, amygdalae-driven shortcut to action. He didn't particularly like my explanation because it made him feel less special. When it comes to understanding coincidences, students of coincidence are best served by looking for conventional explanations first.

But in the next story, which involves my experience with a new colleague at a conference, I'm not sure which set of beliefs to draw from—the facts of current conventional brain science or our probable GPS-like ability to locate need fulfillment in our environment.

Someday, the GPS locating function may be recognized as part of conventional brain science, but currently the dichotomy exists.

I was looking for Carlos Mirapeix at a psychotherapy conference. We had communicated by letter and then e-mail but had never met. The conference was just beginning. I nervously looked around for a place to sit. After settling in at a random place (there were plenty of empty seats), I glanced over at the nametag of the person sitting next to me. It was Carlos Mirapeix!

Had I noted his nametag subconsciously sometime earlier? Did I glance at it as I sought a seat and it registered without my consciously being aware of it? Or was it our mutual desire to find each other that led me to that seat? I don't know. However it happened, I was delighted to find him, and he was delighted to meet me.

In 1989 two well-respected statisticians, Persi Diaconis and Frederick Mosteller, presented a thorough look at coincidences. They admitted that some coincidences are so remarkable that they couldn't find statistical ways to explain them. But they also offered several cautions to coincidence enthusiasts:

1. It is difficult to determine the accuracy of coincidence stories, and whether some of them even happened.

2. The more you think about something or someone, the higher the likelihood that you will encounter that something or someone while ignoring how often you had been thinking about it/him/her.

3. Coincidences are formed in the minds of the observer. Their occurrence depends very much on remembering a specific thought and also recognizing that this thought is reflected outside the mind. Some people have categories in their minds for coincidences and can remember them. Others don't.

4. Cultures influence the degree to which coincidences will be noticed.

5. How similar are the two (or more) events? How much room do we allow for near misses or near hits? Some romantics caught in the throes of love seek out evidence that their union is meant to be. They've been known to stretch similarities in names, locations, vocations, and history to prove they have already been meant to be together.[12]

The statisticians should have added one more item: How close in time must the elements of a coincidence be? Jung started with synchronicity—meaning "taking place together in time." However, some very impactful coincidences are composed of elements very separated in time (for examples, see Chapter 9 for the full-circle coincidences).

Acquaintances and Strangers

Coincidences involving people we hardly know can also draw on intense emotion.

Susan Watkins described an intersection between television and real life: Hugh Wheeler of Elmira, New York, found himself feeling connected to a TV actor named Peter Deuel (also known as Pete Duel), who costarred in *Alias Smith and Jones* from the early 1970s. Deuel seemed familiar somehow. Hugh purchased a large wall poster intending to hang it, but then on December 31, 1971, Deuel was found shot to death in his Hollywood apartment, an apparent suicide. The poster became a source of embarrassment to Hugh, who then stashed it in his closet, still in the tube, and forgot about it.

Twenty years later, Hugh's youngest son, Chad, decided to surprise his father for Christmas by having the poster framed and wrapped. On Christmas day, Hugh was about to rip open the present when the phone rang. Chad answered the phone and returned looking pale and frightened. He reported that someone from a military base had called, refusing to identify himself, who had been given Hugh's number as the place where Jeff Deuel, Peter's younger brother, could be reached!

Of course, the Wheelers had no explanation for how this could've happened. The Deuel family had lived in Rochester, New York, not too far away, but that was all the connection they could make. The area codes were entirely different for Elmira and Rochester (607 and 716, respectively).[13]

Did the energy associated with opening that old emotionally laden poster help set in motion a chain of events that culminated in this exquisitely timed telephone call? For Hugh Wheeler, the memory of Peter Deuel was briefly reignited.

From the Statistical Laboratory at the University of Cambridge comes another tale of telephones and strangers:

When I was a teenager in South Africa in the late '70s, I was travelling to England on holiday with my sister. We were waiting for our flight at Jan Smuts airport in Johannesburg when I decided to phone my best friend in a suburb of Jo'burg called Bryanston. Whilst I was chatting to her from the telephone booth, I noticed that the man in the booth next door was struggling to use his phone so I asked my friend to hold on a minute whilst I helped this man (who I did not know!). I asked if I could help him and he was very pleased and said that he was from England and had just arrived in SA and was trying to call a colleague. I said "Ok, which town does he live in?" He said, "Johannesburg," so I told him what numbers to dial and asked, "Which part of Johannesburg?" He said, "Sandton." I said, "Oh, I'm on the phone to someone in Sandton" and told him what to dial. Then I said, "What part of Sandton?" He said, "Bryanston," and I replied, "Oh, I'm on the phone to someone in Bryanston. Who are you trying to call?" He said

"Julian L." I said, "You won't believe this, but I'm on the phone to his daughter!! Come and use my phone and I'll ask my friend to get her dad!" I went back into my booth and said to my friend, "The man I was helping wants to speak to your dad, can you get him please!"[14]

The base rates for two strangers next to each other in phone booths to be calling the same family at the same time would be hard to determine, especially if one person is going to the country the other person has just left. The young woman asked the right questions. Even if the base rates for the simultaneous phone calls could be calculated, what then is the chance that one person would feel the need to help the other *and* act on it? What made her offer the help? She probably sensed a resonance between the two of them that she could never articulate and *knew* without knowing that she could be of help. Because of this feeling of knowing, it was easy for her to do. And, fun, too.

Kindness and politeness can bring us out of our usual patterns of behavior and sometimes yield fruitful results. Kindness and politeness can bring us out of our usual patterns of behavior and sometimes yield fruitful results. Each of the following coincidence stories illustrates this idea in different ways. The first report comes from the Koestler Foundation collection of coincidence stories. The foundation solicited self-reports over several decades and received thousands of replies.

"John Carr" became deeply depressed when his first serious gay relationship was ending. He decided to commit suicide by starving himself because his lover had liked him thin. On a day he had eaten nothing, the doorbell rang. A woman he knew only slightly handed him a cake "she thought he might like." Her kind gesture became a turning point for him. He began to take care of himself again.

They had met at a cricket match where she was the caterer. He had expressed his appreciation for her efforts. He later asked her why she had brought the cake when she did. She told him that she "had *suddenly* conceived the idea of making and delivering the cake" to him. Her kind gesture became a turning point for him.[15]

How did this woman know where he lived? The report doesn't tell us. What it does tell us is that this woman somehow picked up John's need and responded to it, much as we have seen in simulpathity stories where a close relative feels the need and sometimes can act upon it. John's compliments seemed to have "tuned" the woman to him. This coincidence of need being matched by the action of another demonstrates that casual acquaintances can pick up these feelings, much like a family member or significant other can.

In the next situation, another form of politeness helped to save a life.

Rabbi Samuel Shapira practiced the Talmudic dictum to try to greet a person first when on his daily walks. In 1930s Poland, relationships between Jews and non-Jews were strained. One of the people he met on his walks through town was a farmer named Mueller, who turned away in stony silence when greeted. Day after day the rabbi persisted with his hearty, "Good morning, Herr Mueller," until the farmer began to reply with a tip of his hat and a faint smile. This routine went on for many years, as Mueller also began to reply, "Good morning, Herr Rabiner."

This all stopped when the Nazis invaded Poland. The rabbi was deported to many different concentration camps and finally to Auschwitz. He was forced into a line at the head of which was the camp's commandant, who would swing his baton to the right or to the left to indicate where each person should go. Left meant certain death in the gas chambers while right offered the possibility of survival. The rabbi drew closer. Would the baton go left or right? Despite his terror, he looked directly into the eyes of the commandant.

Their eyes locked.

"Good morning, Herr Mueller."

For a brief moment, the cold eyes flickered. "Good morning, Herr Rabiner," he replied, swinging the baton to the right.[16]

The baton might've gone right anyway, but I choose to believe that the rabbi's persistent politeness stacked the coin flip in his favor.

 TEST THE IDEA THAT politeness increases the likelihood of coincidences.

Like Attracts Like

In 2012, I very much wanted to thank someone, also a matter of politeness, and here is the coincidence that resulted: Russ F. had to cancel lunch with me, so I asked my friend and colleague, the very popular David B., to join me. I was surprised he had the time to join me, as he's a very social guy. We walked to a Greek restaurant on the downtown mall in Charlottesville. We were early for the lunch crowd and Dave picked a table by the window near the entrance where he could see anyone who walked in and they could see him. Sure enough, he smiled a greeting to one person and then another, and then he happily said, "Hi, Russ." My back was to the door, so I was puzzled: Russ? I thought he couldn't make it. I turned around to see another person named Russ. Dave introduced us.

I'd wanted to meet this Russ; I just didn't know his name. A month earlier my wife and I had gone to Saturday morning services at the local synagogue for my father's Yahrzeit, the annual remembrance of a loved one during which the prayer, the Kaddish, is recited. We had arrived late. The place was full; there was nowhere to sit. The usher directed us to a narrow space in the back row and we squeezed in. The bearded man sitting there politely got up as we went in and quietly left, gesturing kindly that we take the space. I very much wanted to thank him, but we left soon after the services and didn't see him. Several times I thought of how I would like to thank him.

That bearded man was the other Russ who walked into the Greek restaurant. I reminded him of his kind gesture; he remembered, and I thanked him. The circle was completed.

One Russ fades, another one appears around the appointed time. Random, you say? The second Russ was meeting his wife and friends for lunch at a good restaurant. He worked downtown sometimes, so the probabilities were there. When I sent an e-mail about this coincidence involving him to the skeptical Russ F. (the friend who'd had to cancel lunch with me), he replied with a fantasy story about having dressed himself up as the other Russ and showing up to fool me. It was a clever story, but when I asked how he knew that I would be seated with my back to the door, he answered, "A grasshopper told me." He constructed this fable to avoid having to think about the coincidence itself. Human beings invent many ways to avoid challenging dearly held beliefs, and so it is with coincidences.

On the other hand, statisticians will complain that I'm remembering only the positive hits, not the many times there was no coincidence. It's true that I have a bias toward convincing myself and others that coincidences are often not just random, and I intentionally and unintentionally select stories to confirm my bias toward the usefulness of coincidences. This bias toward confirmation, or the "confirmation bias," resides deeply in all of us. Political television, radio programs, and websites confirm the biases of their audiences. They tell the audience members what they want to hear so that the audience experiences that positive sensation of having a belief confirmed. So, like the mystery filmmaker Alfred Hitchcock, I'm taking out the boring parts of life to highlight the interesting ones, those compelling, hard-to-explain connections between mind and environment. There are so many of them.

Paul Kammerer, the Viennese biologist who was an early student of coincidence, emphasized another important characteristic of many coincidences we come across repeatedly: similarity. Like attracts like. People become friends because they are similar. Kammerer emphasized this important characteristic of coincidence and developed a theory to explain it based on the science of his time. One of his more dramatic examples involved two strangers who lay wounded in a hospital in Kattowitz, Bohemia, in 1915. Both were nineteen years old, had life-threatening pneumonia, were from the town of Schlesien, were volunteer drivers, and had the same name: Franz Richter. One of them was dying, but by mistake the relatives of the other one were told their Franz was dying. Because the two young men looked alike, the family of the other Franz believed they were staring at their own dying son. Sometime after the burial, their true son announced himself as alive.[17]

The two soldiers had seven common features: age, city of origin, job description, illness, first name, last name, and physical resemblance. Kammerer made nothing personal out of these parallel lives but used the case as one of more than a hundred examples of *seriality*, by which he meant the clustering of similar events in time. He spent hours sitting on benches in various public parks, noting the people who passed by, classifying them by sex, age, dress, whether they carried umbrellas or parcels, and so on. He did the same during the long train rides from his home to his office in Vienna. Kammerer wasn't particularly interested in meaning, only sequences of similar things. His examples include apparently insignificant repetitions of numbers, names, words, and letters. One involved his wife, who was in a waiting room reading about a painter named Schwalbach when a fellow patient named Mrs. Schwalbach was called into the consultation room. Another involved his brother-in-law, who went to a concert and received cloakroom ticket #9, which was the same number as his seat. Shortly thereafter, he and his brother-in-law went to another concert and again his brother-in-law's cloakroom ticket, #21, matched his seat number. A third example involved his friend Prince Rohan. On the train, his wife was reading a novel with a character named "Mrs. Rohan." She saw a man get on the train who looked like Prince Rohan. Later that night, the prince himself dropped by their house for a visit.

Kammerer developed complex categories and proposed a dense theory about why so many similar things seem to cluster together in time. He believed that information could never be destroyed, only dispersed. Under certain conditions, similar forms of information seemed to be attracted back to each other and then observed.[18]

Parallel lives, like Kammerer's two Franz Richters, can be quite startling, and they can also take on a strong personal meaning. For example, Arthur, my cousin's friend, told me about his chance encounter with a man with many similarities to himself.

After graduating from City University of New York in 1966, I was hired by Shell Oil Company for their executive training program at corporate headquarters in New York City in the RCA Building. I was hired by a man named Leroy Drury, who headed the program. In my four years there, I worked for two other men, E.V. and L.T. Although they were located in the heart of New York City, almost all key spots were held by Texans.

In August 1969, I was offered a position in what was to become their new corporate headquarters in Houston, Texas. As L.T. stated, I was "almost as good as his boys down in Texas" (his version of a compliment). They suggested that I go down to Houston and work for a few weeks. I went there in August 1969. Houston in August was totally tolerable only after I figured out how to never go outdoors between the hotel and the office. Oh well, it was tempting, but I passed on this wonderful adventure.

Fast-forward about forty years to a trip my wife and I made to the Canadian Rockies. The trip started in Seattle, Washington. The tour group met on a party ship that toured the Seattle waterways with sites such as the Bill Gates estate. On the ship we were all given a slip of paper with another tour person's name on it. We had to go through the group of people looking for that individual. My individual was a fellow named Mark, whom I found after talking to several other people who were not Mark. This was a clever way of meeting our fellow travelers. If you knew me better, you'd know I found this exercise extremely painful. In any case, Mark and I met, and our initial conversation resulted in the following.

- Mark was recruited by Leroy Drury in 1965; I was recruited by Leroy in 1966.

- He started on the forty-third floor of the RCA Building and worked on that floor until 1970; I started on the forty-third floor and worked on that floor until 1970.

- His first assignment was working for E.V.; my first assignment was working for E.V. one year later.

- He was eventually transferred to L.T.; I was eventually transferred to L.T.

- We both served in the National Guard and received half pay from Shell for six months of active duty in 1967 (which wasn't an easy accomplishment).

- He went to Houston in August 1969 to work there for a couple of weeks to see if he liked it; I went to Houston in August 1969 to see if I liked it.

- He decided to go to Houston and worked for Shell for forty more years; I went on to work for seventeen companies over the next forty years.

- I had met the man who took the offer I turned down.

Arthur saw this meeting as an opportunity to see what his life might've been like had he taken the job in Houston. He confronted the possibility that at each juncture point in our lives, many possibilities exist, as if there are numerous parallel universes each with its own consequences.

The chances were pretty high that two men about the same age and same income bracket would take a tour like this. That Arthur would be given Mark's name to seek out was very unlikely. Perhaps Kammerer was on to something with his theory that like attracts like. Even more unexpectedly, the two Laura Buxtons with their list of similarities were drawn together through a helium balloon. Not only does similarity help keep us connected to each other, as the twin stories tell us, but similarity also helps bring people together who were previously unknown to each other.

Kashmir Hill was creepily surprised when she received an e-mail with a photo of someone who looked almost exactly like her. Three of Kashmir's friends had approached this other person, whose name was Leigh, thinking it was Kashmir. Leigh then tracked down Kashmir. U.K. journalist Sophie Robehmed used crowd-sourcing to locate her facial twin. When Niamh Geany made a video of her meeting with a stranger who looked just like her, the video went viral. There is something amazing about looking at someone who looks just like you. Unlike the two Lauras and Arthur, however, the similarities between Kashmir and Leigh stopped at the superficial level.[19]

DO YOU KNOW A PAIR OF DOPPELGÄNGERS?
What do doppelgängers tell you about the nature of coincidences?

CHAPTER 5

Health Solutions

We alternate between two worlds—sickness and health. Sickness arrives unexpectedly, takes us out of our usual routines, and often alters consciousness through fever, pain, isolation, and worry. During those sometimes silent hours and long, lonely days, the immobility and weakness are harbingers of aging and dying. Sometimes sickness lingers for months and becomes chronic. We become shadows of our former selves, remembering the joy of unencumbered health, learning in various degrees to accept and surpass the new, unwelcomed physical-emotional states.

The transition from health to sickness, the altered states of mind that sickness brings with it, and the vision of being healed provide another fertile breeding ground for coincidences.

Healing the Body

How do you know when to seek medical help? Some people too readily make doctor appointments for minor aches and pains, while others wait until something bulges out of their abdomen or they can't move. Physicians often balk at becoming a patient, as did Dr. Esther Sternberg, until a coincidence pointed her toward helping her body heal itself.

I heard Sternberg's story in March 2010 while attending the Integrative Mental Health Conference in Phoenix, Arizona. Onstage, Sternberg, a researcher at the National Institute of Health, appeared vital, energetic, enthusiastic, smart, and wise. As a neuroendocrinology-rheumatology researcher, she was trying to convince her colleagues that stress could affect the immune system. Sternberg knew that stress makes people sick and that a third of Americans were living under conditions of extreme stress. She wanted to show how stress causes physical illness. As she was promoting these ideas, her mother was dying of breast cancer. Sternberg didn't notice that she, too, was under much stress.[1]

After moving into a new house in Washington, DC, she flew to Montreal for the last three weeks of her mother's life. As she was coming back on the plane, she noticed that one of her knees was swollen. She thought that maybe she had somehow injured herself. After a few weeks, the other knee swelled up. Then other joints began to ache. Here she was: a rheumatologist living with inflammatory arthritis!

The last thing she wanted to deal with was being hospitalized. She was writing her first book and wanted to get it finished. One day, as she was working at the computer in her new home, someone knocked on her door. It was her new neighbors. They welcomed her with some Greek food—moussaka, dolmades, and other delicious, wholesome treats.

Seeing all the words on her computer monitor, they asked, "Are you a writer?"

"Why do you ask?" She didn't think of herself as a writer.

"Because we always wanted a writer to stay in our cottage in Crete."

She soon found herself in Crete and there learned the healing power of place and diet. She was now removed from the stress of Washington, DC, and enjoying the calm of her idyllic island surroundings. She began what became known as the Mediterranean diet, food much like her neighbors had brought her. The diet is composed of olive oil, legumes, unprocessed grains, fresh fruits and vegetables, some dairy products (mostly as cheese and yogurt), fish, a little meat, and moderate amounts of wine. This diet, with variations, has been repeatedly shown to help reduce heart disease and cancer. Her arthritis receded. She also recognized the possibility that a change in environment had accelerated her recovery. She began new research to formally test the untapped power of calming physical location in helping people recover from stress-related illness.

Her research shows how places help people heal by activating the brain's own self-healing abilities. Another researcher studied the outcomes of people healing from gall bladder surgery. Those who had a bed near a window that enabled them to see trees and sky healed a day faster and with less pain medication than those whose bed was next to a wall. Sternberg is encouraging hospital architects to design healing places rather than the stressful environments most current hospitals have become. She advises each of us to find places that soothe us: a certain chair, a certain room, or someplace outside, which for her is a garden on the grounds of Washington's National Cathedral.

Being in her new house facilitated the development of this important message. Sternberg discovered, through her neighbors' generosity, help for herself and potential help for many others. How did it happen? Sternberg believed her mother played a part in bringing her

to that house, which she needed not only for writing but also for healing, just as Jerry believed his deceased father had brought him and
Rita together on the airplane. But is there another possibility? Could
belief in forces outside themselves have helped them activate their
own innate capacities and internal GPS? I believe that Sternberg didn't
consciously know she was seeking help for her inflammatory arthritis
and that she was guided by her *behavioral unconscious*, that part of
our unconscious containing wisdom and information that helps us find
what we need.

The behavioral unconscious of mothers helps them take care of their
children. At age nine, Kent began to suffer much stomach distress. His
parents noticed that his shoe size didn't change. And he didn't get
any taller. They took him to a pediatric gastroenterologist who spent
a lot of time with them. He set Kent up for a procedure that would
peer into his stomach and intestines. The results were ambiguous; any
number of things might be involved. Considering the possibility that
he was suffering from an inflammatory problem, the doctor prescribed
steroids (prednisone). That treatment was brief because Kent became
hyperactive: he couldn't sleep, and he talked a lot. It might've been
funny had he slowed down every once in a while. He didn't. Steroids
can trigger mania in some people, as well as depression, so they dis-
continued that treatment.

He limped through his teenage years, not telling his parents about his
stomach pain or the diarrhea he experienced seven or more times a day.
Then he got a little better and started growing again. A few years later
he had more tests, though they still didn't reveal anything definitive.

By his third year of college, he had had enough. He wanted help.
So his parents began another round of testing with a gastroenterologist
at the university, but the test results were still not conclusive. Then

one day, before receiving the test results, Kent and his mother were deeply immersed in a stomach discussion, trying to figure out what to do. Suddenly, she realized she had a haircut appointment and rushed off. She arrived late, out of breath, and apologetic. In the midst of this frenzy, his mother did something out of character. She told the friendly stranger who cut her hair about her son. This very private mother was now gushing out her anxiety and pain in a public place.

The hair stylist replied with her own story. She had similar problems that went undiagnosed until she found an allergy doctor who tested her and found her to be allergic to several different types of food. Kent's mother quickly got the name of the specialist and made an appointment.

After being tested, Kent discovered that he had food allergies and had to refrain from eating anything that came from a cow—meat and milk. He could eat pizza every once in a while, but he knew the consequences. When he managed his diet well, the symptoms he had lived with for most of his life were negligible compared to the earlier pain and suffering he had endured.

The potential to find help depends on the environment in which a person is searching. The help has to be out there somewhere. A dog searching for a bone is more likely to find one in the forest than in a desert. In addition to heightened emotion, need, and a change in regular routine, the right environment for discovery becomes an important variable in matching need to outcome.

Kent's mom was in a heighted state of anxiety and need because of her concern for him. She was also upset about being

In addition to heightened emotion, need, and a change in regular routine, the right environment for discovery becomes an important variable in matching need to outcome.

uncharacteristically late to her hair appointment. As a result, this private woman talked about personal problems with a relative stranger who happened to have the right information. Was this meeting just a random event? I believe her behavioral unconscious was activated in an opportunity-filled environment. She sensed that she was close to what she needed and began to talk.

Like Sternberg and Kent's mom, many people unexpectedly discover needed medical information, as did the women in the next stories. One of our study participants who was having difficulties with her daughter told us about going to an auction:

> My daughter, who has attention deficit disorder and a major learning disability, was just finishing grade school, reading at a first-grade level. I was pretty upset about the possibilities for failure in her life because of this. Within a month or so I "ran" into someone at an auction in rural Missouri with whom I had worked about seven years earlier. She told me about a program in Kansas City that had taught her son to read, so we investigated it. A couple of years later my daughter was reading a grade level above her age-group. I felt like "fate" or "grace" had put me at the right place at the right time to give us guidance on something that would work for my daughter.

In another story, a woman named Val told Robert Hopcke (the Jungian therapist mentioned earlier in the book) about making a rare visit to her unhappy childhood home. She had gone to her parent's house to relieve her mother from caretaking for her sick, pain-ridden father. Val didn't want to sleep in the house she had fled many years previously but did so reluctantly. She woke up one morning feeling "a powerful message" to drive to a shopping center she had never visited, enter a bookstore, go directly to the natural healing section, pick a specific

book, and open it to a page that described the use of camphor oil and
flannel for pain relief. Mystified, she followed this strong feeling, went
to the bookstore, found the book, and looked up information about
camphor oil and flannel. She bought the book and then bought the camphor oil and flannel and returned home. She encouraged her mother to
follow the directions in the book and massage her husband's painful
areas. Not only was his pain relieved, but, more important, what had
been a negatively charged marital relationship became a loving one
that lasted for the final year of his life.[2]

The natural treatment done with the help of an estranged daughter
through the physical touch of an exhausted wife combined to help a
body and relationship heal. Val knew where to go without knowing how
she knew. Her behavioral unconscious guided her to a specific page
in a book "out there" that turned a painful situation into a loving one.

Less dramatic examples of finding solutions to physical problems
seem to occur fairly regularly. Solutions are floating around us; we
only need to be open to receiving them.

A friend of mine was experiencing twinges in his lower back after
doing some exercises at the gym that were not part of his normal routine. He told me he had been lying on the couch watching TV when he
noticed a movie actor on the screen who was lying on a massage table,
getting massaged. The actor was in the same position my friend used
for his back exercises, which he had forgotten to do. So he got down
on the floor and did the exercises. The pain disappeared. He took the
hint offered to him. Hints like this are out there. We just need to look
for them.

A psychiatrist friend liked paying attention to messages like this,
much to her benefit, it turns out. She had twisted her ankle. Her ortho-
pedic surgeon put a light cast on it, saying it would soon be okay. But

several months later, it wasn't okay. A tennis friend suggested that she see a physical therapist named Brad. The psychiatrist refused; she would wait it out. Shortly after receiving that suggestion, a patient who had severely sprained her ankle, and whom she hadn't seen for several months, came in walking normally.

The patient was wearing the same brand and model of tennis shoes that the psychiatrist had worn when she twisted her ankle. *Well, hello,* the psychiatrist said to herself. She then asked the patient who she had gone to for physical therapy. Her answer was "Brad"! The psychiatrist got the message, went to Brad, and soon her ankle was healing.

 IF AND WHEN YOU ARE CONFRONTED WITH a major medical dilemma, scan your surroundings for possible solutions, sometimes looking in odd places.

One of our research participants intuitively registered the terrible distress of someone nearby whom she didn't know:

Several years ago I was babysitting out in the country in a home that was very secluded. At lunch, I happened to open the blinds on the sliding glass door. At that very moment, I saw a man way out in a pasture on a tractor pulling a plow. In the instant that I glanced at him, the spring broke on the old tractor seat and the man fell off the seat and the back wheel of the tractor rolled over him, then his body got mangled under the blades of the plow as the tractor kept driving. If I hadn't opened those curtains at that very moment to see the man fall, he would be dead today. We were out in the middle of nowhere. The man later said nobody knew he was out in the pasture, and both of his lungs were punctured and rapidly filling with blood, so he couldn't yell for help. He couldn't walk because his legs were crushed and he was rapidly deteriorating. I called 911 and ran out to help him. Had I not seen him in that instant, he would've died. What a coincidence!

She didn't know why she opened the blinds—she just happened to. Perhaps she heard something. Perhaps not.

The tractor rescue by a stranger suggests a human ability to know about physical problems of others in nonordinary ways. Of course, many people die suddenly and alone without someone sensing their impending death and rushing to their aid. Not everyone is rescued by a loved one or a stranger or anyone. Baseball players strike out, financial geniuses make terrible decisions, surgeries go bad, and medications harm rather than help. None of what we try to do helps each and every time. Nor are we always able to pick up when a loved one or even a nearby stranger is in trouble. Yet this ability to sometimes sense the physical problems of others seems to dwell within us. And this sensibility can be developed.

Medical Intuitives

Physicians sometimes surprise themselves when they make diagnoses in nonordinary ways, as happened to primary care physician Ian Rubenstein of London, England. One Saturday Rubenstein had an edgy feeling that compelled him to go the gym. There he found Catherine, a former patient of his whom he had helped with a driving phobia. She told him that her granddaughter Kirsty had swallowed a cap from a plastic ballpoint pen during school the day before. Kirsty was given a drink of water. "With that," Rubenstein wrote, "I had an awful, pressing feeling in my chest. As I experienced this, I developed a strong impression she'd inhaled the pen cap and it had lodged in one of the main tubes of her lungs."

Rubenstein insisted upon talking with Kirsty's mother, Vicky, who reported that her daughter was just fine except that she didn't feel like going to her ballet lesson. He asked Vicky to tell Kirsty to run around the yard and listen to her breathing. Kirsty was wheezing. Then Rubenstein asked that Vicky put her ear to either side of Kirsty's chest and listen. The wheezing was louder on the right side than the left. Since most inhaled objects travel down the right main bronchus, Rubenstein was now convinced that she had inhaled the cap.

Although two chest x-rays were negative, both mother and grandmother insisted upon a direct look into the lungs with a bronchoscope. The pulmonologist agreed to perform the procedure and ended up pulling out the chewed pen cap from her right main bronchus. Because she had chewed it, the plastic cap had frayed, producing little barbs that had embedded the cap into the bronchus wall. Kirsty couldn't have coughed it up. She more than likely would've developed pneumonia or perhaps something worse.

Rubenstein had made a diagnosis through the story of a grandmother about a granddaughter he had never met. Simulpathity-like, he felt an awful feeling in his chest after hearing about Kirsty's swallowing the cap. He then was able to convert the feeling into a visual image of the cap in one of her lungs. That visual image became a diagnostic clue that led to a successful treatment.[3]

My own brush with medical intuition started with my need to earn continuing medical education (CME) credits to maintain my license to practice medicine. From the online Medscape education section, I could select from more than fifty brief courses in psychiatry. For some reason I picked one about sleep apnea, which I didn't know much about. It can present as depression, and I memorized most of its key criteria, including snoring and at least five episodes per hour of sleep during which the person stops breathing. People who are more likely to have sleep apnea complain about daytime sleepiness, are often obese, and have thick necks. The image of a thick neck stuck with me.

The following day, I saw a new depressed patient who had a thick neck, was obese, complained of daytime sleepiness, snored, and, according to his wife, stopped breathing during the night. Did my selection of this topic have something to do with a sense that my new patient would present with these symptoms? I randomly chose obstructive sleep apnea from a long list of possibilities. Depression and bipolar disorder had been my previous favorite CME subjects. It seemed like it was time for a change. Once again, openness to randomness and breaking free of habit opened the gates for an instrumental coincidence.

Making a diagnosis through nonordinary means has drawn enough attention to warrant the creation of an organization of medical intuitives. Begun in 2002, the International Association of Medical Intuitives has a membership listing that includes no MDs and very few people with advanced degrees. They offer diagnosis at a distance, as Rubenstein did with the pen cap problem.

Edgar Cayce, sometimes known as the "sleeping prophet," was said to have made thousands of diagnostic and treatment recommendations for people both in his presence and at a distance while he was in a trance. In the 1920s, he founded several organizations in Virginia Beach, Virginia, which are now known as the Association for Research and Enlightenment and Atlantic University to study and promote what were to become many "New Age" ideas, including alternative and complementary medicine.

Most medical schools disregard the possibility of intuitive diagnosis and healing. Instead they rely more and more upon "evidence-based treatment," which usually means treatments that are supported by double-blind, placebo-controlled studies. Most physicians are dissuaded from sharpening their intuition, although how a doctor can practice medicine without some consideration of inner promptings is a mystery to me. Clinical experience, personal experience with sickness, gut feelings, and inner promptings can and do add to our rational knowledge and help our patients. Cases of simulpathity demonstrate the human ability to know the physical and emotional state of others, at a distance. Some medical research on the subject does exist.

Radiologist Larry Burk has reviewed the scant literature.[4] The research suggests a little more strongly than anecdotally that some people are very good at picking up the medical problems of others at a distance. Unfortunately, most medical intuitives seem reluctant to participate in research because they wouldn't only be helping the patient, they would also be helping the researcher. Apparently the patient's need is the driving force in coming to an intuitive diagnosis. Medical intuition differs from the previous examples of simulpathity by its intentionality. The practitioner deliberately intends to diagnose the medical difficulties of a specific person. So the capacity for simulpathity appears to be within the conscious grasp of some people. This possibility means that physicians and nurses can develop their own simulpathity abilities, and many of the most skilled ones probably do so without realizing it. They then can integrate rational, data-driven decision making with their continuously honed intuitive senses.

Psychotherapy and Counseling Through Coincidence

Psychological help arrives in many forms—from relatives and friends, from experiences both good and bad. Like psychotherapy itself, the two essentials for psychological growth are the recognition that change is needed and a willingness to examine maladaptive patterns of thought and behavior. Sometimes after therapists describe a key pattern to their patients, the surprised patient says that someone close to them (parent, spouse, best friend) has said the same thing. They had been ignoring what their loved ones were telling them. Because they are paying me for help, and because I had no personal benefit in their change, they could listen and begin to take steps. Psychological change through coincidences also requires an openness to seeing maladaptive patterns.

Changing patterns usually proceeds in three steps: giving up the old pattern, beginning the new pattern, and then maintaining the new pattern. Each transition requires a conscious decision, which can be facilitated by coincidences. The example that follows comes directly from psychotherapy and illustrates how coincidence plus the therapist's comments foster the decision to change.

Carl Jung was seeing a highly educated "rational" young woman in psychotherapy. She repeatedly rebuffed his ideas, preferring, according to Jung, to remain highly rational and logical. Jung "attempted to sweeten her rationalism with a somewhat more human understanding" but with little success. He then hoped that "something unexpected and irrational would turn up." As she described a dream about a costly piece of jewelry in the shape of a golden scarab, a beetle that was holy to ancient Egyptians, Jung heard tapping on the office window. He opened the window and caught a scarab whose color and shape closely resembled the insect in her dream. He handed the beetle to the patient, saying, "Here is your scarab." The unexpected had happened just as Jung had hoped. Subsequently, the woman became more open to Jung's ideas. She took the first step toward changing by becoming willing to give up her old ways of thinking.[5]

Jung presented the story of the appearance of the scarab as a mystery to be solved by his theory of synchronicity, but he ignored the vital role he played in the drama. Jung fervently wanted something irrational to happen to help him break his patient's resistance. This intense desire by a very creative, very strong mind helped that wished-for beetle to arrive at Jung's office window at just the right time and for him to notice it. I'm suggesting that his mind may have drawn the beetle to the window. He completed the coincidence by opening the window, grabbing the insect, and presenting it to his patient. Without Jung's desire and alertness, this synchronicity wouldn't have been created. Our personal surroundings can be rich sources of psychotherapeutic coincidences. To see them seems to require some of the same mental states encouraged in the therapist's office—stepping out of your usual routine, heightened emotion, alertness to your own mind, and a desire for change, just like the person in the next vignette.

While on a solo vacation, Ali, who is a psychiatric colleague of mine, encountered a scene rich in metaphors for his personal romantic struggle. Like a friend, colleague, or psychotherapist who reflects back to you what you are thinking, the scene helped Ali decide what to do. He recalls:

I left the central station in Amsterdam and drifted into the city, with intense excitement that eclipsed all other feelings. I rented a solid bike and wandered off into the city. I was intensely exploring and absorbing my surroundings. As I passed the famous city canals, I remembered my recent romance and fantasized about an intimate boat ride with her. The grief of the lost relationship haunted me. I had decided she wasn't elegant enough. I biked faster.

I came across a neat antiques roadside market occupying a block by the river. I savored the relics of a past generation and reflected on their lives. I noticed a shawarma [grilled Arabian meat] stand in the middle of the market and my hunger started to build up. The image of my perfect next meal started to form. I saw myself sitting at a fancy restaurant table, right on a canal, watching the boats slowly go by. I craved something unique from Amsterdam, something that would nurture my intimacy with the city. Nothing spoke more loudly than the shawarma in terms of unique, but the setting was all wrong. Not fancy enough.

I got on my bike and explored further and saw countless restaurants along the way. But this one wasn't on a canal, and that one was just trite Italian cuisine. Another was a Burger King. An amazingly fancy place with tables right on the canal served only drinks.

My hunger grew stronger, and the practical dilemma presented itself. I couldn't continue looking for my perfect scene forever. At some point I would have to eat. Maybe perfection is not the only goal. Nevertheless, I was determined to have a pleasant experience.

I came upon a bridge over a canal—not a glamorous part of the city by any means. But near the bridge, three jazz musicians improvised. A crowd of idling people sat on the base of a sculpture nearby enjoying a mild summer breeze and music. An "aha" moment hit me, and a new picture started to form. I immediately flew to the nearby shawarma stand and rushed the Middle Easterner to provide a sandwich quickly.

I sat down amongst the crowd and enjoyed my well-earned, pleasant lunch with the sound of music and the view of the canal, surrounded by friendly people. My heart jumped at the perfection of the moment. I chatted excitedly with everyone around me. And as the happiness sank in, I remembered the last time I was this happy, and a sad insight hit me. My sadness bridged the two experiences.

I had just left my perfect happiness. I remembered her, the witty exchanges, and the deep conversations. I remembered how affectionate she was, and how affectionate I was, how both of us were addicted to travel and didn't own a TV. The harmony between us struck me in a wave of revelations. I saw how she was all the bits and pieces of what I had always wanted. She was intellectual and reserved, intelligent and modest. She understood me and I her.

But I let her go because my darkness prevailed. Things had to be fancy and perfect. I failed to see beyond her modest beauty because I needed to be seen with a stunning woman as I entered the room. As I basked in the sun of my coincidental heaven, I looked around me. I reflected upon how much happiness I found by the shabby bridge and the asphalt road, only to realize that none of it mattered. My quarrels with the relationship seemed utterly ridiculous. I saw how the world reflected my thought patterns, and as I looked into the mirror, I could see my error. The insight hit me, and I couldn't hold back the tears. I cried at the loss of the happiness. Even though I wasn't looking for her when I found her, I was determined to find her again.

Ali was searching for something to feed his body and his need for love. He found both at a casual scene by a canal in Amsterdam. His conflict was coincidentally mirrored by his surroundings, leading him to resolution. Two years later they were living together and planning to be married.

By noticing and analyzing mind mirrors, these symbolic coincidences, we can find aspects of ourselves in the forms and patterns around us and come away with a new perspective on our place in the world. The tangible helps us to access the intangible.

For some Jungians, Ali's coincidence fits with a sharp definition of synchronicity—the concurrence between a psychological conflict and a symbolic environmental event that helps the person make a significant psychological change. For Jungians, synchronicity implies a yet-to-be understood process by which mind and environment become temporarily connected. Ali's coincidence does not require a mysterious explanation. He was burning with desire to resolve the conflict between appearance and substance. Without clear, conscious intention, his hunger for simple food and resolution of emotional turmoil led him to select the situation that satisfied both needs. He created this coincidence subconsciously.

 WHEN YOU ARE STIRRED UP BY A PSYCHOLOGICAL conflict, look around at the patterns in your surroundings. Some of them may form a mirror of your mind and provide a useful perspective on your choices.

Grief

The objects and living creatures in the world around us can supply symbolic reassurances about the people we lose through death. Sometimes, these aids for grieving come from randomly appearing human creations.

Christine and her family were preparing for her mother's funeral. It had been an emotional and difficult few days, made worse because Christine hadn't seen her mother for many months. Christine lived out of state and wasn't able to get to her mother's bedside before she died. At the cemetery, in the waning hours of the afternoon before the funeral, the family decided to view the plot. An older woman in the nearby parking lot was standing next to a burgundy Buick Park Avenue, the same make, color, and model that Christine's mother had driven many years earlier until she could no longer drive. She'd always loved that car. As Christine and her family drove off, her brother-in-law commented, "Who is that woman staring at us?" Christine looked again. She noticed that the personalized license plates read "Ruby 2." Christine gasped and felt the fog of grief lift; her mother's name was Ruby.

The unexpected appearance of birds and flowers can also become grief-diminishing coincidences. A friend of mine recounted the brief story of a grieving mother whose child had died at the age of five. Shortly after the funeral, at an outdoor brunch, a small bird landed on her breast and stayed there for some thirty minutes, looking around, chirping, and looking at her. The woman finally shooed the small bird away, and with that movement of her hand, she began to let go of her child.

Birds can fly, land smoothly, ride the winds, and find their way over many, many miles. But are they sometimes spirit-like creatures attuned to the needs of human beings, helping us to feel part of the great wonder that they represent? It certainly looks like it.

Despite the existence of many stories like this, I have been skeptical about bird stories and reluctant to include them. These avian flights differ from other coincidences because the grieving person is not thinking about a bird when it shows up. Yet the bird's arrival becomes a mind mirror when its behavior mimics the lost loved one. How could the grief-stricken person not think this flying creature represented the lost person? Evolved from dinosaurs, birds reach for the heavens and sometimes carry us with them. The right bird at the right time helps with the healing process. At least what they do is help unleash our abilities to self-heal. Like placebo medications or unconditional acceptance by a counselor, they help us change the direction we are striving to take.

Flowers can also resonate with grieving. They perform their magic by blooming out of season just when someone needs reassurance. Author Taylor Caldwell's husband was dying after a long illness. Minutes before he died, she clutched his hand and pleaded, "If there is a life on the other side, I beg you to send me a sign. Let me know you are with me." He promised he would.

The next morning she sought comfort in her garden, pleading for a sign. As she approached a stubbornly infertile spot, her gaze landed on a rosemary bush that had never thrived. The day before she had walked these same grounds, seeking relief from her deathwatch and commenting to herself on the sad state of the bush's existence. One day later, it was in full bloom. She had received her message. She now believed that he was still with her. She knew the symbolic meaning of the plant: remembrance, love, loyalty, and fidelity. The bush bloomed where it had been failing the day before.[6]

How does one account for this unexpected yet hoped-for event except by believing that a loved one is sending a reassuring message? The more likely explanation lies with her need to believe that her husband still remembered her. Caldwell's need gave rise to the blooming rosemary. We have three choices here: the story is false, her husband made the plant bloom, or Caldwell's need energized it.

The giving of flowers may have originated from their spontaneous appearances in times of high emotion. Jennifer Hill was taking her grandmother back home after her grandfather's funeral. The grieving woman kept blotting the corners of her eyes with a well-worn tissue, still not able to let the full flood of tears begin. As they approached the house, the place that her grandmother had shared with her husband of forty years, Jennifer noticed a single gardenia blooming next to the entrance. Gardenias don't bloom in November. It was her grandmother's favorite flower. Her grandfather knew that. Jennifer waited for her grandmother to notice its sweet, pungent scent. When she saw it, her tears finally began to flow. The healing began. He had sent her favorite flower. The clipped gardenia, placed in a vase, became the centerpiece for the celebration of their life together.[7]

In each of these stories involving a bird or flowers, the person experiencing the coincidence was in intense transition, high emotion, and very much in need of comforting. How many bird and flower stories do we need to suggest that these common spiritual symbols can and do play active roles in our lives?

A clue to how these coincidences between mind and living symbols take place comes in a simple paragraph from psychiatrist Viktor Frankl, who was writing about his experience in a Nazi concentration camp near the end of World War II in 1945. He was thinking of his wife, long separated from him, and not knowing whether she was alive or dead. They had been married in 1942. That same year he, his wife, his parents, and his brother were all arrested and sent to the camps. His parents and brother had died. His sister survived because she had immigrated to Australia.

"More and more I felt that my wife was with me," Frankl wrote. "I had the feeling that I was able to touch her, able to stretch out my hand and grasp hers. The feeling was very strong; she was there. Then, at that very moment, a bird flew down silently and perched just in front of me, on the heap of soil which I had dug up from the ditch, and looked steadily at me." He felt the presence of his wife.[8]

Like us, birds and plants are tuned in to their surroundings. In their own ways, they sense need, human need, which evokes behavior from them that we can interpret as reassurance. Frankl was tuned in to love, deep into his feeling for his wife, yearning to be near her. Like birds migrating to their annual feeding grounds, some seem able to sense a human feeling that draws them.

Our domesticated animal companions, dogs and cats and others, can sense our needs, too. Dogs lick our wounds, attempt to comfort us when we are distressed, and seem to listen to our complaints. When my son Karlen dislocated the patella of his right knee, his dog Walter took many opportunities to lie across his knee in a seeming attempt to nurse him back to health.

Cats can also have an extraordinary sensitivity to people. There is the well-known story of Oscar, who could sense when someone was dying. The staff of the Rhode Island Steere House Nursing and Rehabilitation Center where Oscar lived relied on his exquisite sensitivity to the person on the brink of death. He wandered the halls like a regular cat until he sensed an impending death. Then he would go to that person, curl up, and purr until the person died. When Oscar singled out someone, the staff hurriedly called the family. He seemed to help the person make the transition from life. His purring and cuddling seemed to be his attempt to comfort the dying person.[9]

 HOW DOES YOUR DOG OR CAT KNOW WHEN YOU NEED COMFORTING? Take a long, deep look at your animal friend. You have a similar capacity.

The capacity for simulpathity exists more deeply within most of us than we recognize. People known as empaths can know the feeling states of others, both in the present and at a distance. As counseling intuitives, they can know the feeling state of another and respond to it. A nurse empath described her experience of conscious simulpathity this way: "Since I'm an empath, I often feel pain, pressure, or discomfort in my own body which corresponds with the area of distress in the individual I'm working on. Often this kicks in without my 'working on' the person, and quite often this is felt in encounters in chat programs over the Internet. In those cases, I have learned to ask if the person involved is feeling this or that in this or that area. I have learned that if

I can help the person to release it, then I get relief right away, so there is an element of selfishness here."[10]

During my work as a psychotherapist, I deeply enjoy picking up information about my patients without their having told me. Sometimes the patterns I see are explained as sophisticated pattern recognition, a skill developed over many years of listening to people and writing about the therapeutic process. Sometimes I, like many of my colleagues, say something, without knowing why, with no preparation and planning, and the patient responds with an amazed smile. "How did you know that?"

I usually have no good explanation, except that like most of us, I know things that I don't know how I know.

CHAPTER 6

Ideas in the Air

All ideas are not created equal. Many thoughts become "cognitive noise," distracting us from tasks and needs. Some entertain us. Others rise into consciousness to influence thought and action. In previous chapters we have seen highly charged ideas like romance, family and friends, and sickness motivate people to engage meaningful coincidences. In this chapter we encounter charged ideas involving libraries, the Internet, pharmacology, decision making, and novels.

Idea Coincidences

Idea coincidences are common because so many ideas are floating in our minds and around us. Some of these mind-environment similarities strike us as interesting in themselves. Their significance lies not necessarily in how they can be used but in raising questions about how they happen. Is this small coincidence God murmuring to me or just another random intersection of thought and context? Or is something else at work? Inconsequential idea coincidences can serve this useful purpose. They become hints that something a little out of the ordinary is going on in our ordinary lives. They sensitize us to the likelihood of more consequential possibilities. And they lead us to examine the range of explanations from statistical clatter to untapped human potential to peeks into mystery, and how they may each contribute.

To systematically test the idea that coincidences commonly occur, we asked questions about them in our coincidence survey at the University of Missouri-Columbia. For example, when asked about the frequency of this coincidence—"I think about a song and then hear it on the radio"—30 percent said "often." Songs become popular because a large number of people are thinking about them, usually because they generate a positive feeling. Our thoughts give songs life.

The timing of a song on the radio led Sissy Spacek to an Academy Award. Sissy never liked being told what to do. So when singer Loretta Lynn started telling gossip columnists and hosts of daytime and nighttime talk shows that Sissy was going to play Loretta in *A Coal Miner's Daughter*, Sissy had to meet this woman. They met for the first time in a parking lot outside Loretta's tour bus in Shreveport, Louisiana. The power of Loretta's personality instantly convinced Sissy to play this woman! But she had misgivings, too. How could she play a real person who was still living? The director then told her she didn't fit the part, but Universal Studios was still pressing her to take the part, as was her agent. Her manager was advising against it.

In the middle of this tense push and pull, Sissy and her husband, Jack, flew to Washington, DC, to visit his mom. Gerri lived in a highrise apartment building and drove a big white Cadillac and didn't like country music. Her car radio was always tuned to classical. She knew little about Loretta. When she understood Sissy's dilemma, she suggested prayer. Sissy jokingly asked for a sign from God.

Watching television later that evening, they saw Loretta tell Johnny Carson that Sissy would take the role. Exasperated, Sissy asked Jack to go for a drive with her. As they drove away in Gerri's Cadillac, the radio started up with Loretta singing "A Coal Miner's Daughter." Somehow Gerri's classical music station had turned into something else. Sissy decided then and there to do the movie.[1]

She won the 1980 Oscar for Best Actress.

We also asked the research participants to rate the frequency of this coincidence: "I think of an idea and hear or see it on radio, TV, or the Internet." Twenty percent said "often." One out of five people reported frequent connections between the media and their minds. Like songs, ideas float around in our cultural mind and into our individual thought patterns. Ideas are energized by editors of print and visual media, as well as by popular interest.

When ideas within and outside our minds coincide, the effect can range from mildly interesting to startling. Some idea coincidences can also be useful. We asked our research participants to rate the frequency of this: "In a desperate search for information, the information amazingly shows up." Eighteen percent said "often." So, intense focus on a specific need for information somehow facilitates that information to appear in an "amazing" way. Library angels and Internet angels flutter unexpectedly into our lives.

Library Angels

Arthur Koestler, who invented the term *library angel*, tells the story of Dame Rebecca West, who was checking up on a certain episode during the Nuremberg Nazi war crimes trials. To her dismay, she found that the abstracts of the proceedings had been catalogued under arbitrary headings in multiple volumes stored on many shelves. After searching for hours, she asked a librarian for help. As she did, she put her hand on one volume, took it out, and carelessly opened it. In doing so, she found the page she was seeking. West was delighted because her search had been completed.[2]

Statisticians will insist that many people seeking needed information in libraries have opened many books to random pages after long, systematic searching and come up with nothing. A few will sometimes find the right page. But this search had unique qualities. West sought the source for many hours through stacks of poorly organized books, asked for help, and then—without *conscious* intention—selected the right book and turned to the right page. It was as if directives outside her conscious awareness had guided her hand movements. She must've been tired from the long, frustrating search and became open to her capacity to find what she needed using abilities we are only beginning to understand.

Statisticians repeatedly remind us that unlikely events will occasionally happen—that is, after all, the definition of an unlikely event. Yet statistics don't explain the characteristics of the person involved in the unlikely event. Once again we encounter the subconscious ability to scan our environment and locate the very thing we need. As with any skill, some people are better than others. This locating ability can be enhanced under the right conditions, often a strong need and an altered state of mind. In this situation, West was tired, frustrated, and asking for help.

On Trish MacGregor's coincidence website, Nicholas Carroll described two library angels involving the Mormon religion:

I was a young sailor stationed in La Maddalena, Sardinia, when I met two Mormon missionaries in 1994 (my third and final year in Italy). I started meeting with them and was seriously contemplating joining. The barracks complex I lived in had a small library. . . . One day, in the freebie box, I found a book called *Secret Ceremonies* by Deborah Laake, which I'd heard about but was not on the library book list. I have no idea where it came from, but I took it and learned a lot about the LDS religion that the missionaries wouldn't tell me. I ended up not joining, because the religion didn't pass my logic test.

However, three years later, I went to Brigham Young University (as a non-Mormon member) for my college education. In 1998 or 1999, I was really struggling with some of the doctrines that were taught in classes, particularly the view on race. In one religion class, I was stunned to hear an African American Mormon tell a class (full of white Mormon students) that he agreed with the LDS ban on black males holding the priesthood because his race wasn't ready for it, a ban that ended in 1978. His comments troubled me, so I wondered more about the history behind the racial ban. I happened to be in the library (which is huge) and in the room with all the magazines. I noticed a book sitting flat on a shelf and I thought that was strange, so I walked up to it to see if it was misplaced. When I picked up the book and looked at the title, I was shocked to see that it was a book about the history of black Mormons, explaining how the policy came to be. I was stunned. I did not even have to go looking for it in that huge library![3]

Carroll was seriously considering becoming a Mormon when the transformative book appeared in the library free books box. He had a *need* (to find out more about Mormonism), was *searching*, and was in *transition* (soon to leave Italy). How the book happened to show up in the small library remains a mystery. He located what he needed perhaps through the habit of looking into the free books box on each visit or perhaps because one day he was drawn to look, much like Rebecca West was drawn to the book she needed.

Carroll might've looked in the catalog for the second book but instead he was drawn to a book lying flat on a shelf that seemed to be misplaced. Far from being misplaced, the book provided the specific information he wanted. His attention was drawn to the misplaced book, which suggests his own subconscious locating ability had been activated.

While libraries and bookstores concentrate books in one place, needed books can also show up in the scenes of daily life. Actor Anthony Hopkins had been invited to play a part in the 1974 movie *The Girl from Petrovka*, so he wanted to read the novel by George Feifer upon which it was based. He couldn't find the book in any of London's bookstores. While waiting for a train at Leicester Square Station, he noticed a book lying on a bench. It was a copy of the novel with notes scribbled in the margins. He mentioned the find to the author, whom he met sometime later. It turned out that the book he had found was the author's copy, and those were his notes in the margins. The book had been stolen from the author's car on a London street.[4]

Hopkins needed the book and was searching for it. Like Carroll's find in the free books box in the library, the book Hopkins needed was out there in London somewhere and he found his way to it. Miraculous? No, it's just more evidence that certain people under conditions of need, searching, and transition can find what they are seeking by utilizing their subconscious tracking potential. These coincidental book finds provide evidence that our behavioral subconscious can assist conscious intentions.

The next story shows how our behavioral subconscious can also guide us to mind mirrors in books. One of my patients, a forty-five-year-old philosophy professor, was struggling to admit that hidden

deep within him was a cesspool of intense anger. He compensated for
that anger by being overly compliant to the demands of others, particularly his ex-wife, their four daughters, and his new wife. Whatever the
situation, he sought to avoid expressing his own anger and anxiously
tried to avoid their anger by doing anything he could to calm them
down. His anxiety about anger, his and theirs, drove him into circular,
obsessive thinking that tended to paralyze him. He was just beginning
to recognize his deeply felt but hidden anger when he sent me this
e-mail because he knew of my interest in coincidences: "I just finished
reading *Dr. Jekyll and Mr. Hyde* by Robert Louis Stevenson. Not sure
why I was drawn to that book, but as I read it—especially Jekyll's
self-narrative—it really hit home how our work is about me finding
my Mr. Hyde, as well as giving him some airtime on a regular basis."

Although he was "not sure why" he was drawn to that book, it is
easy for me to explain. Without knowing that he knew that the story
applied to him, he subconsciously selected the book to see a reflection
of himself in the evil Mr. Hyde. He wasn't consciously doing it, but
outside of his extremely rational mind, he knew he needed to confront
the "evil" inside of himself by seeing it described outside of himself.

Some authors rely on coincidence to help them develop their creative ideas, arranging situations that are conducive to help from their
own library angel. Isaac Bashevis Singer, a renowned Yiddish author,
was once asked how he could work in his cramped and messy office.
Every shelf and ledge in the room was piled with teetering stacks of
paper and books. Singer found the arrangement perfect. Whenever he
needed a new idea, some papers would float to the floor that would
provide the needed inspiration. The spinning vortex of his need seemed
to create a turbulence in his study that disturbed its equilibrium enough
to produce a splattering of paper with inspiring ideas.[5]

The library angel is one of many information angels, those unexpected and most welcome instrumental coincidences in which needed information arrives in some unexpected way. Author Amy Tan was puzzling over an image that for some reason came to her mind. It was a dark valley filled with hundreds of spires made of rocks stacked at oblique angles that seemed to defy gravity. The image seemed to belong in the story she was writing, but she couldn't understand how. Why should her character come upon this strange valley? In the midst of her attempts to place the scene within the story, a friend suggested a walk on a beach she had never visited. On the walk, they ducked under a pier and then saw a longhaired Asian man stacking rocks to create dozens of spires—just like the ones in the dark valley. She eagerly asked him the secret behind why they were not falling over. The man said, "I don't know. I guess with everything there's a point of balance. You just have to find it." Instantly, she knew that this was the meaning of the scene and how the image fit into the story.[6]

As Tan was caught up in her uncertainty about the meaning of her image, she "wrote in circles," unsuccessfully trying to capture its place in her story. That frustration energized her need for clarity and helped to create the circumstances for its resolution. Going to a new geographical location like this previously unvisited beach aided her in discovering the solution.

Maria Popova, editor of *Brain Pickings*, an online collection of random information, deliberately invites idea angels to provide new items for her blog, newsletter, and Twitter feed. She describes her products as a "human-powered discovery engine for interestingness." Her mother studied library science, so she grew up around books. Her paternal grandmother loved books and had a collection of encyclopedias. Popova learned to randomly open volumes to happen upon interesting discoveries of old knowledge. She criticizes the Internet as being biased to the present. Random flipping through encyclopedias provides a serendipitous way of learning about the world. Her Internet productions reflect this random discovery process that is held together by strings of very interesting quotes, photographs, poems, and research findings. The library angel and its new friend, the Internet angel, accompany her and her readers on this enjoyable journey.[7]

TAKE A SECOND LOOK AT ONE OF THE STORIES
in this book that briefly caught your attention.
What does this story say about you? Look for opportunity
in controlled chaos.

Internet Angels

The Internet, this library on steroids, provides many opportunities for idea angels to perform. My friend Dave, a skilled psychologist, had two hours free at his office because two patients had canceled appointments. What would he read? He didn't want to read another psychology book; he wanted something different. He wished he had a book on popular science, one of his favorite subjects. As he was thinking about what to do, he scanned his e-mail. The first one came from his homeless nephew somewhere in Houston. This nephew would e-mail Dave several times each week, almost always suggesting some new technological innovation for his computer and cell phone. Dave always politely told him to stop sending these e-mails, but his nephew paid no attention and kept sending them anyway. In his newest e-mail, the first in a week, his nephew described a very interesting popular science book and had attached the full PDF of the book. It was just what the doctor ordered! The nephew had never sent a book before, nor has he since. Dave experienced it as a gift. And it was.

The best gifts are the ones that show that the giver has observed the receiver well enough to notice what they would like and need. One person's gloves look tattered, and another offers new gloves as a gift— just what was needed, not an obligatory gift like a new bestselling book or popular DVD. Dave needed something to read and the PDF fit his need. He was touched.

How did my skeptical friend explain this coincidence between what he wanted and what he got? "He must've randomly picked this one out," said Dave. "After all, I receive many e-mails with attachments that senders think I'll find interesting. One of them had to hit at the right time."

"Well, Dave," I replied, "randomness and probability are descriptions not causes. How did he happen to pick just the kind of book you like? Perhaps he had heard from other relatives that you like popular science books, and then just happened to see this one and thought you might like it. That connection could've gone on subconsciously."

"Not possible," he replied. "He's not been in touch with any other family members in many years."

"Then the only other explanation," I said, "is that he picked up your interest in some other way. He tuned in to you through your e-mails and your thinking of him. He had specific knowledge of your interests without knowing how he knew it. He just felt that you would like the book. And you did."

"I can almost begin to see that happening," Dave admitted.

Sometimes needed information comes out of nowhere, from unknown persons for unknown reasons. Author Lauren Raine wrote, "I've often had the experience, especially with the Internet, of having information I needed come to me. I even am not surprised any more, having faith in some kind of 'invisible means of support.' I do remember, in 2000, when I was working on descriptions of Goddesses for my book, receiving several e-mails out of the blue, from someone I didn't know, that discussed eloquently the Goddess Saraswati, information I needed. I still have no idea who that person was who sent me those articles, or why, or even where they got my e-mail address from." The needed information came out of nowhere.[8]

Raine believed an outside agency was helping her find what she needed. Her need was helping to create the response she sought from someone tuned to wanting to share and help. Think of the mechanism as a mental version of websites with ads that put together people with reciprocal needs. One person needs information and the other wants to provide it. While Raine's story illustrates the working of the Internet angel, there might be missing details that could provide a more conventional explanation for the appearance of this goddess information. Who was this person? How did she get Raine's e-mail address? What was her purpose in sending the information? Did they share a mutual acquaintance who told the mysterious sender of Raine's project? Many coincidence stories lack the necessary investigative details that can either make the story more mysterious or clarify their more conventional causes.

But coincidence author Brian King didn't need a detailed causal analysis of his Internet angel. King had gone into the British Broadcasting Company (BBC) offices to use a computer for his coincidence story research. When one of the producers asked him what he was doing, King replied that he was looking for more coincidence stories for a book. She said, "Look at this e-mail I've just received from my friend Cathy in Australia." In the midst of the personal details was an excellent coincidence involving lost and then found objects, which King included in his book. Cyberspace is swirling with so many ideas that some of them are likely to materialize on a computer or smartphone screen just as someone is seeking them. But King wasn't the one sitting in front of the computer. The producer was.[9]

Pharmacological Coincidence

The natural world provides many substances that help to heal the human body. We've discovered the medicinal properties of digitalis (foxglove) for heart disease and aspirin (willow bark) for fever and pain. Many highly effective drugs have been discovered by happy accidents, including anticancer drugs, antidepressants, and Viagra. The discovery and manufacture of penicillin stands out as the story with the most astounding series of coincidences.

Bacterial infections took the lives of enormous numbers of people before and especially during World War I. Driven by the desire to stem the tide of deaths, Scottish bacteriologist Alexander Fleming studied bacterial growth and death in his laboratories. In November 1921, he had a cold. While leaning over one of his culture dishes, in which bacteria were growing, a drop of mucus fell from his runny nose and landed in a clump of microbes. A circle of emptiness, or a "halo of inhibition," then formed within the colonies where the mucus had landed. In other words, the bacteria had died where the mucus had landed! The lethal agent contained in the mucus was a lysozyme that couldn't be mass-produced as an antibiotic. But Fleming had a clue.

Nine years later, he was returning from summer vacation to St. Mary's Hospital in London where he had established his laboratory. He had left a pile of petri dishes in the sink while he was gone. He carefully examined the dishes before disinfecting them. He noticed that a fungus had settled on some of the plates where staphylococcal bacteria were growing. He was startled to see that same halo of inhibition, this time around where the fungus had taken hold. That mold was secreting something that was killing the bacteria! He named the mold juice "penicillin" after the fungus *Penicillium notatum*. The mold spores had arrived on his petri dishes because other researchers in a laboratory upstairs had been working with it on a different project. The creaky old building had many cracks in the ceilings and floors, and drafty stairwells that allowed the mold to float into Fleming's research space.[10]

Fleming's mind was prepared to grasp the significance of the halo. In 1945, he shared the Nobel Prize with two of the men who helped prove penicillin's usefulness in treating bacterial infections and who then found ways to mass-produce the drug.

One of the final steps in producing the large quantities necessary to treat thousands of soldiers in World War II was finding the type of penicillin mold that produced the most mold juice. From their laboratory in Peoria, Illinois, the US Army sent out a call around the world for mold samples that could most efficiently produce the antibiotic. But, according to physician and author Morton Meyers, "The army was beaten by Mary Hunt, a laboratory aide who noticed a yellow mold growing on a rotten cantaloupe at a fruit market right in Peoria. She had found *Penicillium chrysogenum*, a strain that produced 3,000 times more penicillin than Fleming's original mold."[11]

Her mind was also prepared to grasp the opportunity. Her serendipitous discovery made commercial production of penicillin feasible. As some of our wise fables try to remind us, what we are seeking is often right where we live.

What we are seeking is often right where we live.

Chance favors the prepared mind. Chance favors the prepared mind. Luck happens when opportunity meets preparation. Fleming was "lucky" because he was prepared to recognize the halo of inhibition from the effects of his runny nose. Mary Hunt was prepared because she knew what the golden fungus looked like from the specimens in the lab. Both were hunting, searching, and ready to seize upon a chance event that their behavioral subconscious may have made them more likely to create.

Both Fleming and Hunt, each in their own way, created their own luck, as did the person who discovered the usefulness of lithium in bipolar patients. Lithium is a naturally occurring mineral. Like Fleming, psychiatrist John Cade knew generally what he was seeking in the late 1940s but had no clear idea what it was: how to slow down the accelerated thoughts, speech, and actions of people with mania. He compared manic-depressive illness (as it was once known) to the two major symptomatic presentations of thyroid disease. Overly active thyroid glands (hyperthyroidism) produce rapid speech, thought, and behavior, while underactive thyroid glands (hypothyroidism) produce slowed, depressed thought and behavior. In other words, patients who had hyperthyroidism often looked manic, while those who had hypothyroidism often appeared depressed. *Maybe,* thought Cade, *something like thyroid hormone was excessive in the blood of manics.* On the basis of this reasonable but incorrect hypothesis, he kept doing experiments and stumbled upon lithium.

To test for the presence of this hypothetical toxic substance, he concentrated urine samples of manics, schizophrenics, and normals because he thought the substance was probably excreted through the kidneys. He then injected the different concentrates into guinea pigs and found that the samples from manics were more toxic than the other two. So he reasoned that the toxic effect was due to urea, the primary chemical in urine. At the time, scientists believed—incorrectly—that uric acid increased the activity of urea and that high levels of urea caused mania. This single wrong idea set the stage for the discovery of one of the major advances in psychiatric treatment: the first specific medication for a specific diagnosis.

To perform the experiment, Cade needed to dissolve uric acid. Uric acid is hard to dissolve, so he used its most dissolvable salt—lithium urate. He then added various concentrations of lithium urate to the experimental injections. Much to his surprise, the normally excitable and jittery guinea pigs became quiet and passive. They could be turned on their backs, and instead of struggling to stand up, they gazed back at him. Further experiments showed that the calming effect was due to the lithium itself, not to the uric acid.[12]

Cade knew what he wanted—a pharmacological treatment for mania. He took a "wrong turn" but still found what he had been hunting for. Like Alexander Fleming, he believed that what he sought was out there somewhere and after intense pursuit found himself, quite by accident, staring at it.

Serendipity

Accidental discoveries like these are often described as *serendipity*. The word originated with an eighteenth-century Englishman named Horace Walpole, who was a well-known author and member of the British House of Commons. Walpole recognized in himself a talent for finding what he needed just when he needed it. He first recorded the new word in a thank-you note to his friend and distant cousin, Horace Mann, the British minister in Florence, Italy. Mann had sent Walpole a portrait of a beautiful grand duchess with whose image Walpole had become enamored. Walpole found a frame but needed the correct coat of arms to display on it. With the help of a library angel, he "just happened" to find the right coat of arms in an old book he was reading. On January 28, 1754, thrilled with this coincidence, he wrote to his cousin Horace, giving the name *serendipity* to his ability to find needed things unexpectedly.

Walpole invented the term from a fairy tale entitled "The Travels and Adventures of Three Princes of Sarendip." Sarendip (or Serendib) is an ancient name for the island nation Sri Lanka off India's southern coast. The king of the fable recognized that education requires more than learning from books, so he sent his sons out of the country to broaden their experience by becoming acquainted with the customs of other peoples. Throughout the story, the clever princes carefully observed their surroundings and then successfully utilized those observations to save them from danger and death.

To Horace Walpole, the word *serendipity* meant finding something by informed observation (sagacity, as he called it) *and* by accident. The appealing sound of the word, its exotic origins, and Walpole's ambiguous definition have invited a range of possible meanings. Its main ingredients now include luck, chance, active searching, and informed observation. It has two major variations: accidentally finding just what you are looking for and looking for something and finding something else that becomes very useful. Serendipity seems to be based on the subconscious ability of the seeker to scan the environment to find the needed person, idea, or thing.[13]

> *Serendipity seems to be based on the subconscious ability of the seeker to scan the environment to find the needed person, idea, or thing.*

Decisions

Idea coincidences can provide information to help sway a decision in one direction or another. Yes or no. This way or that way.

Opening a book to a "random" page in search of guidance has become such a regular part of human decision making that it has received a name: bibliomancy. Holy books are favorites. The Chinese "Book of Changes," the *I Ching*, provides a formal way to find potentially relevant passages in a book. Bibliomancy offers consciously created coincidences. One of our research participants wrote, "I was at a treatment center for alcoholism. One night I went to the chapel alone. I told God that I was sorry and needed help. A Bible was sitting in the middle of the altar and I looked at the open pages. Nothing happened. I then randomly turned several pages at once and came to Psalm 23. I felt that the words of the psalm were meant for me. A feeling of hope and peace came over me. That night for the first time in a long time, I slept all night. I have repeated that psalm almost every day since that time and still find the words very comforting."

Carl Jung was exquisitely tuned to the potential messages in small environmental events. He lived his life with continuing attention to possible coincidental events that could help shape his decision making. He felt embedded in a living matrix of potential meaning that could illuminate his understanding of both himself and those with whom he was involved. He attended to sudden or unusual movements, appearances of animals, flocks of birds, wind, storms, and the suddenly louder lapping of the lake outside his office as possessing possible symbolic relevance for the parallel unfolding of his interior psychological realities.

In 1928, while feeling very isolated, Jung was painting mandalas containing detailed geometric designs that are said to represent the

totality of existence and are used as meditation aids. Some mandalas may incorporate deities, temples, and other timeless images. Jung
found himself painting a mandala with a golden castle in the middle.
He wrote, "When it was finished, I asked myself 'Why is this so Chinese?' I was impressed by the form and choice of colors, which seemed
to me Chinese, although there was nothing outwardly Chinese about
it. Yet that was how it affected me. It was a strange coincidence that
shortly afterward I received a letter from Richard Wilhelm in Frankfurt
enclosing the manuscript of a Taoist-alchemical treatise called 'The
Secret of the Golden Flower,' with a request that I write a commentary
on it. I devoured the manuscript at once." This thousand-year-old Chinese text concerned a yellow castle like the one Jung was painting.[14]

The coincidence between the Chinese-like castle of his mandala and
the castle of the manuscript cemented his decision to review the manuscript and broke his isolation. It strengthened his friendship with Wilhelm and his confidence in the importance of Chinese philosophy. In
1949, Jung wrote an introduction to Wilhelm's German translation of
the *I Ching*, which Jung had studied soon after its publication in 1923
by a different translator. Jung's introduction places a strong emphasis
on synchronicity. The yellow castle coincidence helped strengthen his
confidence in the existence and usefulness of meaningful coincidences.

Without conscious intention, Jung found what he was seeking—it
was both a way to break out of his isolation and a confirmation of his
ideas about synchronicity. Wilhelm found just the right person to comment on the Golden Flower manuscript and later to write the introduction for what became the best-known translation of the *I Ching*.

Most people are not as tuned in to coincidental guidance as was
Jung. Darla (not her real name) joined our research team after much
data had been collected but hadn't yet been analyzed. I needed someone

interested in working out the challenging statistical questions, so I advertised for some help in the Educational Psychology Department at the University of Missouri-Columbia. We received only one applicant: Darla. She was very interested in learning more about statistics but was doubtful about the value of what we were doing. But she needed the job, and I needed her.

Shortly after she began work on the project, Darla came into my office to report what had happened to her over the weekend. At three different times on Sunday, she was greeted with references to the idea of "ripping out the pages of a special book." At a church seminar on movies, called "Reel Theology," the class discussed the movie *Dead Poets Society* (1989) in which an English teacher named John Keating tore out the pages of a book that claimed to present a mathematical way of interpreting poems. Keating was trying to convey to his students that poetry interpretation was highly personal and couldn't be graphed and charted. Later that day, Darla's sister called to tell her about a church class in which the teacher ripped out the pages of the Bible to suggest to the students that each page exists on its own merits. Then later that evening, Darla was reading a popular book on spirituality and came to a reference in which Keating was tearing out the pages in the movie *Dead Poets Society* to once again illustrate the importance of independent thought.

Darla found the experience interesting enough to tell me and grudgingly had to conclude that there might be something to coincidence studies after all. The "ripping out the pages" coincidences had changed her mind. The coincidence had made her stop, think, and reconsider. I was delighted because now she was more likely to enthusiastically engage in the research. As a side benefit, she reported that she became more interesting at parties when she talked about weird coincidence research. Darla was in transition (the beginning of a new job), had heightened emotion (would she like the work and be good at it?), and was seeking (what was this coincidence stuff anyway?)—all factors that increase the likelihood of coincidences. In the two years she worked for me, she never described another coincidence. The gates had closed. But she did great work on the statistics. She provided just what the project needed. I'm very grateful she showed up. For a brief time, Darla had made direct contact with the psychosphere (see Chapter 12 for detailed info on the psychosphere).

In this next example, I didn't know clearly what I was seeking, but when I saw it, I knew that was it. While on the faculty at the University of Washington, I had a colleague named Wayne Katon who was very smart and friendly, but with whom I felt competitive. (I asked him about the competitive feeling years later. He saw me as a mentor and friend. It was all in my mind.) For several years we were running parallel tracks. He was providing psychiatric consultation to the outpatient Family Medicine Clinic, and I was providing psychiatric consultation to the outpatient Internal Medicine Primary Care Clinic. After ten years in Seattle, I was preparing to leave for Columbia, Missouri. Standing in the hallways of the Psychiatry Department for the last time, I was deciding whether or not to say good-bye to him. Politeness and respect urged me to do the right thing despite my competitive feelings. I knocked on his door. On his desk was a paper on the relationship between chest pain and panic disorder. I asked him about it. The researchers had interviewed patients who had undergone cardiac catheterization and found that more than a third of patients with normal coronary arteries fit diagnostic criteria for panic disorder. This finding meant that people with severe chest pain who didn't have heart disease had a good chance of having panic attacks. Wayne had sketched out a one-page research protocol to build on this research. I tentatively asked for a copy, which he kindly gave me. This protocol helped lay the groundwork for his subsequent internationally acclaimed research integrating psychiatrists into medical clinics. With the protocol in hand, I hit the ground running at the University of Missouri–Columbia. With the help of three psychiatry-friendly cardiologists, I began two large studies of cardiology patients with chest pain and no heart disease. These efforts led to my publishing approximately forty papers on the subject. Two of the papers were written collaboratively with Wayne. As a result I was promoted to full professor with tenure and soon became chairman. It all began with my urge to be polite and tap on Wayne's door.

I was in transition (leaving Seattle), in need (of a research project at the new place), and in high emotion (anxious about talking with a colleague with whom I felt competitive, and whom I would see for probably the last time). I was prepared to look and to ask, and found something I didn't know I was seeking. Wayne's protocol turned out to be the key to my academic success.

Writing Matches Reality

The fiction of novels, plays, and movies reflects our daily lives, and fiction relies on coincidences. Describing how to write for the movies, creative writing instructor Robert McKee put it this way: "Story creates meaning. Coincidence, then, would seem our enemy, for it is the random, absurd collisions of things in the universe and is, by definition, meaningless. And yet coincidence is a part of life, often a powerful part, rocking existence, and then vanishing as absurdly as it arrived. The solution, therefore, is not to avoid coincidence, but to dramatize how it may enter life meaninglessly, but in time gain meaning, how the antilogic of randomness becomes the logic of life-as-lived."[15]

Coincidences are part of living life. Every once in a while story-writers become enmeshed with an eerily predictive coincidence. Their written words coincide with real life *after* they have written it. These are not journalists describing what has already happened but rather they are somehow tuned in to information about events that are about to happen. Fiction becomes real life.

Among the most famous of these coincidences involves Morgan Robertson, who wrote a book in 1898 entitled *Futility*. His novel described the maiden voyage of a transatlantic luxury liner named *Titan*. Although it was touted as being unsinkable, the ship struck an iceberg and sank with much loss of life. In 1912, the *Titanic*, a transatlantic luxury liner widely touted as unsinkable, struck an iceberg on her maiden voyage and sunk with great loss of life. In Robertson's book, the disaster took place in April, just as it did in the real event. In the book, there were 3,000 passengers aboard the ship; on the *Titanic*, 2,207. In the book, there were twenty-four lifeboats; on the *Titanic*, twenty.[16]

Statistics are difficult to apply to this remarkable coincidence. Too many details correlate. The author must have been aware that such a ship could be built around the time he wrote the novel and that danger lurked in the cold northern Atlantic Ocean. But something more than logic led him to the richness of detail that correlated with the actual event. He predicted the sinking of the *Titanic* without realizing it. He somehow tuned in to the flow of human arrogance and power to provide a written mirror of the future. He knew something, but he didn't know how he knew. Art unknowingly imitated life.

Another often-mentioned "fiction unknowingly imitates life" story involves New York writer Norman Mailer. When Mailer began his novel

Barbary Shore, he was living at 102 Pierrepont Street, Brooklyn, New York. He didn't plan to write about spies, but as the story unfolded, a Russian spy in the United States was introduced as a minor character. As the work progressed, the spy became the dominant character in the novel. After the novel was completed in 1951, the U.S. Immigration Service arrested a man who lived in the same apartment building as Mailer.

In a 1963 interview, Mailer was quoted as saying, "On the floor below me worked one Colonel Rudolph Abel, who was the most important spy for the Russians in this country for a period of about eight or ten years, and I am sure we used to be in the elevator together many times. I have always been overcome with that. It made me decide there's no clear boundary between experience and imagination. Who knows what glimpses of reality we pick up unconsciously?"[17]

In ways we are just beginning to appreciate, Norman Mailer sensed the presence of the spy downstairs. That sense of his presence infiltrated what he thought was his own creation. He was recording the drama in the rooming house without his knowing it.

Neither Robertson nor Mailer created the events they were describing. Robertson subconsciously predicted the wreck of the *Titanic*, and Mailer subconsciously recorded some of the events that were taking place with a real-life spy who lived downstairs.

They are not alone. A man named Ryan posted a comment on Robert Perry's coincidence website about an incident he had in which writing and reality clashed ominously and instantaneously:

> The audible knocking sound gave me a very weird feeling. It was because of the timing: At that exact moment, I was editing a scene in a story [I had written] where a visitor comes to a door, and I was having trouble deciding whether the story-visitor "rang" or "knocked." I dropped my pen and got up to see who was

providing sound effects. Through the window, I beheld, in flesh and blood, a black male stranger, and I realized I was in a realm of extraordinary synchronicity. [My] story-visitor was a black male stranger too. And when I opened the door, the parallels continued. Like the story stranger, the flesh-and-blood stranger had alcohol on his breath. I smelled it right away when he started to talk. Flesh-and-blood drunken stranger was holding an empty pill bottle, and he was asking for money to fill his prescription, and so the first thing he told me concerned his diagnosis—he had a chronic disabling disease. [The] story drunken stranger was physically disabled, too. The story stranger . . . had survived a near-death experience [NDE]. And so it made me wonder about [the] flesh-and-blood stranger. So I asked. His eyes widened. He had flat-lined in a hospital. "Do you know what it is like to see trees with golden apples? Have you seen a manticore?" he asked.[18]

In January 1995, two weeks before the stranger knocked, Ryan had a dream in which he encountered a stranger who turned out to be an angel. He then had an out-of-body experience, which to him resembled a near-death experience. The novel became a safe vehicle through which to tell his NDE-like story. He thought the fiction would be more compelling if the friendship was unlikely socially—crossing rich/poor, black/white, disabled/able-bodied boundaries. That Ryan's fiction became reality informs us that writing with intense emotions, imagining with great feeling and detail, can sometimes help to produce similar events in the world around us.

Then we have a similar story from Doug Moench, whose experience is described by Jeffrey Kripal in *Mutants and Mystics*: "Moench has just finished writing a scene for a *Planet of the Apes* comic book about a black-hooded gorilla named Brutus. The scene involves Brutus invading the human hero's home, where he grabbed the man's mate by the neck and held a gun to her head in order to manipulate the hero. Just as Doug finished this scene, he heard his wife call for him in an odd sort of way from the living room across the house. He got up, walked the length of the house and entered the living room only to encounter a man in a black hood with one arm around his wife's neck and the other holding a gun to her head."[19]

Just as Moench was writing the scene, the hooded intruder of his fiction entered his house. Moench didn't know whether he had predicted it or created it. He wondered whether or not he should write anymore. He only knew that a story on his page and an event in his life mirrored each other.

The writing comes alive; the imaginings of the novelist come true. The hooded intruder existed before Moench wrote about him, as did the dark stranger before Ryan wrote about him. These two men showed up at each writer's door just as each was writing about them. Somehow, these real-life "creations" were drawn to the house. These fictional characters had real-life counterparts and were not created by the authors.

Under the right conditions we can know things that we don't know we know, and we can sometimes predict events or attract what we are thinking. Our minds seem to generate ideas within a greater field of ideas that is always swirling around us, sometimes matching our inner world. These stories take a seat at the table—along with randomness, the rational appeal of statistics, and the belief of divine intervention—in explaining these types of coincidences. Many of these mind mirror events are most efficiently understood as indicators of a vital human potential lying within our own minds, yet often outside awareness.

We can sometimes predict events or attract what we are thinking.

CHAPTER 7

Timely Money

The idea of money packs powerful emotional clout. Physical survival may depend on it. Self-worth is too often built on it. Politics is driven by it. Organizations thrive on it. Without it, many families disintegrate. Money creates the desire for more of it and the fear of losing it. Money provides the means for many pleasures, for helping and hurting others, for gaining new knowledge and distorting the truth. Competition for money creates winners and losers, self-glorification and self-deprecation. Money can be used to control other people, to isolate oneself from the concerns of others, and to bring people together into loving and caring communities.

Most people desire more money. Too many need more, and too many simply want excessive amounts. This desire inhabits our minds with varying degrees of awareness and energy. When desperately in need of money, people fervently hope that the needed amount will somehow arrive. Sometimes it does arrive in the exact amount required. Statisticians argue that since many, many people seem to desperately need money, some of them will unexpectedly receive it. But this rational-mathematical explanation does not address why the event occurred to one fortunate person over another.

Needed Amount Arrives

Six months after her friend Pete had been murdered, author Amy Tan was worrying about the lack of money coming from her job working with children with disabilities. Her cat Sagwa made matters far worse by jumping out of their fourth floor apartment window and breaking a leg—that was going to cost $383, a lot of money for her in the 1970s. She and her husband couldn't even imagine saving that amount of money in a year.

Driving across the Bay Bridge from Oakland to San Francisco, Tan heard Pete's disembodied voice advising her to take it easy on herself.

"Easy for you to say," she said to Pete. "You're dead. I have real bills."

Their banter was interrupted by a slam to the side of her rickety Volkswagen bus, which sent her swerving across the road. A man rushed to find out if she was okay. She was. They looked for damage and saw a long gash barely noticeable in the already banged-up vehicle. He offered his insurance company information, but Tan refused because her rates would go up even though it wasn't her fault. So the man gave her his card and advised her to get an estimate. His company would pay her directly. She ended up receiving a check for $383.[1]

As the years passed, Tan came to think that the $383 coincidence was a product of her desire to see coincidences. She tried to dismiss the wonder of this vital financial windfall. But she was clearly in a state of transition while driving over that long bridge; she was in great need and wanted help from somewhere. The number 383 was clearly in her mind. Tan helped to create this timely match between her need and its fulfillment by entering into an altered state through her conversation with Pete. This altered state of consciousness facilitated the functioning of her subconscious homing ability. The VW bus was essentially undamaged. She wasn't hurt. The other driver had easy access to sufficient funds. The amount was no more or less than she needed. What can't be explained with our limited information is the reason the other motorist was involved. What benefit, lesson, or need was met for him in this interaction? Or was his part simply to help Tan?

Several of our research participants reported the unexpected arrival of much-needed money. One of them wrote, "I have had several meaningful coincidences but the most recent was unexpected money in almost the exact amount of what I needed. The mortgage payment was due and we were $350 short. I had agonized all day at work about how I was going to come up with the money. When I got home that day, there was a check in the mail from the U.S. Government for $358.49, a refund for overpayment on a student loan that I had paid off well over five years ago."

This was no lottery or TV giveaway show. This person needed the money and it arrived unexpectedly. The deep sense of relief makes the story highly memorable. The participant offered no personal explanation, just the agony of need and then the unspoken relief. The money need timed perfectly with a specific output from the slow-moving wheels of government bureaucracy. It may have felt like divine intervention. But here statisticians have the upper hand. Many people need money. Many people will receive late checks from the government. Sometimes the check will arrive at a time of need of which there are many. The base rate for government money arriving just when needed will not be small. This is a likely kind of event. What makes it somewhat more unlikely is the very close match to the amount needed.

The timing of the arrival of the check made the event memorable. As the rational ones among us like to say—we remember only the odd, outstanding events and neglect the many, many times people who also needed cash never got it. To some people the idea that "very unlikely events occur in large populations" does not seem satisfying enough.

An easier explanation can be found in a money story from another study participant: "My wife and I had an unexpected bill that was too much for us to pay. We prayed to God for us to be good stewards of our money and use what He gave us for His glory, not our own. About ten minutes later, a thought struck me, leading me to our filing cabinet and pulling out an unopened envelope I'd received from a previous employer. It was a dividend check from my old 401k for almost the exact amount of the unexpected bill. Because we'd prayed for God's guidance in being responsible with His money, He hit me with the thought to go to the filing cabinet."

This is a great example of prayer at work, but not necessarily in the way the supplicant thinks. He believed that God guided him to the money. I believe he played a collaborative role with God in finding the money. I suggest that through prayer he entered into an altered state of consciousness in which he could gain access to the location of the dividend check. Their need activated his capacity to know things in non-ordinary ways. He couldn't and didn't access that information from his usual state of consciousness.

A similar story comes from Ema in Eastern Europe who posted it on the website of *The Secret*. In this case, "the Universe" rather than God was asked for help: "The biggest wish for Christmas was to have enough money to buy something for my family members. But I didn't have any! I started thinking what I should buy, and all the details, but then realized that I don't have any money, so I decided to ask the

Universe to give me some money to buy Christmas presents. And guess what? Money came to me from nowhere! I was tidying my room and found a box. I opened it and there was money. I hadn't seen this box for two years. Do you think it was an accident? I was so grateful."

The box was hers. The money was hers. The decision to tidy her room was hers. Yet she attributed the finding to "the Universe." A little later she does take some responsibility. "But what have I learned from this? How important it is to LET IT GO. I tried to achieve money many times and it didn't work. Now I realized why. Because I was concentrated in 'I need money. Give me money. I want money.' But after this I realized that it's very important to forget and let the Universe do the job."[2]

She learned to let go and let the "Universe do its job." I believe she connected with something greater than her usual sense of herself that allowed her to remember and track the location of the desired cash. In other words, like praying, she altered her state of consciousness by asking for help and then *Let It Go*. She let it go into the greater mind, which facilitated access to her own untapped abilities. She collaborated with the Universe to produce the desired result.

Before reaching for divine explanations or settling for statistical simplicity, we need to look for possibilities within ourselves—including the capacity to access knowledge beyond our conscious memory and five senses.

Before reaching for divine explanations or settling for statistical simplicity, we need to look for possibilities within ourselves—including the capacity to access knowledge beyond our conscious memory and five senses.

A clearer example of the simulpathity—like bringing together two people with reciprocal needs, also shared on *The Secret* website, is a story by Senthil in Chennai, India. In February

2008, Senthil needed thirty rupees to travel to another place about fifteen and a half miles away where a check for one thousand rupees was waiting for him. He had no money at all. Sitting in front of his house, he remembered a suggestion from *The Secret*. After calming his mind for five minutes, he asked the Universe, which he imagined as a small golden ball in front of him, for thirty rupees. As he was sitting there, a man came over to him saying that he was looking to buy old bottles and vessels. Senthil looked around his little garden. In one corner he saw an unused, small aluminum bucket. He asked the man how much he would pay for the bucket. "Thirty rupees," was the reply. Senthil now had sufficient rupees to collect the check.[3]

The request for money went out and a person wanting to purchase a vessel just happened to come by for some reason. Senthil had energized the need with imagination. The beams of need seemed to cross, a connection made to bring the two people together.

Each of us has preferred explanations for coincidences that are based on our fundamental views of reality. No matter how many stories, no matter what evidence is presented, we tend to hold tightly to our preferred beliefs. Our research participants made their preferences very clear—divine intervention or a random event were the two most favored explanations. A story from Richard, a literary agent I know, sharply illustrates this point.

An acquaintance asked Richard, who told me this story, for money to get married. The man thought he and his bride had a sufficient amount, but that turned out not to be true. After much discussion, Richard agreed to lend him the money. In front of Richard, the man looked heavenward and loudly said, "Thank you, Jesus. You have answered my prayers." Richard thought angrily to himself, *I gave you the damn money. Thank me!* But the other man *had* picked the right person.

Who was more responsible for the loan, Richard or Jesus? The two men disagreed. The man was most responsible since he decided to ask Richard. Asking the right person at the right time can involve relying on information we don't know how we know.

Sometimes we are better off not receiving money when we think we should get it, as one study participant reported: "One time I was waiting on a large sum of money to arrive. I thought my need was immediate and was devastated when the funds were delayed by two months. During the time, I tried to guess what could be interfering with my plans. When I let go and the money finally arrived, I could see how I would have made some foolish decisions that may have cost me, not only my money, but my heart and peace of mind as well. I could see that I was being protected from my own impulsive ideas the money would have financed."

Late-arriving money, unlike the previous stories of well-timed cash, turned out to be beneficial. The participant does not tell us how the money would've caused trouble. We also don't know how the money was delayed. This person believed he was being "protected" from the expected arrival, as if a divine hand had intervened to slow down the money's journey. Others call on their reliable random explanation. But I wonder about the role played by this person's own subconscious awareness of potential problems in delaying the payment.

TRY PRAYING FOR THINGS THAT ARE WITHIN THE RANGE OF POSSIBILITIES. You may activate your own behavioral subconscious in useful ways.

Doing the Right Thing

The lure of money draws some of us into sticky webs, challenging us to do the right thing. Character can be defined by the sum total of decisions made. Our character is challenged when the possibility of receiving more money or losing money is placed before

Character can be defined by the sum total of decisions made.

us. Plimmer and King tell the story of Allan Cheek, an employee eager to advance, who had to choose between right and wrong. After Cheek's first promotion, his boss congratulated him on his successes and described the next project—to deceive a prospective investor out of a substantial amount of money. Cheek refused, threatening to resign if his boss went ahead with the scheme. The boss insisted. Despite his need for the job, Cheek resigned and then drove 180 miles to warn the unsuspecting victim. The potential victim had trouble believing the accusations. Cheek left, saying that he had done all he could do.

Two years later, Cheek was working for another company that entered into hard times. Money had been foolishly spent and a large debt incurred. The chairman of the board was about to close down the company. Cheek saw a way out, wrote a report describing how the company could prosper, and discussed it with the chairman. After several hours of intense negotiation, the chairman fired the CEO and put Cheek in charge.

With very little cash at his disposal, Cheek's first step was to move out of their expensive offices to less costly ones. He found an advertisement for three small offices over a garage and went to look at them. They were barely adequate, and even at the much lower cost, the company couldn't afford them. He asked the landlord to share his faith in the nearly bankrupt company by allowing him to defer payment.

"What did you say your name was?" asked the landlord.

"Allan Cheek."

"Two years ago, did you warn a man that he was about to be swindled?"

"Yes."

"That was my brother. He would've lost his life savings. Move in when you like and pay me when you can."

Four years later, the company had paid the landlord, paid off its debt, and moved to bigger offices.[4]

Cheek behaved in an ethical manner, true to his own beliefs about right and wrong. His dramatic gesture might've resulted in little more than the satisfaction of upholding his personal code. Yet he did something truly out of the ordinary—he drove 180 miles to warn the potential victim. Most people would've said "no" to the boss's request and simply walked off. Cheek completed the circle of potential betrayal by not only taking himself out of the loop but also warning the target of the swindle.

With his clarity of thought, Cheek made a proposal to the chairman of the board of his new company that was accepted, not only on the merits of the plan, but likely also on the strength of Cheek's character. Upon acceptance of his new role, he quickly proceeded to downsize their office space. His strong need for a less expensive space seemed to activate his behavioral subconscious. He selected a place to rent that was owned by the brother of the potential swindle victim. He found what he needed without knowing how he found it.

I have many coincidence stories in my files about the value of doing the ethically correct thing. There is a hint in such stories that not only is virtue its own reward but also that right behavior can lead to positive outcomes. The phrase "no good deed goes unpunished" does capture a cold, hard fact on the other side of this coin. Sometimes doing the right thing gets people in deeper trouble. Yet these stories illustrate a more enduring lesson—ethical behavior sometimes helps the doer. I said a polite good-bye to someone who I thought was an academic rival, and I was rewarded with a research protocol that significantly advanced my academic career. I'm a believer in the connection between ethical behavior and good outcomes.

Malicious Coincidences

But not all coincidences have positive outcomes. In fact, when they don't, we tend to call them bad luck rather than coincidences. Unfortunately, coincidences can be intentionally created and used unethically. Investment con artist Bernard Madoff lured many of his victims with apparent coincidences.

In his book *Cat's Cradle*, author Kurt Vonnegut coined the phrase "granfalloon"—a false association that is mistaken for friendship. Two people meet somewhere, discover they are from the same place, or in the same organization. The coincidence encourages them to believe that they are destined to become closely connected. Madoff worked the "Jewish circuit" by becoming a member of country clubs and synagogues on Long Island and Palm Beach that were attended by wealthy Jewish people. Because he was Jewish, they trusted him. Because he belonged to the same organization, they trusted him. Their search for good investment returns, coupled with these emotionally laden, granfalloon coincidences, blinded the victims to the questionable details of Madoff's strategy.

Madoff used new money from new investors to pay debts to old investors. The stock market crash of 2008 spelled the end of his Ponzi scheme. He had no new investors with which to pay off the old investors. He was arrested in December 2008, pleaded guilty to eleven criminal charges associated with a $64.8 billion–dollar fraud that went on for about twenty years, and was sentenced to 150 years of prison.[5]

Another financial granfalloon goes something like this: Mr. Lucky receives a financial newsletter, no strings attached, at no cost. He glances at it. The financial advisor announces that there will be a dramatic rise in a specific stock index. And there is. The next newsletter trumpets his clever methods for making this prediction. It also predicts another rise in the index. And there is. Once again, the advisor reviews his metrics for this conclusion but this time forecasts a decline in the index. And down it goes. After several more of these accurate predictions, he asks Mr. Lucky to send $2,000 for future newsletters with a fuller range of trends and a greater potential for earning high returns.

Let's look behind the scenes. By purchasing a list of investors with a net worth of over one million dollars, the financial advisor selected 128,000, half of whom received a newsletter predicting a rise in the index while the other half received a newsletter predicting a decline. To those 64,000 who got the correct prediction, he sent another set of newsletters, half predicting gains and half predicting losses. The 32,000 who received the correct prediction were then sent another set of newsletters, again, half predicting gains and half predicting losses. Mr. Lucky was one of the 16,000 for whom the financial advisor was "correct" three times in a row. He decided to wait for one more prediction. Unfortunately, he received a prediction that was again correct, so he joined many of the 8,000 investors who sent the advisor $2,000 for another variation on a scammer-created coincidence.

Bernard Madoff created coincidences to trap people in his pyramid scheme. The financial newsletter writer trapped people through consecutive correct predictions. Some coincidences are simply too good to be true.

Visualizing Money

Rhonda Byrne's book and video *The Secret* advised people how to consciously create money coincidences by imagining themselves receiving it. In the simplest version, if you want $1,000, draw an image of a $1,000 bill, put it on the ceiling over your bed, and stare at it. The money will come. She invoked "The Law of Attraction" or LOA. What you think is what is attracted to you. Whatever surrounds you is what you were thinking about. If you are poor, it is because you are thinking about poverty. If you are rich, it is because you have been thinking about wealth.

Some coincidences are simply too good to be true.

In a typical LOA story, the person is very depressed and believes that money is bad. Because that person thinks money is bad, the person has no money. One day the person comes across *The Secret* and their life is forever changed. "I manifest money all the time—it comes to me regularly and easily. I win lotteries, get cash gifts." The person thanks Byrne and her books for the transformation.[6]

Tax refunds, bonuses from work, stock market gains, business successes, and financial gains of all kinds have been attributed to the teachings of *The Secret* and its sequels *The Power* and *The Magic*. Byrne advises: Ask, Believe, and Receive. Ask the Universe for what you want. Believe your request will be answered. Expect to receive it. Keep a positive attitude. You must believe. Don't hold on to the wish; let it go. Then, sometime, you will receive. Always be grateful for what you have. At the same time, think of yourself as a "money magnet" by thinking and saying, "I am a money magnet. Everything I touch turns to gold. I am asking for a big fortune. I thank God all the time." A video of affirmations like these promises financial change if watched for thirty days.[7]

Byrne encouraged visualization. Some people look into a flowing stream and imagine money flowing to them. Others create vision boards with stacks of cash on them, or a house perched on piles of $100 bills, or a purse overflowing with money. Some people simply believe and wait and know that their taxes will be taken care of.

The Secret began as a series of video interviews with various gurus of the power of thought. The book followed as an edited version of the video. As a producer of videos, Byrne knew how to produce and market it effectively. The method of her success also teaches us about the law of attraction. Byrne imagined the outcome and put in a lot of work, discipline, courage, and cleverness, coupled with years of media experience. Making dreams come true requires more than high-intensity imagining. Effort is necessary. She proved that.

Making dreams come true requires more than high-intensity imagining. Effort is necessary.

The vast popularity of her books suggests that many, many people sense some truth in what she writes—imagining what you want is very important in getting what you want. Athletes know that success depends upon keeping a goal clearly in mind, as do business people and academics. Success follows an imagined future with certain necessary ingredients. These include positive expectancy, belief in your own ability to accomplish the goal, willingness to invest time and energy, and those pesky, unpredictable events like coincidences.

The coincidence stories tell us that, under certain conditions, what you think may be mirrored around you. We can sometimes find our way to the people, things, and situations we are imagining. Strong emotions—especially those involving needs that are activated during times of transition—seem to increase the likelihood of these mirrors. My research tells us that the people who reported higher numbers of coincidences were restless, seeking, scanning, exploring, and wondering. Those who were satisfied and accepting reported fewer coincidences.[8]

As a psychiatrist-psychotherapist, I help people clear their minds so they can imagine the possible and the needed. They come into the office confused about themselves, trying to find a way out of emotional and interpersonal dilemmas. As their vision sharpens, they appear to themselves to be coming to the end of a long journey through black space and thick clouds. The place they are seeking comes into sharper view. They see where they want to go. Knowing the geography of that desired location helps them get there.

As a prescriber of mind-affecting medications, I help patients imagine the change in symptoms the pill is intended to help them achieve. What are the targets of the medication molecules? Which bad feelings are they intended to alleviate—poor sleep, low energy, high anxiety, difficulty concentrating, social worries, or irritability? A clear target helps mobilize the "pharmacological storehouse" in their own brains to bring about the desired symptomatic improvement.

In both psychotherapy and medication prescribing, I help my patients activate their abilities to imagine and find what they have come to me seeking. These positive changes don't necessarily require a professional helper. Each of us carries within ourselves a self-healing potential that can be activated in other ways. Under the right conditions, all of us can activate our unconscious capacity to guide us to what we are seeking.

How then to consciously help our unconscious abilities bring us together with what we need? Dame Rebecca West not only knew the specific Nuremburg abstract she was seeking, she also *asked* the librarian. Asking out loud may be a way to increase the likelihood of matching idea with object. Like an incantation to the library angel, her request was granted. Similarly, prayer requires clarifying a wish. Many prayers are not answered because the conditions are not right. What is requested can be well beyond current possibilities, or the need is not sufficient, or the attitude and situation decrease rather than increase the probability of a match.

Birthdays mark times of transition and many celebrants make wishes. Maybe the ability to effect outcomes lies unrecognized in this part of the celebration ritual. Speaking the wish out loud or silently may sharpen the functionality of our ability to match thought pattern with environmental pattern.

Byrne recommends drawing what you want and/or acting as if what you want is already in your life. Writing seems to help, too. I often suggest that my patients keep diaries not only of what has happened but also of what they want to have happen. Drawing makes the visual more real. Acting as-if makes what is sought more real. Writing makes ideas more concrete by giving them a place in time and space. These actions also increase the clarity of the intention.

Byrne developed a checklist of thoughts and behaviors that she believes will produce money for anyone who tries them. A logical experiment would test the importance of each of the key variables: (1) ask, believe, receive; (2) imagining; (3) the vision board; (4) letting go; and (5) gratitude.

A study testing some of these ideas was done before *The Secret* was published.

 REMEMBER TO ASK SILENTLY OR OUT LOUD, alone in the woods, or in a field, or by water, to the Something Greater surrounding us. Or that "just right someone" sitting next to you.

The Study of Unexpected Money (SUM)

In the late 1990s, psychology graduate student Mary Kay Landon conducted the Study of Unexpected Money (SUM), the first careful research into this highly speculative area. The study, involving sixty participants, was designed to test the idea that conditions can be arranged to increase the likelihood of a coincidence between conscious intention and receiving cash—that under certain conditions, being receptive to the idea of, or actively wishing for, unexpected money could increase the likelihood of actually receiving it.[9]

For the purposes of the study, "unexpected money" was operationally defined as "money that comes into your hands *surprisingly* and *suddenly* ('out of the blue'), without your earning it, soliciting it, specifically seeking it out, or otherwise expecting it." Finding cash on the street, of course, is one classic instance of receiving unexpected money, and others include inheriting money unexpectedly, winning money in a lottery or contest, and receiving money through an unexpected credit or class action settlement, even windfall capital gains. Return of borrowed monies was considered unexpected money for the purposes of the study if there was "some aspect to their receipt that is highly out of the ordinary." The types of unexpected cash not allowed under the study's definition were "gains from illegal activities" and "awards from litigation or insurance settlements of any kind in which you are an active plaintiff, defendant, or victim."

In Landon's experiment, participants were first asked to record the number of times in the previous month they had received money "unexpectedly." During the following two weeks, they were all asked to simply pay attention to the possibility of unexpected money. Everyone recorded his or her results each day. Then, over the next two-week period, the sixty people were randomly divided into three equally sized groups to see if the way in which they focused their attention influenced how much—or how often—they received.

The first group was asked to just stay receptive. The full instructions included "position an object associated with money luck in a prominent position."

The second group was asked to perform a money-seeking action of their own choosing, such as make a wish, perform some lucky behavior, write affirmations, pray, meditate, or perform money visualizations.

The people in the third group were each asked to burn a green candle and repeat a short optional invocation, which Landon supplied for them, at any point during the two weeks. They were also asked to keep in mind the idea of receiving unexpected money.

The results surprised Landon. Simply paying attention mattered more than performing any of the particular, intentional activities. Members of the group that only paid attention received money more times than members of the other two groups. In comparison to the group that performed any of several money-seeking activities, this difference was statistically significant.

A secondary analysis located an even wider gap: Those who reported at the beginning of the study that they expected to receive unexpected money received money 20 percent more often than those who reported low or middling expectations—a difference that was highly statistically significant. Positive beliefs about attracting money were also positively related to positive beliefs about the efficacy of prayers and luck in financial matters.

After the formal study analysis was completed, Landon informally divided the sixty people into four groups by the ways they approached the study. There were "passive" people who showed up because they wanted to help her out—friends of her parents included—but didn't expect to receive any unexpected money in the course of the study. There were the "curious" people who were open but unattached to the prospect of receiving unexpected money. The "engaged" people were already involved with spiritual practices for manifesting money and wanted to see how participation in the research could enhance their efforts. The "solution-oriented" group simply wanted more cash—they were out of work, or in debt, or had some other need for money.

Although this last group was the most motivated, they were the least successful at finding unexpected money. Some of this group even reported losses during the study period. The curious participants, by contrast, were, on average, the most successful.[10]

The conclusion to be drawn from the lack of success by the solution-oriented people is: Don't hold too tightly to what you are seeking. Let it go; trust in active passivity. It takes energy to restrain urges to over-engage in behaviors related to your goals. Strive to become actively receptive. This finding supports Byrne's emphasis on "letting it go."

Landon's study also suggests that people with high expectations of success had the greatest success.

I've seen the dramatic influence of expectation in my psychopharmacology research. I did a study with a drug called adinazolam, which never made it to the market. It was a cousin to the well-known benzodiazepine alprazolam (Xanax). It was being tested for treatment of two different forms of anxiety: panic disorder (frequent panic attacks) and generalized anxiety disorder (excessive worry). The study was sponsored by the now defunct drug company Upjohn and involved researchers at eight different universities. Each diagnostic group included about 120 people, a good-size study. Half the participants were given a placebo and half were given the active drug.

Upjohn let me add on a questionnaire—"The Stages of Change"—which measured how ready someone was to change. The thirty-two-item survey had shown that readiness to change predicted outcome in many different psychological treatments: smoking cessation, weight loss, and drug rehabilitation. The question had never been asked in a psychopharmacological study.

We found that those who were ready to change changed. Those who received a placebo and were ready to change improved just as much as those who were given the active drug and were not ready to change. Those who received the active drug and were ready to change changed the most.

How does readiness to change and the expectation of change work with medication effects? You can see how being ready to give up smoking or losing weight increases the odds that the person will *do* something different—stop smoking or stop eating so much. But a pill is not something you do beyond taking it. The key is letting the pill work on you, allowing it to initiate that cascade of change that increases brain chemistry harmony. The pill's effect requires active passivity—letting the biochemical changes steer your brain in a more desirable direction. Good results come from letting it happen. My clinical practice in psychopharmacology is deeply influenced by this idea. I want to make sure the patient wants to take this pill and has a good idea what symptoms the pill is intended to help.

What you expect to happen increases the likelihood of that happening, and so it appears to be the case around receiving unexpected money.

 POSITIVE EXPECTATIONS AND CURIOSITY yielded the best results for receiving unexpected money. Keep that in mind!

CHAPTER 8

Jobs, Work, and "Luck"

Advice about finding a job has become an Internet industry. You are told how to construct a résumé and to smartly develop an online persona with warnings about limiting personal information because recruiters are looking at many phases of your online presence. In the distant past, vocational counselors guided people to the jobs that matched their interests and abilities. No more. The job search has, for most people, become a personal, aggressive hunt—scavenging through your connections and the Internet to find the open position that suits.

The participants in our research told us that coincidences played an important role in their career development. In response to the statement, "I am introduced to people who unexpectedly further my work/career/education," 30 percent told us that this had happened for them quite often. In response to the statement, "I advance in my work/career/education through being at the 'right place at the right time,'" 25 percent reported that this, too, happened often.

For reasons they cannot explain, people act in certain ways that net them the prize—they connect with the right person or put themselves in the right place at the right time. Coincidences can be instrumental in helping people find work.

Right Place/Right Time

Going from dead end to dream job can involve all the ingredients that make for a useful coincidence—transition, need, high emotion, and seeking.

Twenty-something Allison left her lifelong home in snowy Massachusetts for sunny Florida with her new boyfriend. Not wanting to freeload until she could find a career in publishing, she applied at a temporary staffing agency and was placed at a job answering phones for a closet design company. The first to arrive, she parked in the closest spot and waited on the step for someone to open up the place. The first employee to arrive graciously showed her around but said she hoped the owner of the company didn't come in because he was "a total jerk."

Sitting down at the switchboard, Allison said hello to the other employees as they filed in, and she heard them all saying the same thing: "I hope the a-hole boss doesn't come today." "I hate it when he's here." *Geez,* she thought, *these people are so negative. How bad could this guy be?*

At that very moment, a large man stormed through the front door, red in the face and shaking. "Who the f—k is the idiot who parked in my spot?!" She looked up to see him fuming, the vein in his head pulsing as he pointed to the idiot's car: her car.

"Um, I would be that idiot," she said, half joking, half embarrassed. Standing up to introduce herself to him, she thought he might laugh or perhaps apologize for calling her an idiot to her face. He didn't crack a smile and his face didn't soften.

"Well, honey, then move it! *Now!*" he bellowed, as he pointed his finger at her car and then extended his arm toward the front door.

Are you kidding me? she thought. *No one talks to me like this! Not for eight dollars an hour, anyway. Sure, I'll move my car—I'll move it right down the street!*

She grabbed her keys and marched to her car. She made sure the boss locked eyes with her and then she smiled, waved, and shot him the double-bird before peeling out of the parking lot. Screw him! She thought. And then she started laughing, imagining his face and the staff's reaction. That'll show him!

But then she realized: She hadn't shown anyone anything. She had no job, no job prospects, and surely this man wouldn't give her a glowing recommendation. *What have I done? I've made a huge mistake!*

In her angst, she missed her exit as her mind began to race. *Oh God, I'm going in the totally wrong direction! I have no idea where I'm going or what I'm doing.*

Just then she looked to her right and saw a strip mall. She caught a sign that said "TEMPORARY STAFFING." *What the heck*, she thought. *I'm all dressed up and my makeup is on.*

She turned into the parking lot.

She opened the door to the ding of a bell and a voice saying, "Allison? Is that you?"

"Um, yes . . . And you are?"

She didn't recognize the cute, perky blond woman standing in front of her. She knew she knew her but couldn't place her.

"Wow," the blond girl said, "it's so great to see you! The last time I saw you was at Jim's place in Boston."

Jim! It all came back to her. Jim was Allison's ex-boyfriend. And she and Jim had broken up because of this blond girl whose name was Brigitte. Her perkiness—and her perfectness—made Allison jealous, igniting a series of fights that ultimately broke up the couple. And now, here she and Brigitte were, twelve hundred miles away from where they first met, where Brigitte was now working at this staffing agency.

"You're an editor, right?"

"Yes," Allison said.

"Well, I have a publishing company right down the street and they are looking for an editor. I know you'd be perfect. They are looking to interview one more candidate today. I won't even make you take the test because I know you'll be great. Do you want to head over there?"

The answer was an obvious yes.

Allison went on the interview and got the job—her dream job. She began as an editorial assistant and worked her way up to an editor position. Fifteen years later she became the editor for *Connecting with Coincidence.*

What if she hadn't parked in the "wrong spot"? What if she had arrived ten minutes later or she chose a different spot? What if the boss hadn't been so mean, but instead asked her in a nicer way or tone to move her car? She might still be answering phones for eight dollars an hour.

Bad timing played a large part in the good outcome of the next story, told by psychotherapist Robert Hopcke. "Elise" was a dedicated professional singer who was gambling time and money on voice, acting, and movement classes for a career in opera. Those who knew her talent encouraged her to do musical comedy, but she was determined to be an opera diva. She bounced along with small parts in small opera companies, always poised for her big break.

After having energetically and meticulously prepared for a leading role in a popular opera, she presented herself at the community center for the last audition of the day. She looked around at the deserted building and realized that a mistake had been made. She anxiously approached a woman packing up papers in the hall marked "auditions" and asked about her 5:00 PM appointment. The startled woman informed her that the auditions were over but that the judges were still there. She offered to ask them if they would be willing to listen to one last contestant. They agreed. As Elise handed her music to the pianist, he gave her an odd glance. The two men and one woman on the panel sat attentively without expression as she launched into her aria, singing in Italian. After her performance, she graciously thanked the judges for staying and prepared to leave. One of the judges asked if she had prepared anything in English. She was surprised by the question. The man told her that this audition was for the musical *Candide*. "The opera audition is tomorrow," they told her.

Right then, she decided to try for a part in the musical comedy. She had to sight-read unfamiliar music for a most difficult part— Cunégonde, Candide's wife. Compared to the three other sopranos they heard that day, she was judged the most capable of performing this demanding role. As a result of being selected for the role, Elise received much media attention through which she received more local and then regional roles—not in opera but in musical comedy.[1]

When asked to explain her mistake, Elise replied that she was being "ditsy." I'm not so sure. She ended up in roles that she should have been in, not the ones she thought she should be in. This belittling of herself ignores the very distinct possibility that she was guiding herself to a better future. Those who cared about her imagined her future in musicals not operas. She fought them. What drew her there a day early?

In times of uncertainty, when the rational mind is jumbled, we can have access to information that is not deduced from known facts. Perhaps she had seen the listing for the *Candide* audition without registering it consciously. Perhaps she knew in other ways what was really the right time for her audition. Without consciously knowing it, she allowed herself to show up at the right place at just the right "wrong" time.

TV talk show host Oprah Winfrey told a more complicated tale about how she got her greatly desired role in a movie. In Chicago in 1982, after she had become the host of a local TV talk show, Winfrey read a review of the novel *The Color Purple* in the *New York Times*. She went to a bookstore and read it. One of the lines immediately caught her attention: "Dear God, I am fourteen years old . . . what is happening to me." The book resonated with her. It captured her life as a poor, abused black female in the South. She identified most with Sophia, a strong and assertive woman. She bought all the copies of the book she could find. Obsessed with it, she patrolled Chicago's Wacker Street Bridge, giving out the book to anyone who hadn't read it.

Musician-producer Quincy Jones had purchased the rights to the book and had persuaded director Steven Spielberg to join him in making the movie. Winfrey wanted to play Sophia. She knew deep within herself that the fit was perfect. To hear her tell the story, nothing in her life was more important than to be selected for this role. Yet she didn't know how to make the connection for an audition.

While passing through Chicago, Jones happened to see Winfrey on television and immediately decided that she would be ideal for the role of Sophia. Soon afterward, Winfrey received a call to audition for a movie called *Moon Song*. "Are you sure it isn't called *The Color Purple*?" she asked. The casting agent said no. When she went to audition, she saw that, yes, it was *The Color Purple*; the name had been temporarily changed. Just as she had imagined, Winfrey was asked to audition for the role of Sophia.

Several months of anxious waiting followed. She called the casting agent, who insisted that she not call again and warned her that she had no acting experience, that others were more qualified. Thinking that she had to do something to make herself more acceptable, she went to a "fat farm" to lose weight. As she was running around the track one day, she began to pray out loud. "I don't get it, but I know you do. Don't know if this is a joke. Thought you wanted me to have this part. I can't thank you. Please help me let it go." An old spiritual came to her mind: "I surrender all. I surrender all. All to thee, my blessed savior, I surrender all." She sang and prayed and cried. She felt herself let the strong desire go and knew it was going to be all right.

Just then someone came to the track saying there was a phone call for her. Spielberg was calling. He said that he heard she was at a "fat farm." He warned her that if she lost a pound, she could lose the part. She quit the weight-loss program and gorged on some junk food. The next day she was in Spielberg's office at Universal Studios and got the part.

The movie was released in 1985, just before her talk show went national. She was nominated for an Academy Award as best supporting actress and received the Golden Globe Award for best supporting actress—all of which helped to propel her TV program into a huge national success.[2]

To hear Winfrey tell the story, the most emotionally important step was giving up her long-cherished goal, the spontaneous singing of the old spiritual, the "letting go and letting God." I believe that spontaneous prayer, crying, and singing was produced by her subconscious recognition that the call was coming, that her intuition had found the beam of information her conscious mind would only later confirm. The old spiritual song's emotional surge prepared her for the call, prepared her for the acceptance not of failure but of success.

The coincidence between her tearful prayer and the Spielberg phone call had been built upon years of work and drive. As a child, Winfrey enjoyed playing at interviewing almost anybody. As a teenager she found her way into radio, honing her sense of what is real and what works in front of audiences. And finally, she had placed herself in a situation where she could be seen—a local Chicago TV program host, while she passionately imagined herself in the role of Sophia. She knew herself so well that she could clearly recognize her excellent fit for Sophia.

Oprah wasn't the only one hunting for the role of Sophia. Quincy Jones's behavioral unconscious led him to find just what he was looking for—by scanning the TV programs in Chicago. Psychic tunnels being bored from two separate minds became connected. Reciprocal needs were fulfilled. Oprah did much work to prepare herself for the nod. She was ready for the call.

 KNOW YOUR CAPACITIES AND LIMITATIONS. Find the image, the dream, that fits you and your circumstances. Stay with what is possible for you. Keep moving, trying, experimenting, and imagining.

The Ask

As I mentioned, luck is when opportunity meets preparation. Sometimes you've got to be prepared to create that job opportunity.

In 2002 Lear deBessonet was a fourth-year student majoring in political and social thought at the University of Virginia. Her idol was theater director Anne Bogart, whom she recognized one day at LaGuardia Airport. DeBessonet engaged Bogart in a conversation at the end of which she was offered a job as Bogart's assistant director at the SITI Company in New York City. That stepping-stone helped launch her career as a theater producer. Theater for her "is just a medium for engaging the larger world, for opening up big spiritual, political and social questions."[3]

Anne Bogart wasn't physically in deBessonet's network, but she was in her mental network. When deBessonet spotted Bogart, the mental network helped establish a real-world connection. LaGuardia can be a busy place. Somehow deBessonet had managed to be in the right place at the right time to recognize Bogart and then have the quick courage to ask.

Being lost, uncertain, and unclear leaves some people open to the potentials around them. San Francisco Giants' broadcaster Ted Robinson benefited from his own willingness to question randomness. "It was just a fluke," said Robinson in 1996. How did he get started? He made the call. He called the Oakland Athletics office and Charlie Finley, the owner, answered. Robinson was ready. He had experience as a broadcaster for college sports and for a minor-league hockey team. When the hockey team folded, he lost his job. He almost quit broadcasting, but his father encouraged him to call the Oakland A's because Charlie Finley had a habit of hiring inexperienced people at low salaries. Ted Robinson seized the opportunity to sell his talents, got an audition, broadcast a few innings, and went on to full-time major-league broadcasting.[4]

If you want the job, make the call (or send that e-mail). People want to help, and sometimes you can hit it right where your vision matches their needs.

Missed Opportunities

We miss many opportunities because we are not able to recognize them, not prepared to move quickly, or afraid to ask.

A journalist I know ran into this ambiguous opportunity at the beginning of his career:

It was the late 1970s and I had moved to New York City looking for my first job in journalism after graduate school. A new magazine was being published called *Omni* and I so much wanted to work for them. The magazine was being published by Bob Guccione, who was also the publisher of *Penthouse* magazine. So I looked in the phonebook, got the address, and decided to visit their offices. It was just a few blocks away from where I lived on the Upper East Side of Manhattan. The address turned out to be a brownstone, not your typical high-rise office building, but I had been to several other magazine offices whose offices turned out to be in brownstones, so I thought nothing of it. When I walked in, I was asked who I was there to see, and I said "Bob Guccione." "Fourth floor," I was told. So I got in the elevator, pressed the fourth floor button, and went up. When the doors of the elevator opened, there was no hallway or reception desk. Instead I found myself right smack in someone's living room lavishly decorated with Persian rugs, large sofas, ornate chairs, huge paintings, a gold-framed mirror, truly sumptuous surroundings. Suddenly it struck me: I was in Bob Guccione's home! Realizing my mistake, and since there was no one in the room, I pressed the first floor button, went back down, and left the building quite flustered. I now wonder: Did I miss an incredible opportunity? What if I had sat down on the couch and waited for someone to show up? Maybe my life would have turned out entirely differently.

What would have happened had he stayed? Would he have been shot by a bodyguard, greeted by a welcoming office manager, or had a chance to meet the publisher and been offered a job on the magazine? He will never know.

The journalist was increasing his luck by moving around, by trying to make connections. But he wasn't prepared for the shock of being in the wrong place that might've become the absolutely right place. Be ready to prepare yourself to let the startle pass from being in the "wrong" place.

Promotion in School

Coincidences can also accelerate advancement in school.

As a lowly member of his high school class, Winston took a preliminary examination to be placed in a much-sought-after position. The exam seemed to require special effort on his part because so many people better prepared had failed it before. He knew that, among other things, they would be asked to draw a map of a specific country. The students didn't know which country, however. The night before the exam, he put the names of all the countries in the world in a hat and drew out New Zealand. He carefully memorized that map. The first question on the exam was, "Draw a map of New Zealand." He received very high marks. The student was Winston Churchill, and the test got him into the military, which provided an essential step toward his becoming prime minister of England.[5]

How did this gamble pay off?

Churchill had called upon the centuries-old mantic (divining) arts to help him with the focus of his studying. He trusted the possibility that the future could be known through controlled chance events. Putting the names for the various countries in a hat and stirring them is much like using the *I Ching*, tarot cards, or randomly opening a holy book for advice. The *I Ching* requires throwing three coins six times to find one of sixty-four hexagrams in the book that are thought to reflect the seeker's current problem and its solution. Shuffling the cards of a tarot deck, drawing the cards, and arranging them according to a predetermined scheme is said to reveal the future. Randomly opening a holy book to a specific page with your eyes closed and putting your finger on a specific line might reflect a solution to a current problem. Winston took his chance with controlled randomness and was paid off with opportunity.

In San Francisco in 1968, I was doing my medical internship at Mount Zion Hospital, getting ready to apply for residencies in psychiatry. Stanford is located south of San Francisco down Route 101, the Bayshore Freeway, so I thought I'd take a shot at a position there. Fred Melges, a psychiatrist on the faculty, interviewed me. Melges, a tall, bespectacled man with deep, inquiring eyes, carefully inspected me. He asked me what I was interested in, what I'd read. I launched into a discourse about George Kelly, a psychologist at Ohio State who had written a book ambitiously called *A Theory of Personality*. Six years earlier, bored with studying, I was wandering in the basement stacks of the Swarthmore College library when I happened upon this book. I was looking for something interesting, and I had found it. For Melges, I recited a key line from the book: "A person's processes are psychologically channelized by the way he anticipates events." Or, said more simply, expectation influences experience. Melges was surprised. "I study George Kelly, too!" That two psychiatrists would be deeply interested in a relatively obscure psychologist amazed Melges. There were three slots left in the residency for my year. I got one of them in great part because of that interview. Melges became, at his request, my advisor.

Of all the faculty members interviewing residents, I got the one who resonated with a serendipitous discovery of mine. Melges was studying and writing about how personal views of the future influence current feeling and action. He was on a leading edge of psychotherapy at that time. Even now, psychotherapists tend to overemphasize the past and the present with little direct focus on personal futures. Yet our views of the future strongly influence what we do and how we feel. Melges's mentorship and his book *Time and the Inner Future* (1982) reinforced my commitment to the study of personal futures. Why had I started talking about George Kelly instead of Sigmund Freud? I had learned about Freudian theory in medical school and knew a past president of the American Psychoanalytic Association, but for some reason when asked to talk about what I knew, I talked about George Kelly. I had intuited the best choice. Somehow I felt, or knew in a nonrational way, that this person might be interested in these ideas. Perhaps I saw, without consciously recognizing it, a book by Kelly on his desk or bookshelf.

 KEEP COLLECTING INFORMATION THAT APPEALS TO YOU.
It may pay off years later.

Doing the Work

Coincidences can also be a big help in doing our work.

One day in 1909 Christopher Sherman, chairman of the Department of Civil Engineering at Ohio State University, was having great difficulty completing his road atlas of Ohio because maps of the southwestern counties were not available or nonexistent. If maps did exist, they had to be in old county atlases located in the counties themselves. Letters of inquiry had failed to yield results from two counties, Pike and Highland. He was also missing a good map of the Ohio River, which bounds the southern portion of the state.

Since all letter writing had failed, he felt compelled to board a train to Cincinnati. There, in the US engineering office, he found an excellent map of the Ohio River. That was a good start! He then took a train to Highland County, stopping in the town of Norwood to wait for his connection to Hillsboro, where he thought he was most likely to find a county map. For some reason he mentioned his quest to the ticket agent who told him about an old book in the back room of the station. Together they found what he was seeking: the *Highland County Atlas*. The ticket agent wouldn't sell the atlas but was glad to lend it to Sherman.

Sherman then boarded a train to Pike County, having to stop in Chillicothe to make a connection. He strolled down a Chillicothe street, intending to surprise an old friend with a visit, but instead found the friend walking toward him as though they had arranged to meet. The friend was on his way to catch a different train. They happily greeted each other.

As Sherman boarded the connecting train, he was greeted by a man who knew him and had sent him a letter the day before. Sherman could now avoid the trouble of writing a return letter by answering the man's question on the spot.

Once in Waverly, the Pike County seat, Sherman wondered if either of the two people he knew there would be in town. One was a mechanical engineering student; the other was a civil engineering student. As he got out of his carriage near the hotel, he saw the mechanical engineer getting out of a carriage in front of him. The engineer had arrived in town just as Sherman was finishing his dinner. He didn't know of any Pike County map but thought his father might.

"Here he comes now!" said the mechanical engineer.

The engineer's father thought the county auditor might have one, and at that moment, they saw the auditor walking down the street. Although it was Saturday night, the auditor invited them to his office, and there behind his desk hung a fine old map of Pike County. Sherman just happened to bring a sheet of tracing paper that fit the map. The mechanical engineer helped him do the tracing.

"I retired that night," wrote Sherman, "with the sensation of having experienced a perfect day."[6]

Sherman wasn't afraid to follow possible leads. He broke his work patterns, allowing new possibilities to enter his life. He had the courage, wisdom, and need to ask—and received what he sought. The remarkable series of coincidences, both personal and professional, indicated that Sherman was in the flow of coincidences.

 WHEN HAVE YOU BEEN in the flow like Sherman?

Need and ethical actions can sometimes yield surprising assistance, as journalist Stephen Diamond discovered when he arrived in San Francisco with only ten dollars to his name and a nervous desire to write down everything he was feeling. Unable to afford even the cheapest notepad, he resolved to shoplift one from a local drugstore. But once there, his conscience got the better of him. Still burning to commit his sensations to paper, he noticed "a pad of paper, face-down on top of a pile of rubbish, clothes, shoes, old books." It was a beautiful medical tablet that had about two hundred clean sheets and a name printed in capital letters at the top of each one: "STEPHEN DIAMOND, M.D."

It was his name. He went on to write a bestseller entitled *What the Trees Said*.[7]

Of all the trash dumps in San Francisco, how did Stephen Diamond find the one he needed? Perhaps Diamond, in his hour of need, was able to call upon his subconscious ability to seek out what he needed from his environment, almost like a guided missile using radar to find its target. We may be less separate from our surroundings than most of us have been educated to believe.

I sometimes have tapped into that connection.

Hiring new people can be a chancy adventure. As head of psychiatry at the University of Missouri–Columbia, I had to find and hire new faculty members. The usual process involved advertising in psychiatric newspapers and making phone calls to colleagues in other cities. My method was different. Most of the faculty I hired just showed up. There were five women whose collective stories were particularly striking. Soon after accepting the position, each of the five became pregnant. The second, third, and fourth each had twins. The fifth had been trying to get pregnant for several years. She, too, got pregnant soon after being hired, but, unlike most of the others, she didn't have twins.

When women of childbearing age find satisfying work, they become more relaxed and more able to conceive children, so having a new job can increase the likelihood of becoming pregnant. The string of twins that occurred here becomes more surprising, however. To follow a basketball analogy: in a single game when a player reaches double digits in points, assists, and rebounds, it is called a triple-double. My department scored a triple-double—three women with twins.

The first woman, who had a single baby, stayed for a few years then took a job that paid twice as much in a warmer climate. Her departure represented a major loss to the department. The fifth woman joyfully raised her single child but stayed with us for less than two years because her husband found a better job elsewhere.

The families of the triple-double stayed. Two of the three women divorced their husbands and went on to make outstanding contributions to the department, as did the third woman, who didn't divorce. The serial coincidence in the "superfertile" environment of our department helped achieve the desired longevity of three excellent faculty members.

Once again, people with reciprocal needs found each other. These women needed a safe, comfortable nest for their planned families, and our department needed helpful, committed faculty members. The three sets of twins sealed each deal. All three women put down their roots and stayed.

Luck

When the emperor Napoleon interviewed candidates for the position of general, he was said to have asked, "Are you lucky?" The people in this series of work stories could be called "lucky." Each was prepared to embrace the opportunity. The study of luck can aid in understanding how to increase the likelihood of useful coincidences.

Psychologist Richard Wiseman conducted a series of experiments to clarify what lucky people do to create their own luck.[8] He found that lucky people persevere, are optimistic, learn from failure, and rely on intuition.

Perseverance

In one of Wiseman's studies, self-described lucky and unlucky people were asked to perform a task. The lucky people persevered in the face of failure. He gave participants a task that wasn't doable but told them that it was possible to complete. Those who thought they were lucky kept pushing ahead through failure after failure much longer than those who thought of themselves as unlucky. So, you become lucky by persevering, by keeping on moving, by continuing to try.

Optimism

Unlucky people stop looking around because they lose the belief that opportunity is out there somewhere to be seized. The world often appears to be random, and in that randomness there is opportunity. It is no coincidence that the word *chance* has two almost opposite meanings. Chance often means random, like a chance occurrence. Chance also means opportunity, as in "give peace a chance." Unlucky people tend toward a cold randomness, while lucky people see opportunity in randomness. Believe that your environment is friendly, accessible, and holds potential for you. Some environments are far richer than others, so lucky people tend to pick the optimizing ones. Without a positive expectancy, unlucky people will just not look around: Why bother?

In another experiment, Wiseman placed money on the ground and provided the opportunity to strike up a conversation with a well-connected businessman by guiding participants in his direction. The "lucky" people immediately noticed the money on the ground and picked it up. They then managed to use the cues to introduce themselves to the businessman seated in the coffee shop where the drama was taking place. The "unlucky" people, those who said things rarely worked out for them, never saw the cash and drank their coffee without any effort to meet the businessman.

Wiseman wondered whether lucky people talked themselves out of possible bad luck. To find out, he presented lucky and unlucky people with some unlucky scenarios to see how they reacted. He asked both groups to imagine that they were waiting in line at a bank. Suddenly, an armed robber enters the bank, fires a shot, and the bullet hits them in the arm. Lucky or unlucky? The unlucky people declared themselves very unlucky—it was just their nature to be caught in a robbery. The lucky people declared themselves lucky because the situation could've been far worse. A few even thought they could sell their stories to the newspapers.

Failure

Failure can be one of life's greatest teachers. The only real failure is the failure to learn from failure.

Lucky people keep moving in the face of failure; they find that cloud with a silver lining and turn stumbling blocks into stepping-stones. Failure can be one of life's greatest teachers. The only real failure is the failure to learn from failure. Success stories are rarely the whole story because "the school of hard knocks" and its lessons about failure help turn problems into new operating principles. When bad things happen, lucky people look for something useful. When you get knocked down, as an old song says, pick yourself up, dust yourself off, and start all over again.

Intuition

The still, small voice within each of us can offer sage advice. Lucky people say they listen, while unlucky people say that they stick to rational thought no matter what their intuition is telling them.[9]

Sharpening intuition requires learning to listen to that inner voice, those inner urgings, those "I just felt like it" feelings. But you then need to be able to determine which hints to follow. Some of them are just bad ideas. Some will lead to excellent new opportunities. Test the advice by using the instruction as a hypothesis. Test it to learn the sounds that resonate with truth and effectiveness.

The word *intuition* comes from a Latin word *tutio* meaning "a looking after, guardianship." It is related to the word *tutor*, the business of teaching pupils.[10] Intuition is our "inner teacher." Our conscious mind is our student. Like most teachers, intuitions have their flaws. Ongoing practice and learning will increase their effectiveness by developing a careful balance with rational thought.

As instructive as Wiseman's experiments are, they miss an important characteristic—for luck in finding jobs to take root, the person has to be qualified. I have a wealthy acquaintance whose father passed the company business on to her, whereupon the company began losing money rapidly. But she was highly optimistic about turning the company around in the face of massive debt. Once she got an idea into her head, there was no stopping her. She persevered and then some. She had the right qualities for luck. But she couldn't manage. She couldn't perform basic business functions regarding the balance sheet and leadership. She was unqualified for the task. No amount of perseverance and optimism could help her through this terrible muddle.

Oprah Winfrey was qualified. The singer Elise was qualified. This businesswoman wasn't. Preparation aided by optimism, perseverance, learning from failure, and

Preparation aided by optimism, perseverance, learning from failure, and sharp intuition can work together to make coincidences more likely and useful.

sharp intuition can work together to make coincidences more likely and useful.

 HONE YOUR INTUITION BY FOLLOWING SOME of your inner urgings to see what happens. Learn the texture and impression of those urgings that provide better outcomes.

CHAPTER 9

Spirituality and the Full-Circle Experience

Coincidences can connect us to something greater, beyond our everyday experiences. That greater something is usually called Nature, the Universe, or God.

A woman finishing the night shift at a factory steps outside the building with her cup of coffee to gaze at the rising morning sun. The sky is filled with gorgeous hues. She sighs with heartfelt gratitude, breathing in its vibrant beauty. As she walks back to the office, she trips on a rock, spilling the coffee over her gray work shirt. The hot liquid forms the shape of a heart, right over her heart. She laughs and enters more deeply into the magical moment.

Hers was a brief spiritual experience—being in the oneness, facilitated by the accidental coffee stain.

Religious Needs Met

Religious rituals connect us across generations and to our cultural past. By performing the behaviors of our ancestors, they remain part of our lives and set in motion religious continuity. The following story tells of a religious ritual that requires a minimum number of people.

An Israeli rabbi and eight of his congregants were flying to Antwerp, Belgium, to celebrate the wedding of one of the congregants. Unfortunately, the plane ran low on fuel and had to land at a small airport in a Belgian farming village. After deplaning, the rabbi asked one of the airport workers if there was a room in which to conduct the evening prayer service. The worker stared at the rabbi in disbelief: "I will show you the room, if you will allow me to chant the Kaddish [the memorial prayer for the dead] for my father." As they entered the room, the worker told the rabbi of a dream he'd had the previous night. His father had come to him and asked that he chant the Kaddish for him since tomorrow was the anniversary of his death. In the dream, his father promised that there would be a minyan (a quorum of ten people, which is necessary to be able to recite the prayer). The worker thought that was impossible since he was the only Jew in the village. And so, they were able to recite the Kaddish.[1]

The worker needed nine other people, and the rabbi needed a room. They met each other's needs. The plane ran out of fuel at just the right time and place. In the worker's dream, his father predicted the availability of a minyan. Strong needs meshed once again, producing a remarkable coincidence.

The need to belong to a religious group and to perform religious rituals lies deep within many of us. In their book *Small Miracles*, Yitta

Halberstam and Judith Leventhal tell a story of religious needs filled by useful coincidences.

Despite her wealth and fame, Linda felt a gnawing emptiness. Her anxiety drove her to consider antianxiety meds, but for her that decision would only mask the problem. As she drove one day to her workplace on La Brea Avenue in Los Angeles, the traffic slowed, due to a broken water main, and was being diverted down a small side street. A handwritten sign in a small storefront church window grabbed her attention: "No God, no peace. Know God, know peace. Everybody welcome."

The next day one of the shops on La Brea had caught fire, attracting numerous fire trucks and policemen. Traffic was diverted down the same side street. Once again the sign caught her attention. What, she wondered, was going on there?

The next day she almost changed routes but decided that if traffic was going to be rerouted down that street again, she had better consider it a sign. This time a major car accident sent her down that street. So she parked her car at the church and asked to speak with the young priest. She ended up joining the congregation. For more than eighteen years since then, she found the peace and serenity she had been seeking.[2]

Linda was looking for something to get her beyond her unfulfilling "wonderful" life and used the series of traffic diversions to find what she sought. Many other cars had been guided down the same street, perhaps as many times as Linda, but she was the one looking. The change in routine became a blessing rather than the inconvenience others must've thought it to be. She found her religious home. The takeaway? Be alert for new possibilities during annoying, unexpected changes in routine.

Be alert for new possibilities during annoying, unexpected changes in routine.

Full Circle

The next story differs dramatically from most other coincidence stories in terms of its timing, but it is by no means unique. Most coincidences involve a thought or need being matched within a short period of time by an environmental event. This coincidence spans decades.

This full circle coincidence involves a woman named Blanche and her eleven-year-old son, who had a learning disability (LD) and panic disorder. None of the schools at that time would accept an LD student with a psychiatric problem, although psychologists told school officials that the dual diagnosis is not uncommon. Blanche campaigned hard for her child's acceptance at the nearby private school specializing in LD education, but they, too, turned her down.

One evening Blanche attended a charity event and happened to sit down next to Barbara, a wealthy and influential person, with whom she was slightly acquainted. When Blanche poured out her heart, Barbara not only listened but also agreed to act on behalf of her son. Barbara lived next door to the director of the school and was a major financial contributor. With Barbara's help, Blanche's son was soon admitted to the school, and for the first time in his life he made the honor roll.

Blanche kept in contact with Barbara, and a bond developed between them. Blanche learned that Barbara had problems with both of her two children: her son was a drug addict and had recently disappeared; her daughter was mildly retarded with many behavioral problems.

A year after meeting each other, Barbara's husband died. At the funeral, Blanche saw a woman about her own age sitting next to Barbara. She looked very familiar. A friend identified her as Nancy, Barbara's daughter.

Twenty-five years earlier in her private high school, Blanche had befriended a mildly retarded girl who had been admitted to the private school because of the wealth and influence of her parents, despite the objections of many in the administration. Nancy was cruelly shunned by most of the students, except for Blanche, who, among other kind gestures, had volunteered to room with her on their graduation trip to Washington, DC. Blanche hadn't met Nancy's mother back then.

The familiar woman at the funeral was Nancy.

Now, as Blanche expressed her warm wishes to Nancy and Barbara in the receiving line, Blanche could appreciate how her help for Nancy had come full circle for her own son.[3]

Perhaps with help from others, we can reach into the future to meet ourselves after we die, or so this next coincidence suggests.

In May 1966, while on his monthly business trip to Montreal, David Brody needed a place to sleep. All the motels were booked solid. Finally, he found a place in a nursing home. As he was leaving, he asked the owner if any of the Jewish residents needed a rabbi's help because he had been ordained. The owner told him that Samuel Weinstein, age one hundred, had died the night before, penniless and without relatives. He was going to be buried in a local Christian cemetery.

Instead, Brody loaded the coffin into his car and took him to New York City to be buried. Unfortunately, the two Jewish burial societies in Brooklyn and Queens owned no burial plots. He was told that a burial society in Washington Heights of Upper Manhattan did have a fund to bury Jews who had no money. Fifty years earlier, a wealthy man had endowed a special fund for this purpose. The society head began to make the arrangements and asked for the deceased man's papers. The director recognized the name, and after looking at the body, he declared that he was the man who had endowed this fund. The burial society gave Samuel Weinstein a place of honor in the cemetery.[4]

No one could've predicted that the wealthy fifty-year-old Weinstein would die a pauper in a nursing home fifty years later, far from his New York City home. A tired businessman seeking a place to sleep initiated a persistent search for a final resting place for Weinstein—the place Weinstein had unknowingly created for himself.

The image of the snake eating its tail, called the ouroboros, can symbolize the endless cycle of life, like spring returning each year through the annual trek of the seasons. It can also refer to a spiral of life—circles moving through time. In coming full circle, Blanche and Samuel Weinstein hadn't come back to the beginning but had cycled through time to meet themselves at two similar points, one past and one present, connecting separated parallel circles in the spiral of life. A simple grandeur emerges when the beginning touches the ending through a series of coincidences.

Connections to Departed Ones

In mainstream thinking, the spirit leaves the body, and the deceased person lives on through the memories of the living. For many people, the spirit of the person continues on and sometimes seems to influence those still walking on Earth, sometimes communicating through coincidences.

The Jungian psychiatrist Jean Bolen tells the story of a young, black fighter pilot during World War II who was being trained on a segregated U.S. Air Force base in the South. During Christmas season, he became especially isolated and lonely, deeply missing the closeness of his family celebrations in Southern California. Also, for the first time in his life, he experienced racial hatred, which was being directed at him by the local townspeople. He became a virtual prisoner on the base.

One day, as he walked around the base feeling increasingly miserable, he heard a Christmas choir rehearsing in a church. He entered and sat in the back row, enjoying the familiar carols. He began to think about his grandfather, a strong, loving Baptist head deacon who enjoyed singing. The hymn he loved best, which wasn't a Christmas song, came flooding to his mind: "In the Garden."

Then, for some reason, he felt a presence and a certainty. He knew that the choir was going to sing it, and it seemed that in the very next moment they began, "I come to the garden alone, while the dew is still on the roses . . . and He walks with me, and He talks with me, and He tells me I am His own." The black pilot cried, feeling tremendous joy and great peace. He felt cared for and no longer isolated.[5]

The song came at the right time to infuse a lonely soul with a feeling of connection. Music evokes strong emotion—especially those songs that are already part of our relationship history. When the right sounds reach us in a moment of need, a lost connection can be reestablished.

Just as music can produce unexpected results, so can sitting down next to a stranger. Squire Rushnell tells the story of a stranger in the next seat who served as an intimate connector to a recently departed loved one. Stasia's father, a famous clown, had died, and she was on a plane to Florida for his funeral. Unlike other clowns who smiled all the time, this Weary Willie always carried a frown, one that was so endearing that he was hard to forget. He never allowed himself to be photographed while smiling, except one time. It occurred during a publicity interview with a photographer. The phone rang and the clown heard, "You're the father of a baby girl!" She was his first and only child. Emmett Kelly, the man in the Weary Willie clown suit, smiled broadly. The photographer clicked. Newspapers around the world picked up the photo.

Stasia had brought that photo with her and looked again at that famous shot of the smiling Weary Willy. She once again realized that he was smiling about her arrival into his life. She began to sob. The man sitting next to her asked if she was all right. "My father died this morning," she explained. Startled, the man who had seen her looking at the photograph told her that he was the photographer who took that picture. Stasia felt instantly comforted and at peace, as if her father were soothing her grief.[6] (As a postscript, in my understanding of the story, the photographer wasn't going to the funeral but was going to change planes to another destination in Atlanta, where she was to board a plane to Florida.)

Strangers do find themselves next to strangers who connect them to birth mothers, future spouses, and sought-for colleagues. The need-driven spinning of the wheel of fortune for seating arrangements seems not-so-randomly to guide people to each other.

Openness to guidance can yield unexpected connections.

Openness to guidance can yield unexpected connections. Trish and Rob MacGregor recount the story of Debra Page, who in 1993 gave birth to a daughter whose rare genetic mutation led to her death after two years of life. Many wonderfully helpful people from the local hospice had come to their home to help care for her daughter. Then, in 2007, Page was looking for a new physician for help with her chronic autoimmune disorder. After several inquiries, she made an appointment with the person who was said to be the best physician for treating this problem. When the doctor read Page's medical history, she began to cry. "I know you both. I worked with your daughter as a volunteer." She had been one of the many hospice volunteers. They hugged. The doctor then told Page she had a daughter who was born on October 9, the anniversary of the day Page's daughter had died.

To Page, this coincidence was a "beautiful gift from the past," as if her daughter had reached out from beyond to help her. For a little while, Page experienced the living presence of her lost daughter.[7]

My Father

The coincidence stories in this book were initiated by my father's love for me. My father died on my birthday as I choked over the kitchen sink in San Francisco while he choked to death in Wilmington, Delaware; this event introduced me to the idea of simulpathity. So I end this collection of spiritual coincidences with a stunning succession of coincidences in which my father once again reached into my life, continuing the cord of love from father to son that he had received from his father, Ludwig, who received it from his father, Isaak, who received it from his father, David.

On my birthday, February 27, 2010, another anniversary of my father's death, my son Arie and my brother Allen went to Sabbath services with me. We recited the Kaddish for my father. Just as we finished lunch on Charlottesville's pedestrian mall, Allen's son Gene called to wish me a happy birthday. Allen and Arie got some cupcakes while I was talking with Gene. Gene told me his new baby son's name was Charles. I told him that Charles is the English equivalent of the German Karl, which was my father's name. Gene was surprised and glad to know that. Then he said that at that moment, he was driving past my father's graveyard in Wilmington, Delaware (Gene lives forty-five minutes south and is not usually in Wilmington). I looked up at the store sign in front of me. It was called "Vivian's," which is

Gene's wife's name. On our way back to the car, Allen started choking on his cupcake, reminding me that our father had choked to death.
These events indicate that we are embedded in a matrix of meaning that
reaches our awareness at special times. To expect these conventionally
unlikely crosscurrents is to tap into our potential for connecting to our
own latent abilities and to the greater mind in which we are immersed.

Part 2

Integrating Coincidences into Your Life

CHAPTER 10

How to Use Coincidences

Now that we have seen how coincidences can occur in all of life's many challenges, we can draw general principles that will help us to better use them. In this chapter, we focus primarily on instrumental coincidences and their two major uses: providing just what you need and helping with decision making. Meaningful coincidences can also affirm loving connections and confirm beliefs about the way the world works. The last section emphasizes how misuse of coincidences can lead to unwanted outcomes.

Believe in the Usefulness of Coincidences

At this time in the study of coincidences, we have numerous stories suggesting that coincidences can be useful. As with so many ideas in life, if you ignore coincidences, you will not be able to maximize their potential. If you believe in the possibility, then new vistas can open.

Believing in the usefulness of coincidences means acting as if the section of reality you inhabit is a you-friendly place. Call it positive paranoia, or *pronoia*, meaning that things will work out in your favor, that "luck" is on your side. The idea that "if you are not paranoid, you are not paying attention" also applies to pronoia. If you are not "pronoid," you are not paying attention to helpful possibilities.

Belief in the usefulness of coincidences develops with experience. In his book, *Cosmos and Psyche: Intimations of a New World View*, cultural historian Rick Tarnas describes a common sequence in developing awareness of meaningful coincidences. At first the person might notice some ambiguous patterns that seem remarkable and even uncanny, but these are usually dismissed as chance events and easily forgotten. Later the person is struck with a blast of convergence between mental and environmental events that becomes life changing. Sometimes this event is accompanied by other startlingly connected coincidences that add to their life-changing significance. After this threshold of awareness is crossed, a new attitude toward meaningful coincidences is achieved—they become an expected part of everyday life. Ideally, a disciplined alertness to them then develops, characterized by a cautious acknowledgment of their existence and a careful interpretation of their meaning and potential usefulness.[1]

My research and the many stories I've read tell us that some people see more coincidences than others. I call these people *coinciders*. The term implies someone who shares an inside view with others as in co-insider. Coinciders are part of a developing group of people who find coincidences important, useful, and intriguing. They, more fluidly than others, make connections between what goes on in their minds and the events in their environment. They are not introverts who tend to live primarily in their own minds. They are not extroverts who focus primarily on others and what is going on around them. They move quickly and easily between events outside and inside their minds.

They may be called "self-referential," meaning that they quickly connect events outside their minds with themselves. The most extreme forms of being self-referential are paranoia and grandiosity. A paranoid thinker concludes that external events indicate negative consequences to them—that people are thinking critical things about them and, in the most extreme form, are plotting against them. Grandiose thinkers believe that they are and should be the center of attention and benefit. All events point to their super-specialness. Coinciders seek the middle path.

Coinciders also score high on intuition. They are able to bypass linear, rational thought to come to conclusions about what is going on around them in ways that can be useful.

Both ways of thinking require practice to perfect. Self-referential thinking and intuition require a regular experimental skepticism to eliminate distorted conclusions and to identify ones that are applicable and useful.

Those who are searching for meaning in life comprise a third group of coincidence-sensitive people. They are trying to connect the events around them with the need to understand where they are in life and where they are going. They are actively searching for answers. Like the proverbial dog who trots about to find the bone, they are moving around and scanning their environment. People who are searching for meaning in life tell us all that to find coincidences requires both moving and looking. Just lying in bed imagining a desired outcome won't do it. Action is necessary.

Two coinciders described themselves in this way: (1) "Frankly, this coincidence thing happens to me *all the time*. It's to the point where my family members are uninterested in hearing about it because nothing surprises them anymore." (2) "I have been aware of these kinds of things my whole life and rate them 1 to 10. One is the least coincidental and 10 is many-layered and complex, and of the highest level I rate."

Activating Your Observing Self

The surprise of a coincidence activates your observing self, which is the part of your awareness that monitors the activity of your mind. The amazing connection between what is in your mind and what appears around you awakens wonder and analysis. You observe your thinking and feelings and try to make sense of this odd juxtaposition.

This process is essential in psychotherapy. I help my patients activate their observing selves by encouraging them to examine their emotional entanglements and to find the patterns underlying the confusion. Through their descriptions of their internal events, I can join with their observing selves to label disturbing interactions and conflicts, and to help them find new perspectives and choices.

Like an incisive comment from a psychotherapist, the jolt of a coincidence opens up possibilities, makes you stop and think, and makes you observe your now-energized mind. What does this coincidence mean? What are its implications? What, if anything, should I do with this? Often this activation of self-awareness passes quickly. Either a conclusion is reached or the incident is forgotten.

This activation of your observing self by coincidences is one of their primary benefits. You become more conscious of the potential for connections between your mind and your environment. The more coincidences you experience, the more fluidly your mind will move between you and your surroundings.

Providing Just What You Need

As many of the previous stories indicate, coincidences can surprisingly offer you just what you need at the moment. As I was preparing the final edit of this chapter, I received a request to connect on LinkedIn from a coincidence colleague who is an excellent editor. I'd just been thinking about finding a good editor who understands coincidence. I now had an answer to my need.

Coincidences can also present new possibilities not even considered, much like an opening that appears in what had been a solid wall. Should you take it? People, ideas, and things can show up in our lines of vision that fit important needs. Romantic needs, employment problems, health issues, creativity blocks, and many other challenges can be met, not only by careful planning, but also by surprising serendipity. Needing a new research direction, I went to say good-bye to a colleague and there, lying on his desk, was a journal article that provided the foundation of my future academic success.

You may need to be ready to act quickly. Like a person passing you in an airport who holds a key to your future, you will need to move or the opportunity may disappear into a crowd.

Insight on a Decision

Caught in a quandary, we look around for evidence to support a decision. Who knows what the future holds? There are so many variables to keep in mind when trying to chart the best course. But when caught in tempests of uncertainty, coincidences can help generate confidence in specific decisions. Some coincidences seem to confirm the decision to marry or divorce, to take a job or not, to go this way or that.

Because I love doing psychotherapy, counseling by coincidences has become intriguing to me. In the midst of a personal psychological quandary, you may look around to find symbols in your life that reflect back your current concerns. This outside perspective can offer you a way out. A university undergraduate was tearing up, feeling very sorry for herself as she walked to class one cloudy spring morning. She knew she was overdoing the self-pity but hadn't found a way out of her sadness. A big, gloppy, wet leaf fell right on top of her head. She pulled it off, looked at it, and laughed. She was just like the leaf! No need to be sad anymore!

Among many Jungians, the primary use of synchronicity is to aid in psychological growth and individuation. To individuate is to become more clearly ourselves—to become more genuine, more authentic, more real to others, and to know with increasing clarity our strengths, weaknesses, and desires. Jung's famous scarab case illustrates how a coincidence during psychotherapy can propel psychological change. You don't need to be in therapy for coincidences to help you grow. As it did for Ali, the bicycle rider in Amsterdam, a coincidence encouraged him to put superficial values aside and ask the woman he loved to marry him.

Applications in Different Professions

Ambiguity and uncertainty at work open the door to the use of coincidences. Artists of all forms—novelists, painters, and musicians—sometimes rely on randomness to produce possibilities they haven't yet considered. Inventors, CEOs, and research scientists rely on coincidences delivered through unlikely channels. Accountants don't need coincidences. They need reliable mathematics and calculations.

The history of pharmacological research is filled with accidental discoveries. Antidepressants, Viagra, several cancer treatments, and many other crucially helpful discoveries have been delivered to us through the serendipity created by the persistence and alertness of researchers rather than strictly controlled hypothesis-based research.

I was talking with a psychiatric novelist about twelfth-century Kabbalist Abraham Abulafia, who meditated on the individual letters of the Hebrew alphabet. Intrigued and excited, he dismissed himself for a few minutes and returned to the manuscript he was working on. He had incorporated these ideas into his new novel. Creativity often relies on selecting an apparently random offering to propel the project forward.

Affirming Love and Connection

Many people tell stories in which a deceased loved one seems to be signaling their presence. These felt communications often generate awe and excitement, and the feeling that loving family bonds continue beyond death. This story was told to me by a colleague.

Jen (not her real name), a woman in her late twenties, was depressed because she had suffered three miscarriages in a row. With each pregnancy, she had gone to the doctors, filled with anticipation to see a fluttering heartbeat, yet each time, all she saw was a black screen. She found herself avoiding her friends' baby showers and feeling resentful when she saw other women pushing baby strollers. Her positive outlook on life was dimming.

Adding to her sadness was that it was Mother's Day weekend—a poignant reminder that her life wasn't working out the way she had planned. She had expected that on this Mother's Day, she'd have a baby who was crawling or maybe even walking. *Maybe I'm just not meant to be a mom,* she thought. This particular year, Mother's Day fell on her birthday. Each year on her birthday, her grandfather, who had died years before, had sent her a sign—a bird at her window or a song on the radio. Although she didn't feel like celebrating her birthday, she decided to fly from Georgia to her childhood home in Rhode Island to visit her family.

As she and her mom were grocery shopping for a barbecue, she told her how much she missed her grandfather. But there had been no sign from him today, nothing. Maybe it was all in her head. While putting their things down at the checkout line, they reminisced about Grandpa.

"Remember all those summers we spent at Alton Bay?"

Her mom nodded.

"Being on Lake Winnipesaukee with Grandpa were some of the best times of my life. I wish he was here."

Just as she uttered those words, she felt someone tap her shoulder.

"Excuse me," a male voice asked, "may I put my things down?"

As she turned around, her eyes glanced at his shirt. Squinting to read the letters, her jaw dropped: emblazoned in bold letters was "ALTON BAY LAKE WINNIPESAUKEE."

The man had crystal blue eyes and long, lean arms, just like her grandfather had. Not only was he the spitting image of how she remembered him looking, she felt a familiar warmth from this stranger standing next to her.

Dumbfounded, all Jen could do was stand there and watch as he put his things down. When she and her mom left the store, she couldn't contain her excitement.

"Mom, did you see that man's shirt? I can't believe it!" They both shook their heads in disbelief: What were the odds that their paths would cross with this man's at that exact moment in time? Alton Bay was a tiny village in the mountains of New Hampshire more than a hundred miles away from where they were. Did he live in Alton Bay? Did he vacation there like they had? And why was he in that particular checkout aisle at that particular second?

Jen had asked for a sign and she received one, and after months of feeling numb, she was tingling with energy and excitement. To her, this encounter was an affirmation that the people we love are never far from us. In her heart and mind, this man was proof that miracles were indeed possible. She savored the feelings of hope and awe—two things she hadn't felt in a very long time.

Confirming Beliefs About How the World Works

The amazing surprise presented by a coincidence can open up new ways of understanding the mystery surrounding us or confirm already established beliefs. Many religions use coincidences to support a belief not only in God but also in their particular vision of how God operates. Many coincidences unveil latent human abilities and not-yet-discovered properties of our world. I look not to God or to the stars but to us and our planet to understand how they work. It's all part of the miraculous, mysterious unfolding of life.

Coincidences can increase your interest in the possibility that they are windows into hidden realities. And they can challenge the dearest beliefs of pseudoskeptics. True skeptics take into consideration all pertinent information and are willing to challenge their own beliefs. Pseudoskeptics challenge and ridicule beliefs that differ from their own.[2] After spending much of his professional life debunking anything but a statistical interpretation of coincidences, pseudoskeptic Michael Shermer's materialist worldview that the brain produces the mind was challenged. On June 25, 2014, his wedding day, he and his wife had an experience he could not explain with his usually reliable conventional science principles.

His wife, Jennifer, had been raised in Germany by her mother, and her grandfather was her closest father figure until he died when she was sixteen. Of all his precious heirlooms, only a 1978 Phillips 070 transistor radio remained. Shermer spent hours trying to revitalize the old technological device. He put in new batteries and tried several maneuvers, none of which yielded a sound from the little box. Sadly, he placed it in a drawer in their bedroom.

The wedding took place in Los Angeles, thousands of miles from Jennifer's home. She wanted her grandfather to be with her. They said their vows in their own home. Afterward she whispered to Michael to come to the bedroom. She wanted to tell him something. As they approached the back of the house, they could hear music playing. They could not find its source outside the bedroom or from any of the electronic devices in the room—cell phones, fax machine, computers. Nothing.

Struck with the sudden possibility that the sound could be coming from the old transistor radio, Jennifer open the drawer and pulled it out. A romantic song was playing. Jennifer felt the presence of her grandfather. Amazed and grateful, she no longer felt alone. She felt that her grandfather was present and approved of the marriage. The radio played classical music throughout the night and stopped the next morning, never again to make a sound.

The timing of the radio activation startled the professional skeptic. On this highly emotional day, an extremely low probability event took place that was directly connected to his wife and his new family. Chance could not be the best explanation. The emotional impact was strong. Something else was going on. Shermer had to rethink his beliefs about coincidences. He writes that the existence of these strange coincidences "suggest the existence of the paranormal or supernatural."[3] At least for a moment, the pseudoskeptic opened his mind to new possibilities.

Most people like to have their dearly held beliefs confirmed. So coincidences become either miracles from God or the Universe or more evidence that statistics provide the best explanations in our random universe. Some find confirmation for quantum nonlocality. For those who, like me, believe in the mysterious interconnectedness of all things, coincidences become clues to understanding this densely woven mental web, the psychosphere.

Expanding Awareness of Personal Powers

Simulpathity recognition propels us to accept what seems to be unbelievable: that we are connected to others across space in ways that need clearer definition.

Each of us may possess the ability to experience the pain of loved ones at a distance. A drug company salesman once told me, much to my surprise, that there were times he felt odd pains and wondered if either of his children were experiencing similar pains. He didn't ask them. Perhaps he should have. Simply confirming you have the ability to sense the pain of your loved ones can empower you; you transcend the boundaries of physical separation. He, like others, may need to learn to discriminate when to be anxious about a pain that seems to be coming from another and when to forget about it.

To feel the painful physical and emotional experiences of a loved one at a distance provides evidence of a connecting cord of attachment that is capable of conducting unknown forms of energy-information.

There are many practical applications. For some couples going through divorce, this cord needs to be severed to free each person from what has become a noxious connection. Sometimes one person is ambivalent, hoping that tranquility and love can be recaptured, while simultaneously knowing that disentanglement of the attachment is necessary. My patients soon discover that they must abandon those kindnesses that are intended to bolster the relationship: generosity, efforts at mutual understanding, and helpful suggestions. These well-intended gestures only maintain the noxious flow of feeling between them. The cord is more readily disentangled when these relationship-building kindnesses are let go.

We also seem to have the ability to occasionally locate specific people, ideas, and things we need. It is not a perfect system and will probably always be subject to unpredictable variations. Yet we can and do find what we need with what seems to be an inborn, brain-related capacity—this human Global Positioning System (GPS). Psychotherapists have illuminated the depth and many variations of the human subconscious. Our simulpathity and human GPS can also be brought to fuller awareness. Experimenting with our abilities to pick up the pain (and joy) of others and to locate needed people, ideas, or things in space can help to bring into consciousness this other aspect of unconscious processing. We can develop and expand these intuitive potentials through practice.

Aesthetics of Some Coincidences

Some coincidences are just warm, positive experiences. You can search for use, and maybe there is a use in the standard idea of getting something or making something happen. Relax. Maybe this coincidence results in a wave of pleasure. A twenty-four-year-old woman, upon experiencing an amazing coincidence without apparent cause and no apparent use, described how it made her feel: "It was like when your mom pulls the sheet all over you, and it settles on you, and you feel you are in the right place."

Helping Others Through Coincidences

Coincidences need not and are not all about just you. A coincidence may facilitate a great outcome for someone else, and your pleasure will come from participating in the coincidence.

A colleague of mine found herself on a plane sitting next to a man brimming over with tears. She compassionately asked him what was wrong. His wonderful, talented twenty-five-year-old daughter had suddenly died from a rapidly expanding brain tumor. And now he was on his way to the funeral of his best friend from high school. As they talked, it turned out that this man's wife was a good friend of the wife of the deceased man who was a good friend of my colleague. This coincidence gave solace and support to the grieving man.

On June 7, 2014, I went out to play tennis. As I started warming up, a woman with two preteens started practicing two courts down. She shouted instructions and compliments to the boy while the girl hit off the backboard. After about ten minutes, Will, my tennis partner, drove up and called to me from outside the courts. He said he had a present in his car for me. He raised a tennis basket in the air—one of those metal cages for carrying lots of balls. I shouted back that I already had one. But then the woman two courts down shouted that she needed one. She said she was going to buy one today to help teach the kids how to play tennis better. Nice fit.

Interpreting Coincidences

After the surprise activates self-observation, our minds seek meaning because symbols of the coincidence seem to be some kind of communication.

Keep a diary. Writing things down will help you get distance from and clarity about an ambiguous coincidence. Write down the compelling and confusing ones. Clearer patterns may emerge with time and distance.

When helping a patient understand the meaning of a confusing personal dilemma or dream, I develop my opinions but have learned through sometimes awkward experiences that I'm not the expert; the patient is. The patient has access to information I don't have. My opinion is usually one of several possible interpretations and not necessarily the best one. So I hold my tongue and ask, "What do you think of this situation?" Usually my patients answer, "I don't know," but with my encouragement, they start generating some good possibilities to which I can add my own.

To interpret coincidences, take the time to step back and let ideas emerge into awareness. You are the expert about yourself. Consulting with a friend or professional can help to activate and maintain the necessary self-reflection, but the primary source of interpretations lies in your own mind.

Remember that coincidences are more like signposts than directives.

Remember that coincidences are more like signposts than directives. As compelling as the suggestion may be, the decision is yours.

Coincidences vary in their degree of symbolism. Sometimes they offer just what you need: the person, the idea, or thing, like a timely editor, a scene that mirrors a current conflict, or a gloppy leaf hitting your head at a moment of indulgent self-pity. You can choose to grasp that opportunity or let it go. Others require connecting the dots, linking ambiguous symbols to find implications. The meaning of symbolic coincidences can be easy to find or obscure. If you feel a continuing urge to make sense of the symbols but cannot find clarity, try coincidence counseling. An objective view by a neutral and caring other person can be a big help.

On one of my walks in the woods in the summer of 2013, I was analyzing my irrational fears concerning money loss and relationships. I wanted to relinquish these fears, and on the walk, I made some good movement in this direction. As I was coming down the mountain and reached the flat, wide trail, I came across something lying straight across the path. I stopped about ten feet away from it, my heart rate accelerating. It was a large snake! Its belly seemed expanded. Had it recently swallowed something or was it just lying in the sun keeping warm? How could I get past it without harm? When I threw a piece of wood at it, its tail went up with the sound of a rattle. A rattlesnake! My heart sped up more. I threw another piece of wood. It coiled up! Ready to strike? I visually measured the distance from the rattling snake to the side of the path. He couldn't reach me with a strike—too far. I managed to walk by it quickly. In the four years I'd hiked this path several times a month, I'd never encountered a snake.

I wanted to tell someone about my "escape from near death," which it wasn't, but it was still pretty dramatic. So I told a friend about it. He asked me what I'd been thinking about (which was the perfect question). He then mentioned that snakes are often associated with fear. That was definitely the case. The snake really scared me. During the hike I'd been meditating on fear. The snake was capable of doing substantial harm to me, but in reality it couldn't get to me. I was similarly threatened by financial and relationship fears that were also not founded in reality. The threatening but harmless snake mirrored my threatening but unrealistic fears. I had managed to get past the snake—and my fears.

Perhaps, like my patients, I could've figured this out myself, but the drama and anxiety prevented me. I needed an outside person to co-observe and find meaning in what was going on in my own mind and the startling event in front of me. I later learned that my snake was a timber rattlesnake and that they don't want to attack. They prefer to scare animals like me away with their rattle and sneak up on smaller prey that they can eat.

Formal coincidence counselors may also be useful. One such person is Freudian psychoanalyst Gibbs Williams. He has a well-defined view of the general meanings of coincidences. He believes that coincidences are created by each person in an attempt to solve problems. He believes that the subconscious mind finds or creates an external situation that then triggers an emotional charge in the person who then tries to understand the meaning. The romance story of Ali riding his bike in Amsterdam illustrates this function of some coincidences. Williams thinks of meaningful coincidences as waking dreams. He then analyzes coincidences as if they were dreams by asking the person to associate to the key elements of the coincidence. Under his guidance, the connections of the elements lead to resolving the conflict.[4]

Williams has part of the truth about analyzing coincidences. Clergy see coincidences from a spiritual, religious perspective. Other coincidence counselors may take your perspective, try to see the coincidence from your belief system, and then together with you find a good interpretation. The first best step is to ask a caring friend to listen.

Formal Coincidence Analysis

Coincidences can also be analyzed by examining their four meanings:

1. *Emotional Charge:* Coincidences usually provoke surprise, wonder, curiosity, or interest. Emotional charge creates a feeling of significance and meaningfulness.

2. *Parallel Content:* Two or more elements of the coincidence signify the same or similar ideas or things. They have a meaning in common.

3. *Explanation:* Coincidences usually trigger the question "What does this mean?" This question can indicate a search for how the coincidence happened, its cause, or its explanation.

4. *Use:* The question "What does this mean?" also indicates an attempt to understand the implications for the person's future, its personal significance. The coincidence implies something about a decision, whether to make it or not, a course of action, or a new possibility.[5]

These different meanings can be illustrated by this story, "The Goddess of Wealth." Actor Mike Myers, who played Austin Powers, among many other roles, met with author Deepak Chopra and produced a coincidence that illustrates all four meanings. In their video clip, Mike is entering Deepak's office when he spots a card pasted to the office wall. Surprised, Mike pulls out a deck of Indian god cards. The one on top is the same card as the one on Deepak's wall—the Goddess of Wealth. On his way out of the house, Mike had impulsively grabbed the deck to show Deepak. Mike said, "If I had made a movie and pasted that card on the wall, no one would believe me." Deepak offered an explanation for the coincidence based on the "interconnection of everything," orchestrated by the two of them. He then offered Mike advice based on the coincidence: "Commit yourself to the Goddess of Wisdom. The Goddess of Wealth will then become jealous and come after you. Money will follow you."[6]

The four meanings in this meaningful coincidence are:

1. *Emotional Charge:* Mike Myers had trouble believing this low probability event actually happened. He was very surprised.

2. *Parallel content:* The two elements of the coincidence, the two cards, had exactly the same meaning. They were the same card.

3. *Explanation:* Deepak suggested that through their shared consciousness, the two of them had created the coincidence.

4. *Use:* Deepak thought that the surprising parallel meant that Mike should stay with his passion and ideals.

The analysis of base rates is another important aspect of understanding coincidences. The next story illustrates the value of attempting to quantify the surprise of a coincidence that comes from a very low probability. The probability is judged by the base rates of the two crossing lines of life of the coincidence.

When Lines Cross

A colleague told me this story, which perfectly illustrates such an intersection of coincidence. A pregnant woman was on her way to an ultrasound appointment. Instead of taking the highway, she decided to take the scenic route because she was running ahead of schedule. As she drove, she felt a mix of excitement and nervousness over the growing life inside her. Would it be a boy or a girl? She might find out today. But one thing was sure: she and her husband had already decided on the name—Kyle if it was a boy. She smiled as she recalled their conversation the night before. "Kyle it is!" At that very second, she looked to her right and her car was passed by a large plumbing truck with the word KYLE emblazoned across the side in large blue and green letters and an image of two smiling babies with angel wings.

Goose bumps radiated up her arms. What were the chances of that particular truck traveling by her at the exact same time she was thinking of her baby's name? There was no way she could've seen the lettering in her rearview mirror because the letters were on the back half of the truck. She smiled, shaking her head at what she took to be the Universe's confirmation of the perfect name for her son.

This woman did, in fact, end up having two babies. And while they aren't always angels like the two on the truck, she did name the boy Kyle. She was literally in transition—driving, pregnant, and taking the alternate scenic route. She had high emotion about seeing the doctor and becoming a mother. She wanted to be confident in naming their child Kyle.

The two crossing lines of life were her thinking about the name on the way to the doctor's office and the truck passing her. Calculating the probability of the coincidence would be done as follows:

For the route:

- The appointment was one of several possibilities that day.
- She chose to leave earlier than necessary.
- She chose an alternate route.

For the truck:

- How many KYLE plumbing trucks were there in that area?
- What are the usual routes for KYLE trucks?

- What is the likelihood of a KYLE truck being on that road at that time?

To estimate the probability, multiply the base rates. The result would be a relatively small number, proving that this was indeed a low-probability event.

Misuse of Coincidences

But just as coincidences can help guide us, we need to be careful. Coincidences can be misused. Perhaps the Trickster is tempting you or challenging you. All cultures have tales of a crafty, cunning creature who mocks authority and breaks rules by playing tricks on both humans and gods.[7] Synchronicity is often touted as positive, as a manifestation of a benevolent Universe. While some terrible decisions can turn out well in the end, some coincidences need to be labeled as foolish diversions from a better course. Some can lead to devastating results. Beware that the Trickster may be behind some of your most emotionally charged coincidences.

A patient of mine overemphasized the importance of a series of coincidences in the area of romance: "I really loved him, like no one else I have ever loved. We seemed to be able to communicate telepathically without being in the same room. When he was in the same building, I could feel his presence. I melted into his arms. His mother's name was the same as my sister's. His father's name was the same as my brother's. I could tell how he was feeling when we were apart. I told him these things because they seemed like evidence that our love was meant to be, that WE should last for all time. After about two years, our relationship was over. The coincidences were meaningful only for the time we were together. They didn't mean forever."

This woman had experienced multiple coincidences with this man. She emphasized her fusion with him but nothing about him as a person. She didn't see his selfishness and unwillingness or inability to care for her. She sadly realized that sustaining a loving relationship takes more than remarkable coincidences.

Like most forces used for good, coincidences can also be used unethically and harmfully. For example, two married people in their forties who work for the same university find themselves attracted to each other. Without knowing it, each one attends a different conference in the same city at the same time. They just happen to run into each other while walking to their respective conferences. Surprise! What should they do with this coincidence? Each one has a choice.

So did Mark David Chapman when he murdered John Lennon. He used coincidences to justify his final decision, as described in the book *Let Me Take You Down*. On December 8, 1980, Chapman was standing outside the apartment building in which John Lennon was living (the Dakota). He had traced a series of thoughts he had interpreted as coincidences: this was the building where the movie *Rosemary's Baby* was filmed, which was directed by Roman Polanski, husband of actress Sharon Tate, who was eight-and-a-half months pregnant with their unborn son when she was killed by the Charles Manson gang; the gang's favorite song was "Helter Skelter," which was written by Lennon/McCartney. As he thought about these things, the actress Mia Farrow, who played the character of Rosemary in the movie, walked by. This meant to Chapman that today was the day to kill John Lennon.[8]

Mark David Chapman had a choice. He chose to use coincidences as support for committing murder. Chapman was probably psychotic, although he refused to allow his lawyers to enter the plea of not guilty by reason of insanity.

Many people fear that their coincidence sensitivity also means they are psychotic. But if you think you might be psychotic, then you are less likely to be psychotic. Because of this fear, mental health patients may be afraid to tell their therapists about meaningful coincidences, even when they are significant and could be informative.

But luckily some do. A hypomanic (lower-level mania) woman described to her psychiatrist many different coincidences. She showed him advertisements for merchandise with prices that were also dates of important events in her life. She found a jacket bearing "her employee number at the thrift store where she worked part-time." Dates and names on TV could be assembled into her dad's name and birthday. As she was cleaning a Wilson Pickett CD, a song of his came on the TV. Her license plate said "3-polar"—recognition that she has something like bipolar disorder but she downplayed her need for medication. She liked the way she thought. She enjoyed trying to find and create meaning in her coincidences. Once her psychiatrist accepted that these mind games of hers were not destructive but entertaining, he became less frustrated with her. She found meaning in life by trying to find meaning in coincidences.[9]

This woman might be called mildly psychotic. The disorganization accompanying full psychosis disconnects people from the web of their ordinary reality into a search for clarity in confusion. Traveling at the boundaries between creativity and insanity brings high risk and possible reward. By e-mail a woman proposed a "research project" to me. She would stop her psychiatric medications, which would allow her to experience the surge of coincidences that accompany her psychotic state. For a fee, she would describe them to me. She knew that in the altered state of consciousness of psychosis, new connections would spring to her mind. Curious but cautious, I didn't accept her offer.

Psychotic thinking is sometimes characterized by overvaluing coincidences. In the midst of experiencing a terrible breakdown in their sense of reality, people in the throes of psychosis can see many coincidences and try very hard to find meaning in them.

In their deeply disturbed and disturbing world, they are trying to find order, guidance, and consistency. They can become anxiously perplexed because they cannot figure out the meaning they feel certain must be there. Because coincidence hypersensitivity is associated with psychosis, some of my psychiatric colleagues view any coincidence sensitivity as a sign of major mental illness.

Some nonpsychotic people get so caught up in the wonder of coincidences that they rely too much on them to guide their decision making. They build their lives around seeking them out and trying to figure out what they mean. This is generally not a good idea. Coincidences are best used as aids to decision making, not as the decider-in-chief.

I know of a professor of medicine who applied for the chair of a department in another state. During the interview with the dean of the other medical school, the professor glanced through a pile of books on the dean's bookshelf and spotted a thin book with a maroon cover and gold edges. The professor blurted: "I know that book." The dean said, "That's my favorite book!" They enthusiastically discussed the Christian theology of that book for the rest of the interview. At the end, they prayed together and gave thanks for their meeting. Subsequently, the dean eliminated all other chair candidates, much to the frustration of the departmental faculty, and hired the professor. The faculty strongly disliked him, although he worked excessively hard to do a fair job. His wife developed debilitating arthritis and couldn't create a positive social network. So they returned to the town from which they had come, wishing that they had never accepted the job.

Decisions usually require multiple considerations for and against alternative choices. Be careful about believing that apparently useful coincidences are divine and loving messages that must always be followed. Sometimes they can be the work of tricksters. They can lead us astray as apparent cosmic jokes we subconsciously play a role in creating. They can offer temptations outside ethical boundaries. They can be entertaining in the short term and deeply hurtful in the long term. Learning to judge this difference requires practice and discernment: which intuitions are good guides for you and what are the potential consequences to those around you and your future?

> *Be careful about believing that apparently useful coincidences are divine and loving messages that must always be followed. Sometimes they can be the work of tricksters.*

Coincidences can be used for self-aggrandizement: "These coincidences are happening to me because I'm so very special. I'm the center of everything and the coincidences prove it. Everything is being designed for me." This me-centered universe neglects the fact that coincidences are everyday realities experienced by many—if not most—people. Some coincidences lay traps for us to walk into—tricking us by our own raw greed and desire into believing what they seem to promise. Money, jobs, romance, ideas—desires can show up at what seems like the right time. Easy cash can be within easy reach, if you are willing to steal it. The idea for an amazing proposal, just what you need, may suddenly appear—on a colleague's desk. Are you willing to snatch it from your colleague and claim it as your own? That great job you have been imagining has just coincidentally dropped into your lap. It requires moving to another city. What about the impact on your spouse? Consider ethics and others as part of the decision to act. The possibility can trap you in lies, seeming to give what you desire, but forcing you to pay for them with guilt, shame, and loss of family, friends, jobs, or money.

Non-coincidences are less harmful. A series of events seem to assure you that a cherished goal—a job, a lover, a publisher—will be reached. Then reality slams home the opposite—nothing happens. Disappointment. Maybe you missed something. Maybe you were relying too much on the coincidence and not enough on reason, ethics, and situational factors. And, just maybe, you were lucky not to get what the coincidence seemed to promise.

CHAPTER 11

How to Increase the Number of Coincidences

To increase the number of coincidences in your life, take a closer look at your mind and the situations that are more likely to produce coincidences. Try to find a coincidence culture and practice ways to increase their frequency.

Your Mind

In this section we examine how you currently think about coincidences and the options for changing how you think about them.

Do You Want Them to Happen More Often?

In all kinds of psychological change, the primary factor is you, the person who is to do the changing. No one can do it for you. Increasing the frequency of coincidences starts with a yes answer to the question of "Do you want them to happen more often?"

A coincidence begins with the improbable intersection of a particular thought with a similar event.

The basics: A coincidence begins with the improbable intersection of a particular thought with a similar event. Thoughts include memories, images, and ideas. Events include people, situations, and media activity. Your observing self makes connections between the activities in your mind and the events surrounding you to produce the coincidence.

To increase them means to activate the capacity of your observing self to make connections between and among the ideas in your mind and the ideas floating in the virtual sea of ideas in which your mind is immersed. Since coincidences are intersections of thoughts and events, increases in either or both will also increase coincidence frequency. Thought production can be increased by deep investigation of some engaging topic—a person or concept or need. Environmental events can be increased by moving around, going to more complex situations. On the other hand, going to quiet places can free up your mind to think new thoughts and to find intimate connections in the natural world (one reason I love hiking in the woods).

Know Your Personality Traits

Take a look at the basics of a coincidence. Two lines of life cross. Usually one line is a thought and the other is an event. A coincidence, then, is the intersection of a thought and an event that shares some similarities.

Those people who think a lot are more likely to find coincidences because they are generating many different thoughts and images. But just being caught up in your own mind is usually insufficient. You have to find environmental matches. So people who move around a lot are more likely to experience coincidences.

Then there are those people who tend to believe there are ongoing connections between thoughts and events. They call themselves spiritual or religious. Our research has shown that those who consider themselves to be spiritual or religious report more coincidences. The same is true for people who are searching for meaning or who are intuitive.

Let Go

Many complex sets of goals and behaviors require this good balance. Athletes, CEOs, and surgeons all require conscious intention aided by finely honed subconscious capacities. If conscious intention interferes, questions too much, doubts too much, or advises too much, subconscious goal-seeking abilities become thwarted. Rather than mentally holding tightly to a desired result, holding it loosely allows subconscious abilities to inform the task.

Prayer can open minds to new possibilities.

Under the guise of giving responsibility to a greater power, we can give the power to ourselves. When people say, "Let go and let God," they are letting go of their conscious ability to solve a problem and, instead, inviting an outside force to take over. That "outside" force is more likely to be our subconscious abilities now released to perform. Prayer appears to give responsibility for outcomes to God when instead we can be releasing our own subconscious abilities. A man needed money, prayed to God, and then found himself going to an envelope in a folder in his house where he found the needed money. He thought Divine Providence had guided him; I think his own behavioral unconscious played a vital role in leading him there. Giving up control to forces outside your conscious control could be called "reducing your resistance to what you hope is possible." Prayer helped him reduce his resistance to the possibility that he could find the much-needed cash.[1]

Any possibly effective prayer needs to be reasonable—meaning within the realm of the currently possible. An old Muslim saying illustrates this idea: "Tie your camel to a post and have faith in Allah." We should be both realistic (by making sure the camel does not amble away) and believe in a favorable outcome.

By looking upward and outward for help, you are more likely to find it. To some, God speaks through coincidences. To others, prayer opens us up to our own hidden capacities, like the pathfinding potential of our human GPS (which I discuss further in Part 3).

Meditation comes in many forms and is done for different purposes. The most common techniques include focusing on an external point, like a candle; repeating a phrase or mantra; and letting thoughts come and go while maintaining an evenly hovering attention. Meditation frees up conscious awareness, allowing attention to alight like a butterfly on newly flowering events. Liberated awareness can more easily find connections between mental and environmental events, leading to a greater sensitivity to coincidences. These mental exercises strengthen your flexibility to look outward and inward to find matches between thoughts and events.

Open a Brain Gate

We've seen that transitions, traveling, and taking chances all help "tear the web of ordinary reality" and let more coincidences in. Meditation and altered states of consciousness can do this as well. Brain science suggests a mechanism by which we can modify this web, this psychophysical boundary.

The two parietal lobes located on the top of the brain help define our bodily sense of self. Damage to the right parietal lobe by a stroke can cause a person to deny that his left arm belongs to him—a condition known as anosognosia. Experienced meditators are able to turn off the activity of the parietals by decreasing visual and proprioceptive (position of the body) inputs to the parietals. The coordination between vision and proprioception is necessary for defining where our bodies are positioned in space.[2] When experienced meditators limit the inputs to their parietal lobes by closing their eyes and tuning out most bodily sensations, they can experience a feeling of floating, of being out of their bodies and becoming one with their surroundings.[3] Altered states of consciousness in transitions and crises may also loosen inputs to the parietals and facilitate more direct connections to our surroundings.

Balance Conscious Intention with Intuition

When asked what made the person in many of the coincidence stories "turn this way instead of going straight," the person usually answered, "I just felt like it." Like the man who was driving with his wife and took a new way home when she spotted their ideal house to buy—he "just felt like" making that turn. As with so many coincidences, they "kind of sort of knew" what they wanted but had no clear idea about how to make it happen. Their subconscious directed them. Let intuition grow as your inner teacher.

Conscious intention coupled with subconscious direction can synergistically contribute to increasing coincidences. As a psychotherapist, I must balance two opposing tendencies within myself: the strong desire to tell my patients what to do while also letting go of the goal I see so clearly within their reach. My aggressiveness and receptiveness need to find their balance points. Similarly, with intentionally created coincidences, an imagined

Conscious intention coupled with subconscious direction can synergistically contribute to increasing coincidences.

goal should be strongly desired and gently released in a balanced way. Aggressive, conscious intention can overwhelm the quiet instructions coming from subconscious guidance. Undisciplined subconscious advice can lead to painful outcomes, like the wrong job, bad medical treatment, a poor romantic partner, or money loss. Both conscious and subconscious processes are best honed for optimal collaboration.

I must be confident in my patients' desire and ability to heal, to become whole. Many patients are surprised when I ask them what they think should be done about their medication dose adjustments: Should we raise the dose, should we lower it, should we stay the same, or change to a different medication? After a little shock, some of them say, "Well, you're the doctor." And I say, "Well, you have more experience with this pill in you than I do." They know more than they think they know. And so it is with our subconscious abilities. We have within us the ability to know how best to proceed. The conscious mind can set goals. The subconscious mind with its GPS-like and simulpathity abilities can provide the detailed means for achieving them in a balanced way.

Curiosity seems to help, as suggested by the outcomes from the study of unexpected money (see Chapter 7). Curiosity brings interest without driving need. It taps into the mind of the child.

Watch Out for States of Mind That Interfere

Certain states of mind can interfere with being able to notice coincidences by reducing your flexibility to move between your mind and your context (by context, I mean the current state of affairs in your life, personally, environmentally, etc.). While my research suggests that positive mood as well as depressive and anxious feelings can increase coincidence sensitivity, from a clinical standpoint, anxiety and depression can also reduce coincidence sensitivity. High anxiety diverts our thoughts to catastrophic futures, taking attention away from what is happening right now. Moderate anxiety helps to promote better performances. Deep depression limits movement and often slows thinking, which may reduce coincidence sensitivity, while moderate depression can motivate some people to seek answers and more coincidences. Anger and resentment tend to pull our thoughts to the past, diverting attention from the present. Being tired reduces alertness, and being hungry and thirsty focuses attention on satisfying those basic needs. Liberated attention seems to increase the likelihood for coincidences to occur.

Energize Ideas with Your Attention and Intention

The benefits of imagining, visualizing, and concentrating on a specific outcome have a long history in human thinking. Could the cave paintings of our ancient ancestors have been ways to invoke the appearance of the desired animal? Petitionary prayer—praying for a specific outcome—is a form of imagining desired outcomes. For those who experience a positive outcome, prayers confirm faith in their religion. When the wishes of a petitionary prayer are not answered, some people of faith may become frustrated. Some may lose their religion, feeling spurned by their Divinity. The art of petitionary prayer requires imagining outcomes that are possible.

If an Eskimo in Nome, Alaska, in the early 1900s prayed for a camel with a gorgeous oriental rug to come to his igloo, he would have very little chance of realizing his dream. Be realistic in what you ask for. No wonder some people lose their faith!

Prayer invokes a personal God while nonreligious visualization seems less clear about a "higher power." I believe that the "higher power" in secular visualization is a combination of our own untapped abilities and our attunement to the energy and ideas outside us and greater than us. In this realm, the psychosphere, the lines between conventional ideas of God and spirituality begin to blur.

Remember that other people may also be energizing ideas they want to bring to fruition. Your imaginings could clash with theirs. Be respect-ful, careful, and clear about how your efforts can be compromised by theirs and how your intentions could influence theirs.

Just how to imagine has many variations. Best is not too much detail, but some good outlines. Focus with some intensity but keep letting it all go. Coincidences romp around in freer mind space, in lesser-known territory, in ambiguity.

Timing is so important and may need to be left to our GPS and simulpathity abilities. We are probably better off keeping the goal con-sciously in mind but leaving many of the details to capabilities outside our direct awareness.

Some goals require much intentional, detailed effort—homework, tax filing, grocery shopping, accounting, and following driving direc-tions. No amount of imagining and letting go will bring about the desired results without detailed effort. Find your balance for specific needs between letting go and detailed action.

Your Context

In this section we examine the contexts in which you are more likely to find coincidences.

Recognize Situations That Encourage Coincidences

Some situations are more coincidence-rich than others. When the everyday web of our reality is torn, coincidences are more likely to appear. Be alert to coincidences during births, deaths, weddings, graduation, sickness, falling in love, divorce, crisis, and traveling, especially if you need something. High emotion during transitions induces altered states of consciousness, which are also linked to an increased likelihood of coincidences. In randomness, in chaos, even in crisis, there is opportunity.

So be alert during major transitions!

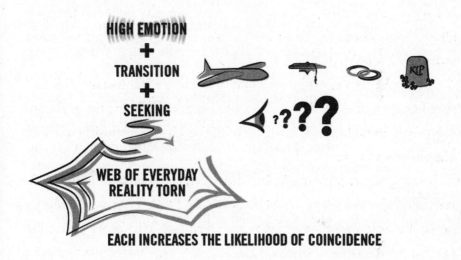

EACH INCREASES THE LIKELIHOOD OF COINCIDENCE

The vast increase in Internet browsing, news, movie, video and music availability, texting, and social media have sped up coincidence frequency. My research, covering more than a decade, shows that people are more frequently connecting to media information. They are thinking something and a song or phrase mirrors that thought. They are asking a question and the answer shows up in their media.

Coincidences are not exotic flowers growing only under special circumstances.

Coincidences are not exotic flowers growing only under special circumstances. They are more like common wildflowers popping up all around us.

They are more like common wildflowers popping up all around us. Once you get used to seeing them under special circumstances, you will be ready to see them in your daily life.

Luck Is When Opportunity Meets Preparation

Louis Pasteur coined this phrase. The famed French microbiologist knew that he would be more able to make interesting findings if he was alert to the possibility. He wanted to find a way to prevent smallpox. He noticed that the milkmaids were less likely to get smallpox. Further investigation showed that they were inoculated with a less pathogenic form—cowpox. He reasoned that a more diluted form of smallpox made into a vaccine might possibly help the body become immune to the disease. He was correct.

Seeing may be believing. Sometimes believing is seeing!

Seeing may be believing. Sometimes believing is seeing!

Be Prepared to Act Quickly

Some coincidences appear in narrow windows of time, giving you only a short time to act. Coincidences are created by matches between the swirling contents of our minds and the swirling images and sounds of our circumstances. Each of these can move quickly. Develop a nimble attention, ready to seize the moment.

The opportunity can present itself and disappear. A person walking by you in an airport, an idea flashing through the Internet, a wrong turn in front of what could be the right door. Using your intuition, learn when to act quickly.

Maybe but not always.

A therapist was seeing a couple who together ran a small tech company. They were co-CEOs. The couple was struggling with whether or not to continue the rapid expansion of the business or slow it down. In therapy they were discussing a new app proposal that would continue to expand their business but take a lot of their time. They had been e-mailing the inventor but had never met her. The husband mentioned the name of the inventor of the new app and the therapist smiled. "She is the therapist in the next office!" At the end of the session, as the couple went to the waiting room, their therapist heard his colleague walk by. He seized the opportunity. He grasped his colleague by the arm saying, "There is someone I know you want to meet," and then introduced them. The inventor and the co-CEOs had an animated discussion and decided to meet sometime in the future. As the conversation ended, the wife remarked that this was quite a coincidence.

Afterward the husband e-mailed their therapist, politely complaining that this introduction was a breach of confidentiality. The inventor now knew the co-CEOs were in therapy together. Although the therapist successfully healed the breach with sincere apologies, the question remained: Should he have seized this coincidental opportunity to help?

This question raises another difficult question. How do you judge the success of a followed coincidence? Do you judge it by a specific person? Which person? The therapist, the inventor, the husband, or the wife? By time? Immediate, short term, or long term? The therapist was pleased with himself in the moment but upset with himself after he heard the complaint. The co-CEOs were uncomfortable with the meeting and perhaps didn't want to expand their business. If not, they were then obligated to tell the inventor there was no future with them—an unpleasant task. The inventor was pleased with the meeting and hoped that something would come out of it.

I believe the couple's therapist should've stayed out of the problem. His task didn't include bringing in business for the tech company. However, in the long run, the therapist may have learned something about his own impulsive need to help. The inventor may have been more able to ease the concerns of the co-CEOs, knowing that they were in couple therapy. And the co-CEOs, after the initial embarrassment, could be more open to acknowledging to others the problems of family members running a business together.

Find a Coincidence Culture

Your social group, religion, and culture have a strong impact on how open you are to coincidences. In societies where people believe that only the five senses provide windows into reality, coincidences are silly amusements. Pseudoskeptics confidently explain them in the statistical language of science. If you are part of a group that welcomes the exploration of strange events, you will gain support for these ideas. Being part of a group of coincidence-friendly people gives you (and me) social permission to see them.

Within many religions are those who believe that God creates coincidences. In our research, people who rated themselves as being religious were more likely than those who were not religious to report coincidences involving money and jobs, affirming their belief that God

Be wary of the use of coincidences to promote specific religious ideologies. They are common to people of all religions.

wants them to succeed financially. Coincidences are reported in ancient Jewish, Christian, and Muslim religious texts, often as a way to promote the religion of the person experiencing them.[4] Be wary of the use of coincidences to promote specific religious ideologies. They are common to people of all religions.

Cultural tides are moving public awareness toward coincidences and their potential usefulness. We communicate to our friends and relatives about so many things—relationships, weather, food, fashion, news headlines, gossip, sports, money. Why not add coincidences to the list? When I bring up the subject, the other person often has a story to tell. When the interest is shared, stories keep on coming. E-mail them, text them, place your stories and pictures on social media and coincidence websites. Each of us can help the other figure out what some of these mysterious events might mean. Someone somewhere is likely to have had a coincidence just like yours and can offer a useful perspective. Crowdsource your puzzlement for a broad-based coincidence consultation. Create a book group that studies coincidences. Many websites provide opportunities to share stories. Websites that also provide a place for posting comments by others would be a useful service. The more you discuss coincidences, the more of them you will be seeing.

Don't Overdo Your Coincidences

Earlier I mentioned a high-energy person who so much enjoyed making coincidence connections that this pursuit became her major obsession, something like video game addiction. For others, that first major life-altering coincidence becomes the reason to look for more advice, support, and direction from them. Coincidence finding and analysis become ends in themselves and lose their capacity to help in life's progress. They become a confusing profusion of suggestions and possibilities because other real-world considerations fade in importance, leaving the ambiguity of many coincidences as the primary guide.

Increase Your Coincidence Capacity

Use specific coincidences to learn more about how you participate in producing them. Practice the methods that seem to bring them on.

Ask Yourself: How Did I Contribute to Making This Coincidence?

Coincidences challenge us to discover our own responsibilities and to expand our own potentials. Sometimes a high base rate can be the only explanation. Others can be attributed to the mystery that has many names, including God and the Universe.

Between statistics and mystery lies personal responsibility, which can sometimes become evident with careful analysis. In psychotherapy and in life, people prefer to look outward for cause, to blame, for example, someone else for their difficulties.

Some personal causes are easy to accept. A woman cuts her finger while trimming the grass at her deceased husband's grave. Treatment requires her wedding ring to be removed, which means to her that her deceased husband is giving her permission to marry her new lover. But she was the person responsible for cutting her finger, not her deceased husband.

One of our study participants was going to a political meeting. She knew she would be asked to be on yet another committee. She didn't want to go, but she decided to go anyway. But her car was out of gas. To this person, it was a sign not to go. Yet this person failed to recognize that she had created the situation by failing to fill up the gas tank.

Both people attributed the cause of the coincidence to forces outside of themselves when actually they had created it. To clarify your own role in creating a coincidence requires your willingness to analyze the situation in detail. Rather than being satisfied with a high base rate or some form of mystery, you have to be willing to consider your own subconscious acts. Some coincidence causes are easy to trace if you look, while others demand assumptions about your own personal power: that you can know the feelings of another person at a great distance from you or that you can navigate your way to needed people, ideas, and things without consciously knowing how. We have greater abilities than we realize, and we seem to be immersed in an information medium more energized and fantastic than we currently understand.

Learn from Negative and Failed Coincidences

When something you really want to have happen is suddenly—with too perfect timing—taken away, I call that a negative coincidence. A friend of mine was on her way to a town two hours away to meet an old friend she hadn't seen in several years. She very much wanted to see her again. Unfortunately, she received a text that her friend's husband had just died, so she couldn't make the planned-for reunion. Great disappointment and sadness followed—a negative coincidence. A colleague of mine submitted an informal research proposal to an old college classmate of his. On the day his packet arrived, the old friend died—a negative coincidence.

What are the messages from these two negative coincidences? Perhaps the new head of the granting agency would be more predisposed to the researcher's proposal. The two friends were months later able to see each other again. Sometimes what you hope for will be delayed, for reasons unknown. If you don't receive money when you expect it, perhaps you are better off without it at that time, as reported by one of our research participants.

If you follow the direction suggested by a coincidence and the results are unwanted, you are experiencing a failed coincidence. If the surgeon, who unexpectedly encountered his old high school sweetheart in a city distant from each of their homes, decides to start an affair, he and she may be creating a failed coincidence. Complication and pain are the likely outcomes.

Train for Simulpathity and Human GPS

Once you believe you may have these abilities, learn to train your subconscious-conscious connection. Look inward as well as outward for information. Try to figure out the circumstances under which your intuitive voice is most useful—usually when the alternatives seem to your rational mind equally good or you just don't know what to do. Some messages will seem like gentle urges, feelings to do this or that, without words. Many coincidences are produced by following a gentle nudge—"I just felt like doing that." Train yourself to know the good nudges from the useless ones by noting the outcomes. Identify the qualities of your intuitive voice that are associated with good outcomes and with bad outcomes. Test your sense of these qualities by consciously acting on intuitive suggestions with those varying qualitative colorings.

Recognize the influences that interfere with accurate, intuitive knowing—being anxious, caught up in work details, being distracted by nonessential desires, worried about problematic relationships, and being fearful of using these abilities. Your ability to be consciously aware of your inner communications needs to be free to seek and respond.

Find ways to mute your rational thinking through meditation, prayer, dancing, music, and drumming to let your subconscious reign more freely, to allow it to associate and connect ideas in new ways.

Practice decision making in ambiguous circumstances by asking for input from your inner guide. Learn from mistaken as well as helpful guidance to know when the impression of your intuitive voice is most likely to correlate with an optimal outcome. Allow yourself to be led by inner urgings while repeatedly challenging their value and usefulness.

Learn to be of two minds—wanting a particular outcome and letting go of it at the same time. Much like raising a child or being a therapist, have hopes and clear intentions but don't hold too tightly to the outcomes.

Create an intention within the realm of possibility, then energize it and allow your subconscious to help carry it out. Keep moving. Remember, the more you do, the more possibilities open up. The dog that trots about in the right places finds the bone.

When you feel something wrong with your body or an emotion that just doesn't fit with the way you expect to be feeling, consider if perhaps this feeling corresponds to the experiences of someone you know and care about. Ask, call, text. Find out if this feeling in you is not from you but connected to someone else.

When you feel the urge to do something different—to go this way and not that, to get lost, to let things happen rather than plan—examine the value, the usefulness, of the urge. Try to determine the specific qualities of these urges that are associated with positive outcomes compared to neutral or negative ones.

Perhaps new smartphone apps will become available to help train your human GPS. The app Crowsflight, for example, which is made for walking through large cities, points you in the direction you want to go but does not give turn-by-turn details.[5] You have to feel your way along—this way or that—all while headed in the right direction. You get to make intuitive choices while keeping your destination in app-sight. Along the way, you're getting a little lost and opening your-self up to coincidences.

Just as
our brains have
developed sensitivity to
threat, to visually attractive
people, to strange noises or
possible criticism, we can
develop sensitivity to
coincidences.

Like any skill, coincidence sensitivity can be increased with practice, practice, practice. We cannot be alert to them all the time. The events of daily life and its problems call our attention. Just as our brains have developed sensitivity to threat, to visually attractive people, to strange noises or pos-sible criticism, we can develop sensitivity to coincidences. A "thought button" can be devel-oped and then easily activated, triggering a shift in attention to coin-cidence evaluation. Your mind then quickly examines the similarity between mental and environmental events and the related emotional charge. Once injected into awareness, the coincidence can then be judged for potential value.

The sequence can be practiced with simple experiments. Guess who is calling or texting; notice a feeling that you might be running into someone, or someone is coming to the door—then examine and note the quality of the feeling that goes with being correct. Notice the little feeling you get when sitting down next to someone; could there be coincidence latent between you? Should you start a conversation? Experiment—you've got to ask. Without asking, many coincidences disappear into possibility without realization.

Advice can come directly from inside your own mind through a still, small voice, almost a whisper; stop and let the feeling-thought enter your consciousness. By being quiet and receptive, you can ask for an opinion to let that small voice speak. Listen to your quiet inner urgings.

Integrate Coincidences into Your Life

The value of coincidences lies less in the guidance from any individual instance and more in what it suggests about your own abilities. Intuition can be honed through coincidence creation. Listening to that still, small voice can only help each of us. Learning to balance aggressive intention with passive letting go can only aid our progress in life. Many useful coincidences do tell us we have latent abilities that can help us experience the feelings of loved ones and help us navigate the sometimes confusing demands of our lives. They also show us the various ways we are intimately connected with those we love and our surroundings. No person is an island, isolated from others and the life around us. Coincidences help to map these connections.

Take the following steps:

1. Decide whether or not you want to increase the number of coincidences in your life.

2. Look for them, especially during times of intense emotion, need, and transition. They also appear in less dramatic periods in daily life. Recognizing the ones occurring in less dramatic times will increase your sensitivity to the full range of coincidences.

3. Remember coincidences are sign posts, not directives. You do not have to accept each suggestion. Tell your relatives and friends about your coincidences. If the message is not obvious, or the suggestion seems problematic, ask them to help figure it out.

4. Speculate about explanations, particularly about how you might be contributing to them.

5. Write down what you find to develop a record. Look for patterns in your coincidences. You may find that you experience a particular kind

of coincidence or that your coincidences tend to involve particular subjects.

6. Read about coincidences to increase their frequency. Reading about them keeps coincidences closer to your conscious awareness.

7. Participate in coincidence websites that help people analyze the meanings of their coincidences.

Part 3

A New Theory of Coincidences

The Psychosphere: Our Mental Atmosphere

The primary purpose of this book has been to confirm the usefulness of coincidences. If this has been your reason for reading it, then you need not go further. But if you are interested in some new ideas about how coincidences are formed, then please come along for additional speculating.

Beyond their usefulness to individuals, coincidences challenge us to recognize explanations beyond our currently accepted notions of reality. You don't have to know how electricity works to flip the light switch and turn on the light in the room. Likewise, you don't have to understand how a coincidence works to be able to use it to improve your life. Yet knowing something about electricity may help you diagnose a problem and

You don't have to know how electricity works to flip the light switch and turn on the light in the room. Likewise, you don't have to understand how a coincidence works to be able to use it to improve your life.

fix it. Knowing how coincidences work can help you use them more efficiently.

I certainly don't claim to know all the factors that make coincidences happen. After all, I'm a psychiatrist, so my interest has primarily been to observe how coincidences can be helpful. But like most people who experience dramatic intersections of thought and event, I'm curious. How do they happen? I've read the major theories of synchronicity and have come to some of my own conclusions.

God-Mystery and random chance are currently the two most popular explanations for coincidences. As coincidence studies develop, we will become more able to assign varying degrees of probability to each coincidence by analyzing their base rates. But probability only sets the stage. It does not explain. As coincidences become more carefully categorized, we will apply a range of potential explanations to specific categories. On one end, explanations will be based on conventional scientific and psychological principles. On the other end, they will still be mysterious, beyond any foreseeable reach of science. There will be many possibilities between these extremes. Psychology and brain sciences may supply new explanations. Quantum physics seems to be a promising source for some answers. Morphic resonance, the idea that "memory is inherent in nature" and that "natural systems . . . inherit a collective memory from all previous things of their kind," may provide clarity.[1] Theories should specify the category of coincidences they are intended to explain.

My theory focuses on two specific and sometimes related coincidence categories: simulpathity and human GPS. Simulpathity tells us that we can connect with the experience of others at a distance without knowing how we do it. Human GPS tells us that we can find our way to people, things, and ideas without consciously knowing how.

Simulpathity plus human GPS gets us to loved ones in distress whose location we don't know.

Sense Receptors

Without knowing why, a brother drove to a place in the woods he had never been. He just went. He found his sister about to commit suicide. How did the brother "feel" the danger? How did he "know" how to get there? How did my dog and I "know" what turns to make to find each other? Somehow the brother sensed his sister's danger. Somehow a boy and his dog felt where the other was. Somehow a map with a GPS-like route popped into their brains, but did so out of their awareness. There must be mechanisms by which energy-information (E-I) like this is converted into electrical nerve impulses the brain can process into emotion and behavior.

We can look for clues to the mechanisms involved by examining our known sense receptors. Sense receptors are specialized structures that convert the energy-information of specific stimuli into neuroelectrical impulses. This conversion process is called "transduction," from the Latin *transducere*, meaning "to lead across, transfer." The receptors transduce photons of light, sound waves, smell, and taste molecules, and touch from outside our body to inside our body, making these stimuli understandable to the brain.

I contend that we must also have receptors that transduce the energy-information involved with many coincidences into neuroelectrical impulses comprehensible to the brain. Our current state of ignorance about these E-I receptors resembles that of the ancient Greeks trying to understand vision. Aristotle believed that the object being looked at in some way altered the "medium" (air) between the observer and the object, allowing the eye to see.[2] He knew that the eye had something to do with recognizing the object but knew nothing about the effect of light on the rods and cones in the retina. And he couldn't have imagined that photons of light touching the vitamin A–derived retinal molecule cause that molecule to change shape, and that this small change in shape triggers a cascade of events that start a neuroelectrical impulse that allows us to see an object.[3] In short, photons of light change the shape of the retinal molecule and start a nerve impulse that the brain can interpret as something visual. A mechanism at least this delicate must be operating on the energy-information that helps to produce useful coincidences. Aristotle didn't understand how vision works, just as we don't know where these E-I receptors are located and how they work.

Most of our other sense receptors use transduction methods less delicate than vision. Hearing, for example, depends on fluid moving the tiny hairs of the organ of Corti in the closed space of the cochlea of the inner ear. The fluid is moved by sound waves beating on the eardrum, which vibrates three tiny bones, the last of which pounds on the oval window of the cochlea, which in turn moves the fluid that moves the hair cells. The moving hair cells initiate nerve impulses. This fluid movement of hair cells seems insufficiently subtle for understanding how the E-I receptors for some coincidences might work.

For taste to register in our nervous system, molecules of food are carried by saliva to receptor cells in taste buds contained in the goblet-shaped papillae—the small bumps on the tongue. Each receptor cell has a taste hair with places for molecules of food to interact. The hair movement triggers a nerve impulse. Again, tiny hair movement initiates a neuroelectrical impulse.

Smell mechanics are more controversial. There are just not enough smell receptors in the nose to account for the thousands, perhaps hundreds of thousands, of different odors our brains can register. According to recent research, the human nose and brain can detect a trillion smells.[4] The established theory is that airborne molecules fit into a receptor the way a key fits into a lock.[5] There is a problem though: two molecules of the same shape can cause different smells.[6] In addition, some odor molecules can activate different receptors and several different molecules can trigger the same receptor. A newer, more controversial theory by Luca Turin employs a quantum physics explanation (quantum tunneling) and relies upon the vibration variations of odiferous molecules.[7] The quantum-vibrational theory has gained some research support.[8]

Touch encompasses several different receptors and sensations. Unlike the other senses, touch is picked up all over the body. Mechanoreceptors respond to mechanical movement, such as touch and vibration. Pacinian corpuscles, one of several types of mechanoreceptors, sense pressure and vibration on the skin. These spiral tissue bodies become slightly distorted when squeezed. The physical distortion is transformed into an electrochemical impulse in the nerves connected to the corpuscle. Hot, cold, and pain are registered in apparently seemingly ordinary nerve endings in the skin versus through highly specialized hairs or receptors. These sensory neurons contain transmembrane proteins that open chemical channels in response to heat, cold, and painful stimuli. Just how this mechanism really works is still a mystery. How can changes in temperature alter a protein that crosses a nerve cell membrane? No one seems to know. This use of free nerve endings has not changed since the most primitive forms of life emerged millions of years ago.

Outside of known human sensory abilities are other hints about how different forms of energy-information might enter our nervous system.

Sharks have ampullae in their skin that detect very small electromagnetic changes in the surrounding water. These energy changes provide information about the location of prey and may help sharks orient themselves to the earth's magnetic field for navigation purposes.[9]

Up in the air, migratory birds may be reading the very small energies of the earth's electromagnetic field to help them navigate. This sensing ability may rely on very tiny pieces of magnetite (iron oxide) that could be responsive to small changes in the geomagnetic field—enough to be transduced into nerve impulses. The mechanism may also involve cryptochromes in the photoreceptor neurons of migrating birds' eyes. These chemicals may activate light-sensitive neurons that allow the birds to "see" the surrounding magnetic fields.[10] Other researchers emphasize the importance of smell (recognizing the smells of the target environment) and vision (mapping well-known routes and following them each migration).[11] Both shark and the migratory bird receptors suggest possibilities for the transduction of very subtle energy-information into electrochemical nerve impulses.

Many people feel "vibes" from other people, a subtle energy emanating from one person picked up somehow by another. I can feel energy changes in my patients before they start to cry or become angry. My sensitivity includes but is more than the subtle reading of nonverbal behavior. Although these feelings are considered "nonscientific," many other therapists informally report similar experiences. Until recently, this supposed energy field has not been measurable, so those of us who talk about it have no scientific support. In our current world, it must be measurable before it becomes "real" or accepted. Oscar the Cat was picking up something from dying patients as if their "light" were dimming.

Researchers have recently developed instruments to measure "biophotons," which are electromagnetic radiations outside the visible range of the human eye coming from living things. At the lower end of our visual range is infrared electromagnetic radiation, which is composed of long wavelengths and lower-frequency electromagnetic waves that are felt as heat by human skin. At the other end of our visual range is ultraviolet radiation, which is composed of shorter wavelengths and higher-frequency radiation, including biophotons, which can now be measured coming from human bodies.

Biophoton emissions from plants and cell cultures have been studied in the past. The development of a sensitive photomultiplier has made it possible now to measure biophotons in humans. An experiment reported in 2012 demonstrated that human intention—that of healers and experienced meditators—can increase biophoton emission from human bodies. But how this energy is registered by another person remains an open question.[12]

All neuroscientists accept that light and sound waves are transduced into neuronal impulses that the brain interprets as images and music. The energy of light and sound waves carries information through tiny modifications in amplitude, length, and intensity of the waves. These tiny modifications are transduced into nerve impulses, along with the energy itself. But an unanswered question remains: How does the brain convert these tiny modifications in nerve impulses into images and music? Neuroscientists can tell us what happens in the brain when people are listening to music or watching movies, but they have yet to tell us how the brain makes light and sound waves into pictures and words. We also don't yet know how the energy-information involved with many coincidences is converted into feeling and behavior.

E-I Receptors

Like receptors for light, sound, taste, smell, and touch, our hypothetical E-I receptors should transduce simulpathity-GPS stimuli from
outside the body into neuroelectrical impulses within the body. Where
are these E-I receptors? Of what are they composed? How do they
transduce energy-information into neuroelectrical impulses?

We can make some educated guesses about the nature of these hypothetical structures. The gaps in our knowledge about known sense receptors open the door to other possible receptor activity that is currently
unknown. Here is an example of scientific ignorance regarding vision.
Until the 1990s, scientists thought that light waves stimulated only our
rods and cones in the second layer of the retina. Then scientists discovered blue-light sensitive ganglion cells in the third layer of the retina.[13]
This recent discovery involving supposedly well-known receptor mechanisms once again tells us that there are more discoveries to be made.

Mystery still surrounds our odor receptors, as well as pain, heat,
and cold receptors. Smell sense has been understudied compared to
vision, perhaps because it is so primitive and so little used in humans
compared to vision, which has been much more carefully studied. The
heat, cold, and pain receptors in our skin haven't changed through
evolution, and, as far as I could determine, their transduction methods
haven't been well explained. These smell, heat, cold, and pain receptors
are almost always available for stimulation, just as E-I receptors probably are. Even single-cell organisms respond to chemical, light, and
electromagnetic radiation in order to maintain optimal states. And like
single-cell organisms, our skin may contain sensors for subtle forms of
energy and information. Scientists recently discovered odor receptors
in the skin![14]

As vision evolved to become our primary means for knowing the world around us, these primitive smell and heat-cold-pain receptors have kept operating. Perhaps they also pick up other forms of energy-information. The coincidence stories may be indicating that our primitive sense receptors have retained an ongoing ability that we may be rediscovering. If quantum mechanisms can better explain how we register smells, then perhaps there are E-I receptors for coincidence information that work on quantum means.

Just as food smells much better when we are hungry, so E-I receptors are more likely to be open and operating during periods of need, transition, and high emotion—which would then increase the likelihood of useful coincidences during these times. E-I receptors could help to explain how I came to be choking uncontrollably as my father was dying. But they are only part of the story about how my lost dog and I found each other.

> *Just as food smells much better when we are hungry, so E-I receptors are more likely to be open and operating during periods of need, transition, and high emotion—which would then increase the likelihood of useful coincidences during these times.*

Human GPS

The mother who rushed to her small daughter by the deepwater quarry got to her without consciously knowing where she was and how to get there. My dog made the correct turns to find me.

A starting place for understanding how our human GPS might work comes from the human ability known as proprioception—the capacity to know what our arms, legs, and head are doing. The word *proprioception* comes from the Latin *proprius*, meaning "belonging to the individual," as in property. Proprioception provides the brain information about the location of parts of our bodies in space.

To know the precise locations of our hands, feet, knees, elbows, heads, and torsos requires a huge amount of simultaneous information processing. Luckily, most of the processing is done unconsciously so our conscious mind is not overwhelmed with "Oh, I just moved my thumb over to the space bar on the keyboard." Without this massive, unconscious, rapid-fire information processing, we would spend most of our waking life using vision to guide our body movements: to put our feet in the right place as we walk or guide our fingers while texting.

Here is how proprioception works. The vestibular system of the inner ear provides information about head position. The organs of the vestibular system transduce head movements and changes of position relative to gravity through the stirring of tiny hairs very similar to those that register sound. The vestibular system works with the visual system to keep objects in focus when the head is moving. Detailed information about limb position comes from muscle spindles that run in parallel with muscle fibers and report changes in muscle length. Golgi organs in the tendons convey changes in muscle tension. Delicate pressure receptors in the skin intermittently add detail. This second-to-second information is reported to neurons in the spinal column, each of which integrates thousands of inputs before firing. Inputs from the spinal column are assembled and reassembled in the brain's posterior parietal area for continual updating of the body's position in space. Without this constant and rapid input of position data, we wouldn't be able to move with smooth coordination.

Proprioception demonstrates the brain's ability to process huge amounts of information outside our awareness. This ability suggests the possibility that other forms of information are also being massively processed second by second in ways well beyond the awareness of our conscious minds.

A newly discovered batch of neurons, called "grid cells," may provide the neural maps for the territories of our lives. Located in the entorhinal cortex, which is near the hippocampus, they define, along with "place cells," where we are in space, something like the way GPS can locate us in space. As with our proprioceptive maps of body position, we seem to be continually updating our maps of our positions in our surroundings.[15] We also may have grid cells in the anterior cingulate, a part of the brain that plays an important role in human emotion.[16] This emotional aspect of grid cell mapping could make particular locations more highly charged in our brain-based maps. Like the maps used in GPS navigation, these maps could then help us find pathways to emotionally important people, things, and situations.

How are these pathways created? The mother could not only localize herself in her surroundings but also her daughter, who was in danger. Grid cells help us localize ourselves in our environment, but how can they help localize someone else *and* provide a path between the two of them? How did the mother mimic the technological GPS capacity to provide information about how to get from where she was to a place she had never been?

Implications of the E-I Receptor Theory

I believe that our physical being seems to have emerged from a primordial soup, a rich mixture of energy (perhaps electricity) and information (perhaps simple molecules). These ancient mechanisms—light-sensitive molecules, electromagnetic-sensitive magnetite, and thermal receptors—provide clues to coming full circle to the primordial oneness. In the Greek Minotaur myth, Theseus ties the end of a ball of string to the door of the Minotaur's vast labyrinth and unwinds the ball as he plunges into its depths so he can find his way back home. Deep inside the twisted tunnels, he kills the half-bull half-man Minotaur and uses the string to find his way back. Like the string of Theseus, these ancient receptor mechanisms may be leading us back into a recognition of the oneness of which we are a part.

Where the E-I receptors are located and the specifics of how they work remain to be discovered. But this should not be surprising considering that even the mechanisms behind the *known* sense receptors remain something of a mystery.

I imagine there are probably many different receptor types for these subtle forms of energy-information. Some are relatively permanent and have perhaps been with us through much of our evolutionary history. Some are specialized for tuning in to loved ones. Others help us find situations that provide useful mirrors for our conflicts. The function of a specific subtype of receptor may tell us more about the composition of various forms of energy-information.

Perhaps we can create specific receptors through intentions, the way a properly programmed 3-D printer can make so many three-dimensional objects out of plastic and other dust. Even pizzas can be formed by 3-D printers using powdered dough and oil.[17] Currently, 3-D printers can extrude concrete to construct walls for buildings while also embedding conduits for electrical wiring and plumbing.[18] By thinking of some need or goal, by having an intention, consciously or subconsciously, perhaps we can create the necessary receptor out of yet-to-be-defined materials. If you've ever seen a Batman movie or comic book, you may remember the Bat Signal. In times of great need, the police of Gotham City turn on a searchlight that projects a bat symbol on the sky over Gotham City to communicate their need for Batman. During our own times of need, great and small, perhaps we project a receptor that's shaped in a way that resonates with the needed energy-information.

As a psychiatrist, I regularly participate in observing with my patients the interactions between mind and brain. I give them molecules (medication) that attach to brain receptors, and then I often have the pleasure of watching their emotions and thinking become more normalized. I see how their attitudes toward the medications seem to shape their responses. How each of us thinks about the medication seems to influence how their receptors function. Perhaps our intentions and expectations can also mold new receptors or change the sensitivity of existing ones.

One deeply respected colleague tells me that there can be no such thing as signal transduction for simulpathity and GPS. There is no evidence, he and others claim, for the signal. No one knows how the coincidence information is carried to and arrives in our brains. As you have seen, there must be receptors of some kind to transduce this subtle external information into brain-friendly information. Therefore, there must be some kind of external information carrier.

Maybe the idea of E-I receptors is a step in the advancement of our understanding of ourselves. But no matter which theory turns out to be closer to the truth, a good theory of instrumental coincidences should sharpen our understanding of them and provide a framework for systematic study.

Our Mental Atmosphere

Where is this energy-information coming from? E-I receptors must be receiving inputs of energy-information from somewhere through some undefined medium. I believe this medium—the dynamic product of our minds, nature, and technology—surrounds us. One way or another, our minds are like fish in water, immersed in some unknown medium that carries energy-information. Some call this vast information medium the "Big Mind" or the "One Mind." Many people envision it as a unifying, intentional energy—God or "the Universe" or "Consciousness"—an active force in our lives.

Since it is difficult enough for me as a psychiatrist to understand the workings of the human brain, my concept of Big Mind tends to stay right here on Earth with just us people. I invented the word *psychosphere* to indicate my intent to limit the medium to our terrestrial environment. The psychosphere is something like our atmosphere—around us and in dynamic flux with us. We breathe in oxygen, nitrogen, and water vapors, and we breathe out carbon dioxide, nitrogen, and more water vapors. We receive energy-information from the psychosphere and release energy-information into the psychosphere. Our thoughts and emotions contribute to the psychosphere and our thoughts and emotions are influenced by it. The plants and animals surrounding us give and take from it. The technologies we invent reshape it and are products of it. We are in dynamic relationship with it.

Support for the existence of the psychosphere comes from several sources. People all over the world say they feel something very subtle that is much greater than each of us, of which we are all a part. We sense something beyond the reach of our five senses, an extended mind. For those who call this subtle greater something "God" or "the Universe," the concept of the psychosphere is a small step toward understanding how this great intentional mind might work. And for those who call it "Consciousness," the psychosphere offers scientists a bounded version of an unbounded idea. By studying the psychosphere, we could be examining a small version—a microcosm, a holographic representation—of the One Mind, of Consciousness, of the Universe, of God.

Of what, then, is the psychosphere made? In a well-known tale originating long ago on the Indian subcontinent, several blind men (interpret blind as ignorant) were inspecting an elephant. Each one felt a different part and declared that he had the whole truth—the leg is a pillar, the tail is a rope, the tusk is a pipe, the side is a wall—while they actually had only a piece of it.

And so it is with arguments about the psychosphere.

The Psychosphere Is Spirit

The parallel between atmosphere and psychosphere has been recognized for thousands of years in many different cultures. Each of the following words originally meant both breath and spirit in different languages: *prana* (Sanskrit), *ruach* (Hebrew), *pneuma* and *psyche* (Greek), and *spiritus* (Latin). *Chi* or *Qi* in Taoism refers to universal energy or life force, both outside and inside the body. Its most literal meaning is "breath" or "gas." We inspire air, food, water, relationships, and spirit and expire carbon dioxide, ideas, and spirit. To be inspired is to be urged to higher levels, to embrace life. To expire means to let go of the vital bodily energy, to die. Hindus developed words specifically for vital energy—Shakti, the surrounding feminine energy, and Kundalini, its manifestation in the body.

The Psychosphere Contains All the Information That Ever Was and Ever Will Be

Some think any information is always available to each of us if we can tune in to the depository of human and extrahuman knowledge, which has been given various names, including the Akashic records and Idea Space. By its vast accessibility to huge amounts of information, the Internet is approximating this old idea.

Jung proposed the existence of the collective unconscious, which he contrasted with the individual unconscious. The unconscious minds of individuals stand apart from each other, giving the impression of separateness. The collective unconscious contains basic information and modes of behavior that are potentially accessible to everyone and that influence all individuals everywhere. The collective unconscious is shared by all human minds.

Jung called the basic information and modes of behavior "archetypes." In trying to articulate the functions of archetypes, Jung seemed to rely on the origin of the word *pattern*—from the Old French *patron*, which was derived from the Latin *pater*, meaning "father." To Jung, archetypes were enduring patterns that existed outside the ebb and flow of life—they father the patterns by which life is formed. Its contents appear in myths, dreams, works of art, and fantasies. To Jung an activated archetype is also associated with all meaningful coincidences.

British biologist Rupert Sheldrake focuses more on the introduction of new patterns. When a group of animals initiates a new pattern, any similar animal exposed to a similar stimulus will learn the task more easily. To Sheldrake, a new "behavioral field" is reinforced by "morphic resonance." "Morphic" refers to having a particular form or pattern. "Resonance" is similar to sympathetic resonance—strings will respond to the external vibrations of a tuning fork when sufficient harmonic relations exist between their vibratory capacities. Once the new shape "morphs" into existence, other beings with similar resonating capacities will more easily pick up the pattern.[19] Sheldrake has no theory for the "behavioral field" within which the morphic resonance occurs, but I believe that the psychosphere provides a starting point for the idea of morphic resonances. Ideas at all levels of energy are present and available in the psychosphere.

The Psychosphere Is Full of Living Energy

Russian biogeologist Vladimir Vernadsky (1863–1945) and French Jesuit philosopher Pierre Teilhard de Chardin (1881–1955) used the term *noosphere* for the envelope of mind in which we are all immersed. According to Vernadsky, the noosphere emerges from the biosphere, which is composed of all living things and ranges from the ocean depths to the upper regions of the atmosphere. Powered by the sun and intimately connected to the earth's geological processes, the biosphere converts the cosmic radiations of the sun into electrical, chemical, mechanical, thermal, and other forms of energy. From the biosphere, wrote Vernadsky, a region of rationality, the noosphere, is developing that will intelligently guide evolution. The noosphere of Vernadsky is fueled by the growth of scientific understanding and the behavior of human beings related to this understanding.[20] Teilhard shared Vernadsky's belief in science and technology as universal, peaceful, and civilizing forces but believed the noosphere emerged through the interaction of all human minds. Although he died before the Internet was created, he envisioned technological advances that would increase the rate of the interaction between human minds and the density of the noosphere.[21] The Internet seems to be doing just that.

Teilhard's concept of the interaction of all human minds in the noosphere suggests a space in which the interaction of energy-information occurs. This space is somehow both psychological and physical. An increasingly dense web, likely fostered by billions of Internet connections, seems to support a matrix for the movement of energy-information. The energy-information can also well up into negativity with resulting social damage. You can picture the thoughts and emotions of individuals as drops of water evaporating into the psychosphere and accumulating into a heavy storm cloud (the collective negativity) that then unleashes its violent torrents (crime, war) onto the earth.

Sometimes science fiction and comics reflect current and near future ideas beyond generally accepted science. References to the energy-information psychosphere are made in science fiction, such as the "Force" in *Star Wars* movies and in comic books like the *X-Men*. Here the energy of the psychosphere is often used for destructive, violent purposes rather than self- and human evolution.

That the psychosphere is equivalent to spirit, contains all information that ever was, is composed of all human minds, and is full of living energy may be aspects of the greater "elephant." More direct evidence for this Mind of Our Minds comes from several sources, as shown below.

Groups Acting as One

A group may share unrealistic beliefs that result in mass hysteria. Thoughts of danger and illness reverberate through highly connected communities like schools, small towns, and factories.[22] In 2012, strange symptoms resembling the neurological disorder Tourette's syndrome spread through a group of mostly teenage girls in Le Roy, New York. In the mid-1940s, the "Mad Gasser" of Mattoon, Illinois, caused fiery lips and throats, and paralysis all through the town. There are always other possible explanations (real villains and toxic fumes) but when not verified, spiraling reverberations within the group mind becomes a plausible explanation.[23] These shared physical symptoms echo the simulpathity of twins and other closely connected people.

Rage also spreads like wildfire through crowds of like-minded people. Polite, pleasant, family-oriented individuals can mass together to form an unthinking, cruel, destructive mob. They attack the Other, the people who are "different"—of a different religion, race, or political party. They burn houses, shoot and hang people in a frenzy of destructive actions, and then recede into their normal lives as if their participation in the primal horde never happened. Like a pack of hyenas attacking a wildebeest or a swarm of locusts descending on a wheat field, the individuals act as one. Simulpathity-like, they share an intense emotion accelerated by their physical closeness.

Smaller groups can be similarly affected. "Groupthink" can isolate them from reality by creating reverberating circuits of self-reinforcing, misleading thoughts. Groupthink punishes independent perspectives in favor of group harmony and often against the "threats" of outgroups. In the early twenty-first century, US foreign policy makers engaged in groupthink by uniformly believing Iraq to be a military threat. Based on this false idea, the group initiated the United States attack on Iraq. Political and military realities were ignored in favor of mutually reinforced shared beliefs. Again, their proximity and emotion energized a belief that created a single-minded creature.

Unified group intention can also yield positive effects. Political action by large numbers of people with shared intentions can help reduce discrimination against minorities and stop wars. Crowdsourcing can help small businesses get started by gathering and focusing on micro-investors. Individual minds working together on difficult problems can find solutions in novel ways. The FOLDIT game invented at the University of Washington relies on the collective energies of video gamers to figure out the specific biologically active 3-D shape of flexible protein molecules. Computer algorithms cannot account for all the possibilities. Gamers can be directed into effective packs of real-world problem solvers.[24]

The human capacity to energize ideas in groups of varying sizes seems to me to represent processes related to the E-I-filled psychosphere.

Simultaneous Discoveries

Another hint for the existence of the psychosphere comes from simultaneous discoveries. Scientists, inventors, and artists often make the same discovery at about the same time without having communicated with one another. The list of examples includes the 1858 announcement of the discovery of evolution by Charles Darwin and Alfred Wallace, and, on February 14, 1876, the same-day arrival of patent applications at the U.S. Patent Office from the inventors of the telephone, Alexander Graham Bell and Elisha Gray.

A comprehensive list of simultaneous discoveries was put together in a 1922 journal article. The authors, William F. Ogburn and Dorothy Thomas, found 148 major scientific discoveries made by two or more people around the same time.[25] They suggest that every generation produces curious, intelligent, motivated individuals who try to shed light on mystery and help make life easier for others. They work in cultures and societies rich with the ideas of those who have preceded them. They stand on the shoulders of giants to find solutions for current problems. But they haven't communicated directly with one another. They work on the leading edges of the evolving group mind that contains the necessary ideas. By integrating the products of previous thinkers with their current knowledge and enthusiasm, they lead the rest of us to the next discovery. They seem to be tuned in to the evolving edges of our collective conscious mind, which may somehow be related to the E-I-filled psychosphere.

To bring the story closer to home, I was having coffee with a few friends at a local Charlottesville coffeehouse when two women known to two of my companions walked in. They sat down and eventually we talked about coincidences. One woman had been a literary agent and smilingly recounted the struggles of several groups of potential authors. "One time five different authors sent me book proposals centered around the same specific idea," she said. "Each one asked me to be sure not to tell anyone else about this idea." An example of a zeitgeist, ideas floating around in the air, floating in particular areas of our group mind.

With the arrival of the Internet, information has been flowing at lightning speed. We can no longer find an individual thinker isolated from the activities of other creative thinkers in another city or on another continent. Within the noise of gossip, fake news, toothpaste preferences, and animal tricks, videos go viral, technology speeds ahead, and new ideas blossom. Ideas build upon ideas as new combinations are tossed around in the minds of individuals and groups. New inventions and discoveries are produced.

In this quiet maelstrom of idea energetics comes a simple basic principle: *If I am thinking it, someone else is also thinking it.* This simple maxim means that what you are thinking has probably already been thought by others. If you want to check out the possibility that your idea is not original, do an Internet search.

Imagine clouds overhead. You can see their movement from your left, yet there is a line from a tree branch to the edge of the clouds that the bank does not cross. Movement from the rear is unceasing, yet the edge goes no farther. And so it may be with our evolving, curious, discovery-seeking collective mind. Movement from the rear continues to alter the content at the edge. At the edge are those curious, driven, seeking, talented individuals trying to grasp new ideas in their areas of interest. The edge keeps changing, just as the cloudbank keeps pushing forward to its edge with new clouds. Curious individuals see the contents of the edge and report it to the rest of us around the same time, creating simultaneous discoveries.

We are all participants in the collective human mind, that evolving set of ideas and feelings conveyed to us through our rapidly expanding methods of social communication. Each of us in small and large ways makes a contribution to this collective mind. We are in a continual, reciprocal relationship to it. The collective mind is also conscious of itself through our own awareness of what is going on around us now, recently, and into the near future. This gathering of our individual awareness of the psychosphere becomes our collective awareness of the psychosphere. By writing about the content and functions of our collective mind, I'm trying to expand our collective awareness of the psychosphere. As you read this, you are becoming aware of the psychosphere and contributing to the collective awareness of it.

Social Network Effects

The spread of personal qualities through social networks adds yet more evidence for the existence of the group mind and, by extension, the psychosphere. More specifically, people you don't know can affect how you feel and behave—a very quiet variation on mass hysteria.

Fowler and Christakis studied more than five thousand people enrolled in the Framingham Heart Study between 1971 and 2003, and the thousands of people with whom they had relationships—spouses, relatives, neighbors, close friends, and coworkers. This study was done *before* the introduction of Internet social networking. (Because of Internet social networking, this study can never be replicated; the Internet adds a major new dimension to the definition of social networking.) They studied many personal variables, including happiness, depression, sadness, obesity, drinking and smoking habits, and thoughts about suicide. To give you an idea of the number of relationships involved, their findings on happiness were based on data from 53,228 social ties.[26]

They reported that the happiness of an individual is associated with the happiness of others whom they don't know but with whom they are connected through others: "Happiness . . . is not merely a function of individual experience and individual choice but is also a property of groups of people. Indeed, changes in individual happiness can ripple through social networks . . . giving rise to clusters of happy and unhappy individuals."[27]

Perhaps happy people are more helpful or financially generous or kinder or exude a contagious positive emotion. Yet the effects the researchers measured reached beyond individual contact, spread from one person through a friend to that friend's friend, and then on to another friend—through three degrees of separation. The effect diminishes with increasing interpersonal distance.

Happiness doesn't seem to spread among coworkers. These findings suggest that emotional connections seem to facilitate the spread of happiness and other emotional states, an apparent variation on simulpathity.

The authors found similar results about obesity with data that was compelling enough to be published in the *New England Journal of Medicine*, the premier medical journal in the United States. Again, in addition to the effects one person has on an intimate other, obesity seems to spread through social networks to people who don't have contact with the originally obese person but to whom they are connected through mutual friends. The effects also decrease with physical distance.

The mechanisms by which depression, alcoholism, smoking, and suicidal thinking spread through social networks are open to speculation. Yet here is additional evidence of our human interconnectedness, of influence without direct contact. Perhaps behavioral copying is involved. But there is more. Our minds share thoughts and feelings through the psychosphere. Social network research tells us that closeness in space and in emotion augments these effects. This research provides an early map of the psychosphere, which suggests that spatial and emotional distances influence communications through the psychosphere.

Experiencing the Psychosphere

We are fishlike, immersed in the ethereal waters of the psychosphere. Currents move through it. Some currents passing through us contain information about who we are, where we have been, and where we are going. "Tunnels"—the only word I can think of that expresses the connection that occurs—open and close, extend and shorten. Through these tunnels, resonating minds can connect with each other. Through these tunnels, places and objects at a distance can be known. This out-of-awareness medium carries vibrating patterns of energy-information, perhaps the way air conducts sound. These patterns can engage similar patterns with which to resonate, amplifying the life span of the original pattern.

Researcher Frederick Myers called the E-I sphere the "subliminal self"—that part of each of us below the threshold (*limen* in Latin) of awareness. It has layers or strata: "They are strata (so to say) not of

immovable rock, but of imperfectly miscible fluids of various densi-
ties, and subject to currents and ebullitions which often bring to the
surface a stream or bubble from a stratum far below."[28]

The "strata" also create regions that closely aligned minds share.
Through these shared regions, mothers can know the problems of
their children, wives know the romances of their husbands, and
friends "coincidentally" run into each other without prearrangement.
Simulpathy-GPS coincidences are windows into the psychosphere.

This is my theory anyway. If it's a good theory, then it should show
us more clearly how deeply we are connected to those we love and how
to enrich our decision making. It should also help to clarify the theories currently being developed formally and informally by thousands
of other people about how each of our minds is not as separated from
other minds as current conventional ideas would have us believe. Call
it God, the Universe, the Greater Mind, or the Unus Mundus, each of
our minds is part of something greater. Our individual minds can, as
many coincidences demonstrate, connect to this something greater. The
psychosphere provides an earthbound understanding of how to activate
and consciously experience our mind-to-mind connections as well as
the connections to our surroundings.

May you connect comfortably, clearly, and effectively and have
fun doing it!

It is my hope that you have gained insights and understanding
about how to harness the power of coincidence in your own life. With
this newfound radar to the psychosphere, may your mind be open to
new possibilities, and may you spark meaningful connections with
increased curiosity.

Acknowledgments

Book writing resembles a marathon, not a sprint. The energy, intellect, and support of many people helped this one reach the finish line.

The Division of Perceptual Studies (DOPS) at the University of Virginia became the essential incubator for ideas that had been floating around in my head for many years. After I arrived in Charlottesville in 2009 and began attending its weekly meetings, I became immersed in its encouraging, helpful, and highly informative atmosphere. So many of the apparently strange ideas I had been entertaining were commonly discussed here.

This book on coincidence was itself the product of many coincidences. I wanted to write a book on the subject but needed the help of a developmental editor. Into DOPS one day walked Patrick Huyghe, who had just moved to Charlottesville from New York. Patrick is the editor and publisher of Anomalist Books. After hearing one of my talks on coincidence, he asked me to write an article for *EdgeScience*, a magazine he edits for the Society for Scientific Exploration. I then asked him to help me with this book and he agreed. Over the many months that followed we had many amazingly helpful discussions about sharpening my ideas and their expression. He's been a wonderful help.

Then Patrick, three other DOPS members, and I formed the Mynders, a gathering for several hours on a random Friday afternoon, where we spun out our stories and experiences and honed our thinking on each other's minds. Frank Pasciuti, a great guy and psychotherapist from Newark, New Jersey, and I met regularly for lunch after DOPS meetings and deepened our friendship while helping each other develop our DOPSian ideas and our practices of psychotherapy. Mike Grosso, wise philosopher and teacher, is a storehouse of intriguing, scholarly ideas and human kindness. And Ross Dunseath, the hard-wired electrical engineer whose mind can also float to the strangest places. What a group.

Bruce Greyson, longtime head of DOPS, welcomed me so very graciously and helped to steady my entrance into this new society. Taking over when Bruce retired, Jim Tucker has continued his interest and support. Both Bruce and Jim always welcomed my requests to speak at DOPS meetings, which further developed my ability to conceptualize sometimes elusive concepts. Bruce and Jim are also psychiatrists, which helped normalize my interests in ideas outside the psychiatric mainstream. Ed Kelly, the consummate academic scholar at DOPS, is a fountainhead of well-considered knowledge and information. He regularly guided my fluid mind back into more reasonable streams of thought.

Many others contributed along the way. Thank you, Dave Morris, Dan Lederer, Tara MacIssac, Howard Peelle, Dave Waters, Trish MacGregor, Mary Kay Landon, Julia Altamar, James van Pelt, William Rosar, Angie Miles, and many unnamed patients.

Allison Janse has been a marvelous editor—allowing me a great deal of freedom in the context of wise counsel as well as contributing her own stories. Cathy Slovensky is a superb copyeditor who caught biases I did not know I had. She strengthened my ability to keep the reader's mind in mind.

My son Arie's amusement with my interest in the subject encouraged me to make it more relevant to him. I appreciate his healthy skepticism. He also contributed a good story. My son Karlen enthusiastically supported the project and provided many insightful comments and examples.

And Paula.

Appendix:
Weird Coincidence Scale

Please rate the following statements based on your experience:

	Never	Seldom	Occasionally	Often	Very frequently
I think of calling someone, only to have that person unexpectedly call me.					
When my phone rings, I know who's calling (without checking my cell phone screen or using personalized ring tones).					
I think of a question only to have it answered by external media (i.e., radio, TV, people) before I can ask it.					
I think of an idea and hear or see it on the radio, TV, or Internet.					

	Never	Seldom	Occasionally	Often	Very frequently
I think of someone and that person unexpectedly drops by my house or office or passes me in the hall or street.					
I run into a friend in an out-of-the-way place.					
I experience strong emotions or physical sensations that were simultaneously experienced at a distance by someone I love.					
I need something and the need is met without my having to do anything.					
I advance in my work/ career/education through being at the right place at the right time.					
I am introduced to people who unexpectedly further my work/career/education.					
Meaningful coincidence helps determine my educational path.					
After experiencing meaningful coincidence, I analyze the meaning of my experience.					

For each statement rating, give the following numbers:

Never = 1
Seldom = 2
Occasionally = 3
Often = 4
Very frequently = 5

Add them up.
Now rate your coincidence sensitivity:

Above 43: Ultra-sensitive
39–43: Very sensitive
35–38: Sensitive
27–34: Average
23–26: Insensitive
22–19: Very insensitive
Below 19: Ultra-insensitive

If you scored in the sensitive to ultra-sensitive range, you are very likely to be regularly using coincidences for decision making and for psychological change. This book will help you strengthen your already active use of coincidences.

If you scored low, you may be in a certain routine or pattern of living in which the conditions are not ripe for coincidences. Or you may be experiencing only one certain kind of coincidence. This book can help you to expand the range of coincidences available to you if you remain alert, open, and seeking.

Notes

Introduction

1 *Psychiatric Annals,* Vol. 39, Issue 5, May 2009, and *Psychiatric Annals,* Vol. 41, Issue 12, December 2011.

Chapter 1

1 Ian Stevenson, *Telepathic Impressions* (New York: American Society for Psychical Research, 1970).

2 Jean Bolen, *Tao of Psychology* (New York: Harper Collins, 1979), 32.

3 Robert Hopcke, *There Are No Accidents* (New York: Riverhead Books, 1998), 158–160.

4 S. L. Coleman, B. D. Beitman, and E. Celebi. "Weird Coincidences Commonly Occur." *Psychiatric Annals* 39 (2009): 265–270.

5 Ian Stevenson, *Telepathic Impressions* (New York: American Society for Psychical Research, 1970), 17–22.

6 Guy Playfair, *Twin Telepathy,* 3rd ed. (Hove, UK: White Crow Books, 2012), 37–38.

7 Brett Mann and Chrystal Jaye, "'Are We One Body?' Body Boundaries in Telesomatic Experiences," *Anthropology & Medicine* 14, no. 2 (August 2007): 183–95.

8 *http://www.nytimes.com/2011/05/29/magazine/could-conjoined-twins-share-a-mind .html?_r=1&hp.* Retrieved 5/25/11.

9 B. Inglis, *Coincidence: A Matter of Chance—or Synchronicity* (London: Hutchinson, 1990), 202.

Chapter 2

1 *http://www.menshealth.com/sex-women/best-places-meet-women.* Retrieved 5/8/12.

2 Aaron Smith and Monica Anderson, "5 Facts about Online Dating," Pew Research Center, *http://www.pewresearch.org/fact-tank/2015/04/20/5-facts-about-online-dating/.*

3 Adam Davidson, "The Purpose of Spectacular Wealth, According to a Spectacularly Wealthy Guy," *New York Times* online, *http://www.nytimes.com/2012/05/06/magazine /romneys-former-bain-partner-makes-a-case-for-inequality.html?_r=0*.

4 Squire D. Rushnell, *When God Winks on Love* (New York: Atria, 2004), 137–141.

5 Robert Hopcke, *There Are No Accidents: Synchronicity and the Stories of Our Lives* (New York: Riverhead Books, 1998), chapter 1.

6 Ibid., 50–52.

7 Squire D. Rushnell, *When God Winks on Love* (New York: Atria Books, 2004), 59–64.

8 Joseph Jaworski, *Synchronicity: The Inner Path of Leadership*, 2nd ed. (San Francisco: Berrett-Koehler, 2011), chapter 13.

9 Squire D. Rushnell, *When God Winks on Love* (New York: Atria Books, 2004), 45–48.

10 Yitta Halberstam and Judith Leventhal, *Small Miracles: Extraordinary Coincidences from Everyday Life* (Holbrook, MA: Adams Media, 1999), 18–20.

11 Robert Hopcke, *There Are No Accidents: Synchronicity and the Stories of Our Lives* (New York: Riverhead Books, 1998), 69–71.

Chapter 3

1 Sally Rhine Feather and Michael Schmicker, *The Gift: ESP, the Extraordinary Experiences of Ordinary People* (New York: St. Martin's Press, 2006), 131–2.

2 M. A. Cameron. "Synchronicity and Spiritual Development in Alcoholics Anonymous: A Phenomenological Study" (St. Louis, MO: St. Louis University unpublished dissertation), 2004).

3 Robert Perry, *Signs: A New Approach to Coincidence, Synchronicity, Guidance, Life Purpose, and God's Plan* (Sedona, AZ: Semeion Press, 2009), 28–29.

4 Sally Rhine Feather and Michael Schmicker, *The Gift: ESP, the Extraordinary Experiences of Ordinary People* (New York: St. Martin's Press, 2006), 133–35.

5 Jean Bolen, *The Tao of Psychology: Synchronicity and the Self* (San Francisco: HarperSanFrancisco, 2005), 42–43.

6 Ruben, "Is a Coincidence a Message from Fate or an Opportunity?" *discoveraid*, July 21, 2008, *http:www.discoveraid.com/self-help-personal-growth/is-a-coincidence-a-message -from-fate-or-an-opportunity.html*. Retrieved 6/6/12.

7 Yitta Halberstam and Judith Leventhal, *Small Miracles of the Holocaust: Extraordinary Coincidences of Faith, Hope, and Survival* (Guilford, CT: Globe Pequot Press, 2008), 60–63.

8 Squire D. Rushnell, *When God Winks at You: How God Speaks Directly to You Through the Power of Coincidence* (Nashville, TN: Thomas Nelson, 2006), 4–6.

9 Thomas Fields-Meyer, "Lost, Then Found," *People* magazine, May 20, 1996, *http:// www.people.com/people/archive/article/0,,20141337,00.html*.

10 Understanding Uncertainty Project, *Understanding Uncertainty*, *http://understanding uncertainty.org/user-submitted-coincidences/public-phone-box*. Retrieved 9/17/13.

11 Ibid. Retrieved 9/17/13.

12 Rupert Sheldrake and P. Smart. "Dog That Seems to Know When His Owner Is Returning: Preliminary Investigations," *Journal of the Society for Psychical Research* 62 (1998): 230–232.

13 Sally Rhine Feather and Michael Schmicker, *The Gift: ESP, the Extraordinary Experiences of Ordinary People* (New York: St. Martin's Press, 2006), 121–123.

14 L. Wu and J. D. Dickman, "Neural Correlates of a Magnetic Sense," *Science* 336 (May 25, 2012):1054–1057. *http://www.sciencemag.org/content/336/6084/1054.abstract*. Retrieved 1/21/14.

Chapter 4

1   Laura Buxton, "A Very Lucky Wind," NPR's *Radiolab*, *http://www.radiolab.org/story/91686-a-very-lucky-wind/*. *Laura Buxton (blog: http://www.67notout.com/2010/05/red-balloon-coincidence.html)*. Retrieved 7/7/12.
    (video: *http://www.youtube.com/watch?v=A_j3bVYwAp4&feature=player_embedded*)
    (*http://www.radiolab.org/2009/jun/15/*). Retrieved 7/14/12.

2   Ibid.

3   Robert Hopcke, *There Are No Accidents: Synchronicity and the Stories of Our Lives* (New York: Riverhead Books, 1998), 10–12.

4   Matthew Hutson, *The 7 Laws of Magical Thinking* (New York: Hudson Street Press, 2012).

5   Yitta Halberstam and Judith Leventhal, *Small Miracles of the Holocaust: Extraordinary Coincidences of Faith, Hope, and Survival* (Guilford, CT: Globe Pequot Press, 2008), xiv–xv.

6   Winston Churchill, *My Early Life* (New York: Touchstone, 1930), 280–281.

7   Yitta Halberstam and Judith Leventhal, *Small Miracles of the Holocaust: Extraordinary Coincidences of Faith, Hope, and Survival* (Guilford, CT: Globe Pequot Press, 2008), xiv.

8   Susan Watkins, *What a Coincidence! The Wow! Factor in Synchronicity and What It Means in Everyday Life* (Needham, MA: Moment Point Press, 2005), 6–8.

9   Rolf Gordhamer, "Destiny," in *Coincidence or Destiny? Stories of Synchronicity That Illuminate Our Lives* by Phil Cousineau and Robert A. Johnson (York Beach, ME: Conari Press, 1997), 203–204.

10 Erica Helm Meade, "Renewal," in *Coincidence or Destiny? Stories of Synchronicity That Illuminate Our Lives* by Phil Cousineau and Robert A. Johnson (York Beach, ME: Conari Press, 1997), 126–127.

11 *Understanding Uncertainty, http://understandinguncertainty.org/user-submitted-coin cidences/happening-algarve.* Retrieved 1/20/15.

12 Persi Diaconis and Frederick Mosteller, "Methods of Studying Coincidences," *Journal of the American Statistical Association* 84, no. 408 (December 1989).

13 "Hugh and Me and Phone Calls Agree," Chapter 6 in *What a Coincidence! The Wow! Factor in Synchronicity and What It Means in Everyday Life* by Susan Watkins (Needham, MA: Moment Point Press, 2005).

14 *Understanding Uncertainty, http://understandinguncertainty.org/user-submitted-coin cidences/telephone-advice.* Retrieved 1/20/16.

15 Brian Inglis, *Coincidence: A Matter of Chance or Synchronicity* (London: Hutchinson, 1990), 52.

16 Yitta Halberstam and Judith Leventhal, *Small Miracles: Extraordinary Coincidences from Everyday Life* (Holbrook, MA: Adams Media, 1999), 81–83.

17 Paul Kammerer, *Das Gesetz der Serie.* (Deutsche Verlagsanstalt: Berlin, Germany, 1919). Translation and updated by Arthur Koestler, *The Case of the Midwife Toad* (New York: Vintage: 1971), Appendix 1.

18 John Townley and Robert Schmidt, "Cause and Coincidence: The Serial Structure of Reality" (unpublished, copyright 1991–2009, used with permission).

19 Kashmir Hill, "How My Doppelgänger Used the Internet to Find and Befriend Me," *Fusion,* June 5, 2015, *http://fusion.net/story/121797/how-my-doppelganger-used-the -internet-to-find-and-befriend-me/.*

Chapter 5

1 Sternberg story in March 2010 while attending the Integrative Mental Health Conference in Phoenix, Arizona. *http://www.youtube.com/watch?v=mxtxCjbWMM.* Retrieved 4/19/11.

2 Robert Hopcke, *There Are No Accidents: Synchronicity and the Stories of Our Lives* (New York: Riverhead Books, 1998), 195–196.

3 Ian Rubenstein, *Consulting Spirit: A Doctor's Experience with Practical Mediumship* (San Antonio, TX: Anomalist Books, 2011), 22–25.

4 Larry Burk, *Let Magic Happen: Adventures in Healing with a Holistic Radiologist* (Durham, NC: Healing Imager Press, 2012).

5 Carl Jung, "Synchronicity: An Acausal Connecting Principle," in vol. 8 of the *Collected Works of C. G. Jung,* Jung Extracts (Princeton, NJ: Princeton University Press, 1973), 109.

6 Yitta Halberstam and Judith Leventhal, *Small Miracles: Extraordinary Coincidences from Everyday Life* (Holbrook, MA: Adams Media, 1999), 143–144.

7 Jennifer Hill, "Synchronicity and Grief: The Phenomenology of Meaningful Coincidences as It Arises During Bereavement," Institute of Transpersonal Psychology, Palo Alto, California, March 14, 2011 (unpublished doctoral dissertation) 71–72.

8   Victor Frankl, *Man's Search for Meaning* (Boston: Beacon Press: 1959), 64.

9   David Dosa, *Making Rounds with Oscar* (New York: HarperCollins, 2010), *http://www.nejm.org/doi/10.10565/NEJMp078108*. Retrieved 9/7/12.

10 *http://www.huffingtonpost.com/margaret-ruth/intuitive-scanning-for-he_b_188744*. Retrieved 8/16/12.

Chapter 6

1   Sissy Spacek, *My Ordinary, Extraordinary Life* (New York: Hyperion, 2012), 180–185.

2   Alister Hardy, Robert Harvie, and Arthur Koestler, *The Challenges of Chance: Experiments and Speculations* (London: Hutchinson, 1973), 162.

3   Rob MacGregor and Trish MacGregor, *Synchrosecrets*, *http://blog.synchrosecrets.com/*.

4   David J. Hand, *The Improbability Principle: Why Coincidences, Miracles, and Rare Events Happen Every Day* (New York: Scientific American, 2014), 1.

5   Martin Plimmer and Brian King. *Beyond Coincidence: Amazing Stories of Coincidence and the Mystery and Mathematics Behind Them* (New York: St. Martin's Press, 2006), 8.

6   Amy Tan, *The Opposite of Fate: A Book of Musings* (New York: Putnam, 2003), 262.

7   Maria Popova, *Brain Pickings*, *http://www.brainpickings.org/*.

8   Lauren Raine, *The Masks of the Goddess: Sacred Masks and Dance* (eBook), *www.laurenraine.com*.

9   Martin Plimmer and Brian King, *Beyond Coincidence: Amazing Stories of Coincidence and the Mystery and Mathematics Behind Them* (New York: St. Martin's Press, 2006), 134–135.

10 Morton A. Meyers, *Happy Accidents: Serendipity in Modern Medical Breakthroughs* (New York: Arcade Publishing), 59–69.

11 Ibid., 75.

12 G. Parker, "John Cade," *American Journal of Psychiatry*. 169 (2012): 125–126.

13 J. Austin, *Chance, Chase and Creativity* (Cambridge, Mass: MIT Press, 1978), 63–69.

14 Carl Jung, *Memories, Dreams and Reflections* (New York: Vintage, 1963), 197.

15 Robert McKee. *Story: Substance, Structure, Style and the Principles of Screenwriting* (New York: Regan Books, 1997), 356.

16 R. Robertson, *Futility, or The Wreck of the Titan* (New York: M.F. Mansfield, 1898). *https://en.wikipedia.org/wiki/Futility,_or_the_Wreck_of_the_Titan*.

17 Martin Plimmer and Brian King, *Beyond Coincidence: Amazing Stories of Coincidence and the Mystery and Mathematics Behind Them* (New York: St. Martin's Press, 2006). 149–150.

18 *Robert Perry Blog*, "Sign Posts," *http://www.wemeionpress.com/signsSignPosts/?p=216*.

19 Jeffrey Kripal, *Mutants and Mystics: Science Fiction, Superhero Comics, and the Paranormal* (Chicago: University of Chicago Press, 2015), 3.

Chapter 7

1 Amy Tan, *The Opposite of Fate: A Book of Musings* (New York: Putnam, 2003), 56–57.

2 *The Secret* website, *http://thesecret.tv/stories/stories-read.html?id=16844*. Retrieved 11/11/12.

3 *The Secret* website, *http://www.thesecret.tv/stories/money-in-urgent-need/*. Retrieved 1/20/16.

4 Martin Plimmer and Brian King, *Beyond Coincidence: Amazing Stories of Coincidence and the Mystery and Mathematics Behind Them* (New York: St. Martin's Press, 2006), 116–117.

5 P. Sullivan, "The Rules That Madoff Investors Ignored," *New York Times*, January 6, 2009, *http://www.nytimes.com/2009/01/06your-money/06wealth.html?pagewanted=1&r=3*. Retrieved 11/10/12.

6 Rhonda Byrne, *The Secret* (New York: Simon and Schuster, 2006); *The Secret* DVD (extended version), 2006, 91 minutes.

7 "Wealth and Abundance Visualization," *Secret-Law-of-Attraction.us*, February 15, 2008. *http://www.youtube.com/watch/?v=2fyVOVsBJUY*. Retrieved 12/17/12.

8 S. L. Coleman and B. D. Beitman "Characterizing High-Frequency Coincidence Detectors," *Psychiatric Annals*, 39 (2009): 271–279. "Agreeableness Is Associated with Fewer Coincidences." 276.

9 M. K. Landon, "On Receiving Unexpected Money: A Theoretical and Empirical Investigation of Anomalous Mind-Matter Interactions with Archetypal Fields" (dissertation, San Francisco: California Institute of Integral Studies, 2002).

10 Ibid.

Chapter 8

1 Robert Hopcke, *There Are No Accidents: Synchronicity and the Stories of Our Lives* (New York: Riverhead Books, 1998), 97–98.

2 See *http://www.youtube.com/watch?V=KYFINGCsr0k*. Retrieved 1/20/16.

3 A. Gabel, "Lear DeBessonet," *Virginia Arts and Sciences Magazine*, Fall 2011. Vol. 29, 41 (2011).

4 K. E. Mitchell, A. S. Levin, and J. D. Krumboltz, "Planned Happenstance: Constructing Unexpected Career Opportunities," *Journal of Counseling and Development*. 77: 115–124, 118.

5 W. Churchill, *My Early Life* (New York: Charles Scribner, 1930), 18–19.

6 Martin Plimmer and Brian King, *Beyond Coincidence: Amazing Stories of Coincidence and the Mystery and Mathematics Behind Them* (New York: St. Martin's Press, 2006), 219–220.

7   A. Vaughn, *Incredible Coincidence: The Baffling World of Synchronicity* (New York: Harper and Row, 1979), 80–81. Cited in F. Joseph, *Synchroncity and You* (London: Vega, 2002), 13–17. Stephen Diamond, *What the Trees Said*, 2nd ed. (Ossipee, New Hampshire: Beech River Books, 2006).

8   R. Wiseman, "The Luck Factor," *Skeptical Inquirer* 27. *http://richardweisman.files. wordpress.com/2011/09/the_luck_factor.pdf*. Retrieved January 26, 2014. R. Weisman, *The Luck Factor* (New York, Hyperion, 2003).

9   R. Webber, "Make Your Own Luck," *Psychology Today*. Published on May 1, 2010. Last reviewed on July 28, 2011. *http:www.psychologytoday.com/articles/201005/make-your -own-luck*. Retrieved 3/2/11.

10   "Intuition," *Online Etymology Dictionary*. *http://www.etymonline.com/index.php ?allowed_in_frame=0&search=tuition&search=none*. Retrieved 1/26/14.

Chapter 9

1   Yitta Halberstam and Judith Leventhal, *Small Miracles: Extraordinary Coincidences from Everyday Life* (Holbrook, MA: Adams Media, 1999), 173–174.

2   Ibid., 140–142.

3   Ibid., 9–14.

4   Ibid., 195–200.

5   Jean Bolen, *The Tao of Psychology: Synchronicity and the Self* (San Francisco: Harper San Francisco, 1979), 96–97.

6   Squire D. Rushnell, *When God Winks at You: How God Speaks Directly to You Through the Power of Coincidence* (Nashville, TN: Thomas Nelson, 2006), 60–63.

7   T. MacGregor and R. MacGregor, *The Seven Secrets of Synchronicity* (Holbrook, MA: Adams Media, 2010), 33–34.

Chapter 10

1   Rick Tarnas, *Cosmos and Psyche: Intimations of a New World View* (New York: Viking, 2006), 55–56.

2   Tara MacIssac, "What Is Unhealthy Skepticism?" *Epoch Times*, *http://www.theepoch times.com/n3/603148-what-is-unhealthy-skepticism/*. Retrieved 1/21/16.

3   Michael Shermer, "Anomalous Events That Can Shake One's Skepticism to the Core," *Scientific American*, *http://www.scientificamerican.com/article/anomalous-events-that -can-shake-one-s-skepticism-to-the-core*. Retrieved 1/21/16.

4   Gibbs A. Williams, *Demystifying Meaningful Coincidences (Synchronicities): The Evolving Self, the Personal Unconscious, and the Creative Process* (Lanham, MD: Jason Aronson, 2010).

5   Roderick Main, "Synchronicity and the Problem of Meaning in Science," in *The Pauli-Jung Conjecture and Its Impact Today*, ed. Harald Atmanspacher and Christopher A. Fuchs (UK: Imprint Academic, 2014), 223–224.

6 "Iconoclasts (S3): Mike Myers + Deepak Chopra Coincidences Clip," *YouTube*, April 2, 2012, *https://www.youtube.com/watch?v=zai_qbA5OSc*.

7 A. Combs and M. Holland, *Synchronicity: Through the Eyes of Science, Myth and the Trickster* (New York: Marlow and company, 1996).

8 Jack Jones, *Let Me Take You Down: Inside the Mind of Mark David Chapman, the Man Who Killed John Lennon* (New York: Villard, 1992).

9 B. D. Beitman, and A. Shaw, "Synchroners, High Emotion, and Coincidence Interpretation," *Psychiatric Annals*, 39: 280–286. 3-Polar patient.

Chapter 11

1 E. L. Mayer, *Extraordinary Knowing* (New York: Bantam, 2007), 173.

2 Shimada K. Hiraki and I. Oda, "The Parietal Role in the Sense of Self-Ownership with Temporal Discrepancy Between Visual and Proprioceptive Feedbacks," *Neuroimage* 24: 1225–1232. *http://ncbi.nlm.nih.gov/pubmed/15670700*. Retrieved 4/1/13.

3 A. Newburg, A. Alavi, M. Baime, P. D. Mozley, and E. Aquili, "The measurement of cerebral blood flow during the complex cognitive task of meditation using HMPAO-SPECT imaging," *Journal of Nuclear Medicine*, 1997, 38:55.

4 Alfred Guillaume, *Prophecy and Divination Among the Hebrews and Other Semites*, (New York: Harper and Brothers Publishers, 1938).

5 Crowsflight. CW&T Studios. *https://itunes.apple.com/us/app/crowsflight/id444185307?mt=8#*. Retrieved 1/20/16.

Chapter 12

1 Rupert Sheldrake, *The Presence of the Past: Morphic Resonance and the Habits of Nature* (Rochester, VT: Park Street Press, 2012). Also see the article "Rupert Sheldrake: The 'Heretic' at Odds with Scientific Dogma," *Guardian*, February 2012, *http://www.theguardian.com/science/2012/feb/05/rupert-sheldrake-interview-science-delusion*. Retrieved 1/20/16.

2 D. M. Szaflarski, "How We See: The First Steps in Human Vision," Access Excellence Classic Collection. Atlanta: National Health Museum, *http://www.accessexcellence.org/AE/AEC/CCvision_backgoundphp*. Retrieved 2/24/13.

3 Wikipedia, "Visual Photo Transduction," *http://en.wikipedia.org/wiki/Visual_cycle*. Retrieved 5/31/13.

4 Sarah C. P. Williams, "Human Nose Can Detect a Trillion Smells," *AAAS*, March 20, 2014, *http://news.sciencemag.org/biology/2014/03/human-nose-can-detect-trillion-smells*. Retrieved 1/20/16.

5 J. R. Minkel, "Is Sense of Smell Powered by Quantum Vibrations?" *Scientific American*, December 12, 2006, *http://www.sciam.com/articlecfm?articleID=885622AA-E7F2-99DF-3859D89E5980A4B2&sc=I100322*. Retrieved 1/20/16.

6   S. Dowdey, "How Smell Works," *Howstuffworks*, Atlanta: A Discovery Company. *http://science.howstuffworks.com/life/human-biology/smell2.htm*. Retrieved 1/28/14.

J. Clark, "How China's Pollution Sniffers Work," *Howstuffworks*. A Discovery Company. *http://science.howstuffworks.com/environmental/green-science/pollution-sniffer1 .htm*. Retrieved 1/17/14.

7   L. Turin, "The Science of Scent," TED. Filmed February 2005. Posted November 2008.

8   Jennifer C. Brookes, Filio Hartoutsiou, A. P. Horsfield, and A. M. Stoneham, "Could Human Beings Recognize Odor by Photon Assisted Tunneling?" *Physical Review Letters* 98, no. 038101 (2007); L. Zyga, "Quantum Mechanics May Explain How Humans Smell," *Phys.org* News. February 1, 2007, *http://phys.org/news89542035.html*. Retrieved 5/15/13.

9   "Ampullae of Lorenzini," *Wikipedia. http://en.wikipedia.org/wiki/Ampullae_of_Loren zini*. Retrieved 1/28/14.

10 D. Heyers, M. Manns, H. Luksch, O. Gunturkun, and H. Mouritsen, "A Visual Pathway Links Brain Structures Active During Magnetic Compass Orientation in Migratory Birds," In Iwaniuk, Andrew. PLos ONE 2(9): e937.Bibcode: 2007PLoSO...2..937H .doi:10.1371/journal.pone.0000937. PMC 1976598.PMID 17895978).

11 "Explainer: How Do Homing Pigeons Navigate?" *The Conversation*, April 23, 2014, *http://theconversation.com/explainer-how-do-homing-pigeons-navigate-25633*. C. T. Rodgers, and P. J. Hore, "Chemical magnet reception in birds: the radical pair mechanism," *Proceedings of the National Academy of Sciences of the United States of America* 106 (2) (2009): 353–60.

12 W. T. Jones, S. B. Bauman, and J.G. Druth, "Electromagnetic Emission from Humans During Focused Intent," *Journal of Parapsychology*, (2012) 762, 275–294.

13 A. Losi and W. Gartner, "The Evolution of Flavin-Binding Receptors: An Ancient Chromophore Serving Trendy Blue-Light Sensors," *Annu Rev Plant Biol*, 2012, June 2; 63:49–72. doi: 10.1146/annurev-arplant-042811-105538. Epub 2011, Nov. 15, *http://www.ncbi .nlm.nih.gov/pubmed/22136567*. Retrieved 5/17/13.

14 Alex Stone, "Smell Turns Up in Unexpected Places," *New York Times* online, October 13, 2014, *http://www.nytimes.com/2014/10/14/science/smell-turns-up-in-unexpected -places.html*.

15 E. L. Mosler, E. Kropff, M. B. Moser, "Place Cells, Grid Cells, and the Brain's Spatial Representation System," *Annu Rev Neurosci*, 2008;31:69-89. doi: *10.1146/annurev .neuro.31.061307.090723.http://www.ncbi.nlm.nih.gov/pubmed/18284371*. J. Kubie, "Human Grid Cells," *BrainFacts.org*, August 15, 2013, *http://blog.brainfacts .org/2013/08/human-grid-cells/*. Retrieved 1/28/14. M. B. Moser and E. Moser "Crystals in the Brain," *EMBO Molecular Medicine*, 3 (2011): 69–71. *http://www.ncbi.nlm. nih.gov/pmc/articles/PMC3377059/*. Retrieved 1/28/14. J. Jacobs, C. T. Weidemann, J. F. Miller, A. Solway, J. F. Burke, X. Wei, N. Suthana, M. R. Sperling, A.D. Sharan, I. Fried, and M.J. Kahana, "Direct Recordings of Grid-like Neuronal Activity in Human Spatial Navigation," *Nature Neuroscience*, 16 (2013): 1188–1190, *http://www.nature. com/neuro/journal/v16/n9/full/nn.3466.html*. Retrieved 1/28/14.

16 K. Bailee, "Penn Research Helps Identify New Brain Cell Involved in Navigation," *Health Canal*, 12/8/13, *http://wwww.healthcanal.com/brain-nerves/41759-penn-research -helps-identify-new-brain-cell-involved-in-navigation.html*. Retrieved 1/28/14.

17 D. Chow, "NASA Funds 3D Pizza Printer," *Space.com*, May 21, 2013, *http://www .space.com./21250-nasa-3d-food-printer-pizza.html*. Retrieved 1/28/14.

18 M. Wall, "3D Printer Launching to Space Station in 2014," *Yahoo News*, May 24, 2013, *http://news.yahoo.com/3d-printer-launching-space-station-2014-215719508.html*. Retrieved, 5/25/13.

19 Rupert Sheldrake, "Rat Learning and Morphic Resonance," *http://www.sheldrake.org /about-rupert-sheldrake/blog/rat-learning-and-morphic-resonance*.

20 J. Oldfield and D. J. B. Shaw, "V.I. Vernadsky and the Noosphere Concept: Russian Understandings of Society-Nature Interaction," *Geoforum*, 37 (2006): 145–154. ISSN 0016-7185. *http://eprints.gla.ac.uk/6820/1/6820.pdf*. Retrieved 5/13/13.

21 "Noosphere," *Wikipedia*, *http://en.wikipedia.org/wiki/Noosphere*. Retrieved 5/14/13.

22 A. N. Wilner and B. S. Stetka, "A History of Mass Hysteria," *Medscape Psychiatry and Mental Health*, New York: WebMD.

23 Ibid.

24 D. Baker, "UW Medicine Donors Try Their Hand at Protein Folding," Local Health Guide: Seattle: Local Health Guide. Seattle: Local Health Guide.10/23/2012. *http:// mylocalhealthguide.com/2012/10/23/uw-medicine-donors-try-their-hand-at-protein -folding*. Retrieved 5/1/13.

25 William F. Ogburn and Dorothy Thomas, "Are Inventions Inevitable? A Note on Social Evolution," *Political Science Quarterly* 37, no. 1 (March 1922): 83–98.

26 James H. Fowler and Nicholas A. Christakis, "Dynamic Spread of Happiness in a Large Social Network: Longitudinal Analysis over 20 years in the Framingham Heart Study," *BMJ* 2008;337:a2338.

27 Ibid.

28 F. W. H. Myers, "The Subliminal Consciousness," Chapter 1: General Characteristics and Subliminal Messages. *Proceedings of the Society for Psychical Research*. 7 (1892): 298–327, 307.

About the Author

Bernard Beitman, MD, is the first psychiatrist since Carl Jung to attempt to systematize the study of coincidences. He is a Visiting Professor at the University of Virginia and former Chair of the Department of Psychiatry at the University of Missouri-Columbia. He attended Yale Medical School and completed a psychiatric residency at Stanford. Dr. Beitman has received two national awards for his psychotherapy training program and is internationally known for his research into the relationship between chest pain and panic disorder. He has developed the first valid and reliable scale to measure coincidence sensitivity, and has edited two issues of *Psychiatric Annals* that focus on coincidences. Dr. Beitman is the founder of Coincidence Studies.

Visit his website at: *www.coincider.com* and his *Psychology Today* blog at *https://www.psychologytoday.com/blog/connecting-coincidence.*

Index